The Educational System
Its Nature and Logic

SOA — follows chapters

- A system or pay attention to those we are not honoring

The Educational System
Its Nature and Logic

Philip A. Cusick
Michigan State University

McGraw-Hill, Inc.
New York   St. Louis   San Francisco   Auckland   Bogotá
Caracas   Lisbon   London   Madrid   Mexico City   Milan
Montreal   New Delhi   San Juan   Singapore
Sydney   Tokyo   Toronto

This book was developed by Lane Akers, Inc.

This book was set in Garamond Book by Publication Services.
The editor was Lane Akers;
the production supervisor was Denise L. Puryear.
The cover was designed by Carla Bauer.
Project supervision was done by Publication Services.

The Educational System
Its Nature and Logic

2 3 4 5 6 7 8 9 10 11 12 13 14 BKMBKM 9 9 8 7 6

ISBN 0-07-014972-0

Library of Congress Cataloging-in-Publication Data

Cusick, Philip A.
    The educational system: its nature and logic / Philip A. Cusick.
      p.   cm.
    Includes bibliographical references (p.) and index.
    ISBN 0-07-014972-0
    1. School management and organization—United States.   I. Title.
LB2805.C865   1992
371.2'00973—dc20   91-3144

About the Author

Philip A. Cusick is a professor of Educational Administration at Michigan State University. He has been a junior high school and senior high school teacher and a central office and university administrator. He is the author of *Inside High School* (Holt, Rinehart and Winston, 1973) and *The Egalitarian Ideal and the American High School,* (Longman, 1983) and a coauthor of *Selling Students Short,* (Teachers' College Press, 1986). He has conducted several research studies and authored numerous articles and reviews.

Contents

9 *Conclusion* *210*

Preface

Handwritten annotations:

X① Elucidate what "the system" is

② What can & cannot be did

- Consistency
- Predictability
- "System" from the separate efforts

Over several years of doing, reading, and reviewing descriptive studies of schools and educational issues, it has often occurred to me how consistent events are. The way students behave, the way teachers and students interact, and the way administrators handle their communities repeat themselves across the years and across schools. Consistency is not restricted to schools and classrooms. Federal and state education efforts, even as they grow and take on more functions, also behave predictably, as do education's reform movements and the reasoning and rhetoric that accompanies reform movements. Thus the book's argument is that there are common and predictable elements that work within and across schools and within and across education's system, which do not change even as times and people change. These stable and enduring elements, it will be argued, are the substance of the educational system. The purpose of the book is to elucidate these elements and, in so doing, describe the system.

The book is built around several descriptive studies. This is an honorable technique, one that George Homans used effectively in *The Human Group*, as did Crane Brinton in *Anatomy of Revolution*. Homans took studies of small groups and described in general what groups always do. Brinton took three national revolutions and showed how predictably they unfold. Similarly, this book works from reliable, descriptive studies to see what always happens in schools and everywhere else the education business is carried out. *[handwritten: always happens]*

It is a good time to combine and examine education's descriptive studies, because in the past few decades there have been several good ones. The studies range from the classroom to the White House, from students making trouble to the President making policy. Using studies of classrooms and schools, we can describe what students, teachers, and administrators always do. Using studies of federal and state efforts, we can describe what politicians, policymakers, and bureaucrats always do. And with close reading of the sources, we can describe *[handwritten: always do]* how the efforts of the former overlap onto the efforts of the latter and vice versa. That overlapping is most important. It is what turns serial situations into an intelligible whole. It is what makes a system from the separate efforts.

This is also a good time to undertake a description of the education system, since the system is currently subject to a multitude of improvement efforts. Amid the suggestions for improvement are the quiet and not-so-quiet assertions that the system does not work or the system has to be changed, or that the system is failing. My effort is not to either agree with or take issue with the

①

criticisms, but rather to elucidate first, what the system is, and second, what of the system can and what of the system cannot be changed. This may not only be a useful contribution to reform efforts, but is one that will place reform and reformers in the context of the system and so help us understand what part they take in the system and what contribution they make to the system. So, stimulated by several descriptive studies, models from honored authors, and current efforts to reform education, I offer this account of the educational system.

Several people helped in this endeavor and I would like to acknowledge them. My editor, Lane Akers, along with Janice Earle of the National Science Foundation, helped with the initial idea. Early versions received cold but helpful scrutiny from Fred Carver, University of Georgia; Gerald Grant, Syracuse University; Ann Hart, University of Utah; Cecil Miskel, University of Michigan; Rod Ogawa, University of Utah; Chris Wheeler, Michigan State University; and Don Willower, Pennsylvania State University. Ideas were honed in chance and sometimes not-so-chance conversations with my colleagues at Michigan State University: Brian Rowan, Gary Sykes, Sam Moore, David Cohen, Judith Lanier, and Barbara Markle. Full and critical readings were made by Ted Okey, Mt. Pleasant, Michigan Public Schools; Dannelle Stevens, Whitman College; and Chris Wheeler, with whom I undertook a study used in Chapter 8 and who allowed me to include his work in my account. Finally there are the authors of the several works from which the book was written. My effort is a tribute to the care and attention they gave to their own.

PHILIP A. CUSICK

1

The System → Commonalities(2)

A Descriptive not theoretical (4)

INTRODUCTION

Education, or more particularly the educational system, is a popular topic of social reformers. Most favorably considered, the system holds the solution to personal success, social equality, and economic competition. Less favorably, the system is viewed as functional but inefficient and somewhat unresponsive to social concerns. Least favorably, the system is viewed as an overblown bureaucracy interested primarily in its own survival, reproducing rather than resolving social problems. The question that reformers might ask, and the question this book addresses, is "what is the educational system?" To answer the question, the book will take the system apart, from top to bottom, to look closely at what goes on inside, to see what the system is and is not, and to determine what it can and cannot do.

If the system is to mean anything, it has to mean something to the way people behave. This account of the system will therefore proceed from descriptions of the ways students, teachers, administrators, parents, and state and federal staffers and policymakers behave. The object is to describe what these people do, what problems they face, and how their efforts overlap. Most important, the book will describe the elements of their behavior that are most common and enduring, those that show up across schools and across the years. The predictable essence that runs through the center of the combined behavior, that guides and limits the behavior, is the educational system, and the educational system is the subject of the book. *elements of Behavior*

The book proceeds from descriptive studies of the system's varied groups. Among the groups are those with formal status: students, teachers, administrators, and those who work in state and federal agencies, for example. Also included are those without formal status: parents, legislators, policymakers, and special interest groups. Those with and without formal status are often spoken of dichotomously, as if they were distinct, as if the latter were part of the background or provided the setting in which students, teachers, and administrators operate. That is inaccurate. The descriptions will show that each classroom, school, district, agency, and reform effort is created and sustained by a combination of people from inside and outside the formal organization. Informal groups of students show up in classrooms; parents show up in schools; legislators and interest groups show up at district, federal, and state levels. Everybody from the President

1

on down shows up in school reform. Not only do groups outside schools influence groups inside schools; those inside and those outside are mixed together into a single system. To understand how education works in the United States, one has to view it as a network of interlocking and overlapping groups, some with and some without formal status.

The earlier chapters are arranged around district groups, that is, students, teachers, and administrators. The later chapters are arranged around state and federal agencies and broad efforts that connect groups from the different levels. The earlier chapters illustrate how schools operate, day to day. The later chapters illustrate the breadth of a system that includes the President, the Congress, and federal and state agencies that deal with education, and a multitude of individuals and special interest groups, without formal designation, who enter the educational scene on their own terms.

There are three levels of description. The first describes groups operating separately. The second describes groups overlapping their efforts with contiguous groups. The third describes the common elements and understandings that run through and across the groups, through and across their overlapping. There are differences in groups and in the ways groups overlap, and these differences will be described and explained. But the book is not about differences; it is about commonalities and its purpose is to elucidate and explain the commonalities that characterize the educational system.

The descriptions have been drawn from studies done over a period of sixty years, from the late 1920s to the late 1980s; the motivation for this being that important aspects of the system, e.g. the behavior of students, the classroom interaction of teachers and students, and the way administrators accommodate their communities, are constant and predictable. Federal and state agencies have changed over the years, but even they behave predictably. Their reforms are wrapped in similar rhetoric, seek similar ends, take predictable forms, and evoke similar responses up and down the system. The problems of translating social ideals into things that teachers teach and students learn are constant and predictable. Combining accounts of multiple and overlapping groups from different times into a single description will allow examination of how events recur, problems persist, and realities endure. It will enable us to see the system as an intelligible whole—as a piece with a nature and logic, a long memory, a discernible past, and a predictable future.

THE APPROACH

The idea of joining descriptive studies into a story of the total system has interested me since 1968, when I read two such studies, Jackson's *Life in Classrooms* (1968) and Smith and Geoffrey's *The Complexities of an Urban Classroom* (1968). The two books are quite different. Jackson joins descriptions from several elementary classrooms; Smith studied one teacher, Mr. Geoffrey, as he ran his own classroom. The two books tell a similar story from different viewpoints, but together they tell more than either alone tells about the way elementary classrooms work. Later when I started doing my own studies, and had read others, I saw the same events over and over. The times, places, and people changed, but the problems and solutions recurred. I came to understand that an accurate portrait of the total system could be created by combining studies that range across the entire educational scene, from student groups to federal policymakers.

Scenes and actors change but themes and behaviors persist. In 1990, I listened to the high school principal in Caseville, Michigan, recount his problem with the open lunch period. Caseville's policy allowed students to leave the building for their lunch hour. Students were happy with the freedom; teachers were equally happy to have students out of the building, and downtown merchants were happy with the students' lunch business. But the citizens who lived between the school and downtown did not like students racing their cars and strewing their fast-food wrappers around the streets. The police were concerned about speeding and safety, the board was hearing from everybody, and the superintendent wanted the principal to quiet the matter down.

Caseville has its own identity and its people have their own personalities. Yet the basic script, with freed-up and fast-moving adolescents, downtown merchants, nervous householders, pressured board, worried superintendent, and principal in the middle, could have come from Hollingshead's (1949) Elmtown in the 1930s. A similar account came from Vidich and Bensman's (1958) Springdale in the 1950s. And for reasons similar to Caseville's, Horatio Gates Senior High, which I studied in 1969, closed its lunch period (Cusick, 1973).

Caseville's principal resolved the issue. However, there is a difference between addressing an issue and eliminating a problem. Matters and issues are addressed; problems persist over the years and throughout the system. Discipline and attendance are never finally "solved." Nor are tensions between school and family or school and community. Nor, from the state and federal view, are issues of control, reform, quality, and equality. These problems manifest themselves differently according to situations and time, but they are always present; they always demand attention, and however temporary, demand some resolution.

Another problem that recurs with great frequency is the clash between the school and children from the lower social classes. Ted Okey (1990) in the spring of 1990 interviewed parents of school dropouts and listened to their versions of their children's behavior and attendance problems. The parents also expressed the view that the school disapproves of their children and marks them for failure before they enter because of who they are. "They just look at the students and they'll pick out the so-called low class students. And they'll put them in special class . . . 'cause we're ADC [aid to dependent children], we're low class" (p. 84). The words are reminiscent of Agee and Evans' 1936 account of an Alabama tenant family and their children's schooling:

> The Ricketts are spoken of disapprovingly, even so far away as the county courthouse, as "problem" children. Their attendance record is extremely bad; their conduct is not at all good; they are always fighting and sassing back. (1960, p. 276)

Poor people, bad school behavior by their children, school disapproval, and parents who are convinced the school prejudges their children: the people and problems persist; the words are almost interchangeable. This book illustrates common themes, problems, and behaviors within classrooms, schools, communities, state departments, and federal agencies. It shows the connections between the efforts of students and teachers, teachers and administrators, and administrators and the varied publics.

A central argument of the book is that the actual business of education is carried on by small, more or less cooperative associations of people who arrange themselves around roles and issues. Within these collectivities, individuals interpret events, reach consensus, and initiate action. The actual business of education is conducted as Wolcott says, "not by the organization but by more responsive and closely knit subunits" (Wolcott, 1978, p. 27). Or as Kidder (1989) reminds us, "the task of universal, public, elementary education is...usually being conducted by a woman alone in a little room, presiding over a youthful distillate of a town or city" (p. 53). These subunits into which participants are arranged or arrange themselves are the system's building blocks. Inside the blocks are people making judgments about their situation and about how to behave. Studies describe the system as these insiders see it and as their combined actions create it.

Many excellent works are available from which to draw descriptions: studies of students, teachers, classrooms, schools, and communities; federal and state initiatives and broad reform efforts that link policymakers to classroom teachers. Each study concentrates on particular groups in a given place and time and describes the participants' problem-solving efforts. This book begins with students, moves on to teachers and students, to teachers and administrators, and to federal policymakers. After the pieces are in place, the book moves back to schools and classrooms and describes how federal and state efforts are played out.

Although that seems to be a "begin at the beginning" approach, given the circular view of the system and the fact that influence can come from several sources, the beginning point is arbitrary. The educational system is open, circular, and elastic. It has both established and emerging groups that form and re-form around particular problems that are never solved in any final sense, but the efforts to solve them take predictable patterns. The purpose of this book is to create an explanation of the system by combining the descriptions of the groups, problems, and efforts to solve them.

SOME CONCEPTS

The book is intended to be descriptive, not theoretical, but a few central concepts are needed and require definition. The first is *system*, and for purposes of this book, which describes the system as its participants create it, Parsons' (1949) definition of social system, "a network of collectivities, side by side, overlapping and larger-smaller" will be used (p. 101). A second concept, "collectivity," also needs definition. Again from Parsons, "among a set of actors, a collectivity is the sharing of common value patterns…a sense of responsibility for the fulfillment of obligations…a solidarity among those mutually oriented to common values" (p. 41). Within that idea of collectivity is the notion of an individual taking a role in order to join with others in the endeavor. A role is "what the actor does in his relations with others seen in the context of its functional significance for the social system" (Parsons, p. 25). The role taken by the individual as a member of a collectivity; the collectivity (sharing) among individuals of perceptions, values, and responsibilities; and the system that results from the combined and overlapping collectivities are the conceptual vehicles that will carry the accounts.

Central to the notion of system is the overlapping. The way students behave among themselves overlaps the way teachers behave with students. The way administrators behave with students and teachers overlaps the way they behave in their communities. The efforts of reformers and policymakers are tempered by the assessment teachers and administrators make of their efforts. Problem-solving by one group cycles into problem-solving and problem-creating by contiguous groups.

The notion of "problem" is also needed. A problem is the dynamic around which collective action is oriented. It is the situation presented to a set of individuals. It requires consensual definition and concerted action. Some problems are presented by the formal organization. The school's bureaucracy demands order, so establishing order becomes a problem for teachers. At another level, problems are imported to the schools from the social and political arenas. School-community conflicts over adolescent freedom as exemplified in Caseville, teachers vying with student peer groups for time and attention, and the hostility between the schools and the lower classes all come from the school's place in society.

Other problems emanate from the school's responsibility for improving society. Following the argument of Burnham (1964), social problems become educational problems because of the liberal belief that evil is rooted in ignorance, and education can eradicate ignorance. Hence when evil arises in the form of inequality, injustice, racism, poverty, crime, or even close economic competition, national leaders often formulate educational responses. These leaders constitute an additional collectivity designed to make the formal organization respond to a national concern such as foreign competition.

Problems are retranslated as efforts move down and into the system. In the case of foreign competition, state governors form associations with business people and educational interest groups. Continuing further, state departmental and district administrators plan more job-oriented schools and try to integrate job orientation with other school activities. Building administrators then meet with teachers to see if they can cram more vocational classes or skill-training into the schedule. Teachers worry that the effort will push out favored electives. Finally, the whole business comes to the students whose personal goals may or may not include anxiety about getting a job. At each level the problem gets retranslated, new considerations and realities are added, and proposed solutions are altered by succeeding groups.

Worms
eye
view

The book takes a worm's-eye view and builds the system from inside out by examining studies of its constituent collectivities' efforts. It illustrates how problems change and are retranslated at secondary levels. For instance, the National Institute of Education emerged, as Sproull, Weiner, and Wolf (1978) describe, from President Nixon's desire to reduce the federal role from funding and surveillance to generation of knowledge. The President and his advisors needed an educational initiative that matched their philosophy of government and did not cost too much money. Federal educationists had to accommodate Congressional appropriations committees and some young and ambitious researcher/bureaucrats who were anxious to change the system. As the initiative moved down, it included district administrators wanting to demonstrate forward-thinking and competence, building administrators who had to reconcile school schedules, and teachers who had to interact with students. At each level the problem was worked anew, interpretations were added, behaviors varied, outcomes changed.

interdep of
problems
↓
conflicts

Although particular problems are commonly perceived throughout the system, often what is perceived as a solution by one group will be some other group's problem. Units tend to define their own problems, and often the solutions that they work out include means of resisting problem-definition by those at higher levels. Attempts by higher levels of the organization to define and suggest solutions for the lower levels are endless sources of conflict. Among the examples cited in the book are several in which administrators attempt to improve the efficiency of teachers or the behavior of students, who, in response, adopt means to protect themselves from their well-meaning but unwelcome superiors.

An additional consideration basic to juxtaposing studies from the 1920s to 1980s is that education is a developed system that behaves consistently. The studies confirm this. They show students, teachers, administrators, and community groups working in the same way and on the same issues across the years. Contexts and issues change; problems and solutions endure. Students' tendency to separate themselves into class- and culture-based groups is wonderfully

Structures

predictable. Equally predictable are the problems that student groups cause for teachers. School-community conflicts and community suspicion of schools and administrators who work to keep disruptive community influences at bay are also predictable. The same stories come from east to west, from the 1920s to the 1990s.

There are of course differences between the schools of the 1920s and the schools of the 1990s. There are many more students now, and many who in former times might not have come or might have been discouraged out if they had come. But fundamentally, the system has not changed as much as it has continued to fulfill its commitment to universal education and egalitarian ends, commitments that were built into the system from the beginning. The bureaucratic means to address those ends were also built into the system from the beginning.

Because the system is envisioned as a set of overlapping groups, the descriptive studies, which form the basis of the book, focus on groups solving problems and on overlapping. The dialogue will move along two parallel lines, first with descriptions of individual groups, second with how the efforts combine into a total system. The system will emerge as accounts of groups accumulate. The groups have goals and so does the system; the groups have persistent problems and so does the system. The group's task is to make sense of its environment and actions. The system is a corporate enterprise with interests that stretch across units. As the book progresses, increasing attention is given to the system as an entity. The conclusion will describe the system, the relations between its parts, and its potential and possibilities.

THE STUDIES

Over the past decades, several researchers have conducted field studies in educational settings. Some of these studies concentrate on individuals, some on groups. Others concentrate on a situation that involves several groups and a particular issue. The argument of this book is that these studies describe the same system and will therefore be combined and offered together as if they also described the same point in time. This approach will enable us to wash out issues that come and go, issues that may change the schools, but that do not change the system. It appears that restructuring will be the issue in the 1990s. In the 1980s the issue was excellence; in the 1970s it was accountability; in the 1960s it was equality; in the 1950s, national defense. Each of those was and remains important in its own right. Each left its mark. But even as we explain these issues and account for their effects, our purpose is to wash them out, to eliminate their topicality, and to see what endures when they have gone and before the next issues arise. Our interest is in the system, and "the system," says Tom Green (1980), "is precisely what doesn't change" (p. xv).

The research methods used in the studies are participant observation, observation, and interview. As research techniques, they are quite modest. In general, the researchers begin with such questions as "what are these people doing in this place?" and "how do their actions reflect their view of their activities and of themselves?" The studies encompass the system's parts. Everhart (1983), Johnson (1985), and Willis (1977) described students; Cuban (1975), Hentoff (1966), and Hollingshead (1949) described parents and communities; others describe federal and state efforts, and still others describe the effect of those efforts on students, parents, and communities. Some of these studies concentrate on single groups. Everhart's *Reading, Writing and Resistance* (1983) describes a set of junior high school students as they go through their school year. Cusick's *Inside High School* (1973) is similar. He joined a group of senior boys in a working-class suburban school and attended classes with them on a daily basis.

Some studies focus on particular events such as change or reform. Wolcott's *Teachers versus Technocrats* (1977) documented an effort in which people from the U.S. Office of Education and from a research and development agency at the University of Oregon, and administrators from a local district attempted to implement a classroom management model. The story tells of that effort, the teachers' reaction, and the eventual reversal of the effort. Barry Gold and Matthew Miles (1981) studied the community-school conflict that erupted over a school staff's attempt at implementing the "open classroom" concept in an elementary school. *Whose School Is This Anyway?* is an important part of Chapter 5 on administrator-community relations and shows how, for a time and around a given issue, a collectivity of parents resisted a staff effort to create an open school. The story, including the firing of a teacher and the resignation of an administrator, tells of the parents forcing the staff to retreat to (the use of) self-contained classrooms. The book also describes how the remaining staff united to protect themselves against the parents.

Other studies center not on an event but on a concept. Johnson (1985), an anthropologist, began his study of West Haven Elementary School with the notion of culture. He wanted to describe the "social and cultural reality of everyday classroom life and to note the conditioning effect of...elementary schooling on children" (p. 3). Achievement, deviance, and ideas on punishments and rewards are explored as Johnson's classroom descriptions unfold.

Sometimes the studies are not of schools or school situations but of broad efforts to effect educational change. Bailey and Mosher (1968) described the emergence of the Elementary and Secondary Education Act of 1965. Their book, *ESEA: The Office of Education Administers a Law,* is the story of President Johnson's efforts to use education to solve national problems of poverty and racism. It documents the change that was wrought in the Office of Education as a result of the President's effort. More importantly, it demonstrates how an array of groups at the federal level combined their efforts and forced change on the schools. Chapters 7 and 8 examine how those changes were retranslated as they moved down into the schools.

Murphy (1974) continued the story of the ESEA with his *State Education Agencies and Discretionary Funds,* a study of the way state departments used funds obtained through the ESEA to build their own bureaucracies. A sequel to both Bailey and Mosher's ESEA story and Murphy's story is provided in Sproull, Weiner, and Wolf's *Organizing an Anarchy* (1978), on the National Institute of Education (NIE). That agency emerged from President Nixon's efforts to redirect the role of the federal government in education away from the ESEA's direct funding and surveillance and instead toward research and development. Also told is how this newly conceived NIE had to find a place for itself despite indifference and even hostility from Congressional appropriations committees who were angry about the bureaucratic excesses and unfulfilled promises of the ESEA. An additional book is the personal account by Terrell Bell (1988) of his years as President Reagan's Secretary of Education. In *The Thirteenth Man,* Bell documents his efforts to find a new role for the Department of Education in the face of the Reagan administration's efforts to abolish it. Juxtaposing these studies of separate but related and sequential events elucidates the federal role in education and the recurring problems faced by federal policymakers.

Studies of several parallel groups operating in a single effort are central to Chapter 7. In the mid-1970s there was a federal effort to improve rural schools and the Office of Education's Experimental Schools Program spent $55 million in eighteen rural school districts. The concept was "comprehensive reform," focusing on research, demonstration, experimentation, documentation, and evaluation. Part of the funds were used to hire field researchers to document the activities of teachers, administrators, communities, and federal-liaison people working in those communities. Five of those accounts will be used to illustrate the way federal efforts are retranslated at local levels.

Several studies concern place-bound units such as classrooms and schools. Others concentrate on particular people as they went their way through a school and the larger district. Wolcott's *The Man in the Principal's Office* (1978) is one of the latter. Ed Bell, the principal of Freedom Elementary School, moves through his daily round of meetings with custodians, teachers, students, parents, and district administrators. A similar situation but with a different focus, on community influence, is described in Hentoff's *Our Children Are Dying* (1966). The story centers on Elliott Shapiro, an elementary principal in New York City's Harlem, who allied himself with dissatisfied parents to force the system to improve conditions at his school.

In addition to the central character or central collectivity, each study describes contiguous groups. As Willis (1977) and Everhart (1983) describe deviant students, they also describe teachers and administrators dealing with deviant students. Grant (1988) describes rights-advocating students and their rights-advocating parents, both interacting with the school. Popkewitz, Tabachink, and Wehlage (1982) describe a single change effort, Individually Guided Education, among several schools. Their book includes administrators, teachers, parents, and students. Lightfoot (1983) details both school administrators enforcing compliance with rules and teachers coping with those administrators. The studies contain descriptions of central units and of contiguous units. They portray the way education's participants engage in simultaneous, multiple, and overlapping groups.

The studies are drawn from different schools, different times, and different places. In Chapter 2 of this book, Kidder's *Among Schoolchildren*, published in 1989, is placed alongside McNeil's *Contradictions of Control*, published in 1986, and Moore's *Realities of the Urban Classroom*, published in 1967. The studies are not juxtaposed to argue that "nothing really changes," but that certain fundamental issues are at work in the classroom and everywhere else in the system. Change occurs but it does so in response to predictable problems with predictable solutions. The task is to explicate both the system's enduring realities and the way it changes and adapts. Drawing together studies from different times and places around common units is at the center of the thesis that public education has a stable but dynamic system that makes predictable adaptations to variations on recurring themes.

The book is not a review of literature; it is a story of education's system based on what this author judges to be good descriptive studies conducted by knowledgeable educational researchers. Most of the studies have been well-published, well-received, well-cited, and are reasonably well known among people who do such studies or who interest themselves in the workings of the system. There are two exceptions: one of small-town principals and the other of a reform effort in two school districts. These studies were not widely published but will be included because they were conducted by this author and had a lasting effect on his ideas.

Regarding selection of the studies, there are two caveats. First, the book does not include quantitative studies that could contribute to the story of the system. My reason for not including those works is related to my conception of the system as a set of overlapping collectivities. A field researcher studies a collectivity and by including only studies of collectivities, their actions and their overlapping, the method will reflect the central concept. A second reason for limiting the selection to field studies is that they describe behavior, and a basic premise of the book is that if the system is to be meaningful, it has to both reflect and influence the way the participants behave: the way they talk, act, and play their roles. Personal behavior is the subject of field studies and the goal is to explain the system as the interlocking and overlapping of personal behaviors. For those two reasons the data are limited to that offered by field studies. A second caveat has to do with the studies that were not but might have been included. My apologies to the authors of those works: I was not interested in reviewing the literature, but in selecting only enough studies to describe the system.

The methodologies differ. Classroom studies concentrate on a few people who spend time in face-to-face interaction and thus develop a coherent social unit. Among the participants, communal relationships arise naturally and one can develop an intelligible and encompassing story around their interactions. The stable locale lends itself to participant observation. Personal relationships between researcher and subjects tend to be an important part of such studies. The researcher comes to regard the group's behavior as reasonable and to sympathize with the subjects, particularly in their conflicts with other groups. For instance Everhart (1983) and Willis (1977) take the part of their lower-class and deviant students as they work out their relation to the school, teachers, and administrators.

That identification is not a mere by-product of the method. Often one of a researcher's important purposes is coming to share the group's collective perspective so that he or she can describe it accurately. Single group accounts frequently go beyond the educational issues into individuals' lives and thereby provide insight into the limits of the system and into the ways individuals use the system to pursue personal ends. Other authors try to present a balanced view of some event or concept. In my own *Egalitarian Ideal* (1983), I tried to take such a view of the racial troubles in two urban high schools. I was not personally involved with either black or white students or teachers. The divisiveness there was such that if the researcher became too allied with either a black or a white faction, it would have meant exclusion from contact with the other. Something is gained and something is lost by either approach. In this book, both types of studies have been used; both contribute to the story of the system.

Beyond the school level, collectivities are more fluid and individuals less place-bound. Frequently, studies beyond the school are not of particular groups, but of issues, movements, and thrusts around which individuals align. The studies tend to focus on a single issue such as a reform effort as perceived and acted on by multiple groups. The studies emphasize formal and associative rather than personal and communal relations. The researcher follows the issue, not the individual or the group, and uses methods of observation and interview rather than participation. Such studies are particularly useful for the way they describe issues and individuals who overlap several groups.

As the book moves from group to group and from groups to issues, several of the studies have been used repeatedly. For instance Grant's (1988) account of Hamilton High includes several good stories, the main one being how an affluent suburban high school of the 1950s became a crucible for policy makers to conduct a thirty-year experiment with integration, student rights, mainstreaming, bilingual education, and community control. Because it is a story of students participating in and adapting to the changes, it is part of Chapter 2, which focuses on student groups. On another level, it is a story of teachers adapting to those same changes and also adapting to the changes among students—so it is relevant to Chapter 3 on students and teachers. On still another level, it is a story of administrators and parents trying to accommodate changes fomented by the students, and so will be used in Chapter 4.

Similarly, Smith and Geoffrey's *Complexities of an Urban Classroom* (1968) tells of a single classroom with students and teachers. The study has several stories: one of teachers among themselves and a second of teachers with administrators. It also tells of the community and its interaction with the school. The stories focus on individuals as they participate in contiguous collectivities in the same setting. A student is a member of a peer group and a member of a formal classroom; a teacher is a leader in the classroom, a colleague on the faculty, and a subordinate, sometimes an opposer, to administrators.

Each story describes several groups that overlap, and thus each illustrates how the system's elements overlap. Because the intent of the book is to describe both the separate collectivities and their system, it makes sense to select studies that illustrate both. Using the same studies increases the book's coherence; it provides a more unified information base from which to consider the entire system. A limited number of studies also allows the reader to become better acquainted with fewer situations and reduces the need for scene-setting.

RESEARCH THEORIES

As well as describing school situations, each study carries an argument or thesis about the meaning of the descriptions and about the place of participants in the overall system. The concepts or theories used by the researchers are central to the studies. Everhart (1983) and Willis (1977) needed their theory of resistance to explain their errant students' behavior. McNeil (1986) needed her argument that "control" is the school's real agenda in order to pursue her descriptions. Wolcott (1978) needed his idea of moiety, or half, to describe the dispute between teachers and technocrats. Grant (1988) needed the notion of "ethos" to explain how its absence wreaked havoc at Hamilton High. Lightfoot (1983) needed her concept of "good" school in order to make sense of her multischool study. Each book has its own central idea, sometimes a social theory and sometimes a concept or a few presuppositions. For this book based on the descriptive part of the studies, the question was, what to do with those accompanying explanations.

The answer is that these studies have been selected for the quality of their descriptions, not for their theoretical arguments. This is not a theory book. A few central concepts are used to convey and analyze the descriptions. Among the concepts are system, collectivities, roles, and problems. In the last chapter, it will be useful to provide a sketch of some current thinking about school bureaucracies, their tight and loose coupling, their resemblance to modern corporations and the way they survive in an open society. Some notions about the relations between individuals, groups, and organizations have been taken from the economist, Mancour Olson, Jr. (1965). Some of these ideas have already been explained; others are explained as they come up and as they contribute to a particular discussion. When judged appropriate, the theories will become part of the discussion, but to survey , critique, or discuss them in detail would require too many detours and would take away from the book's central purpose—to describe the educational system.

Good descriptive studies, such as those selected, contain enough substance to both argue a thesis and allow the reader to supply alternative theses. They allow another to use the data even if she or he disagrees with the accompanying explanation. Accepting Willis's (1977) and Everhart's (1983) excellent descriptions of student behavior does not obligate one to accept also their view that the students are trying unsuccessfully to resist the hegemony of the state. Nor does accepting McNeil's (1986) descriptions of social studies classes in four high schools obligate one to accept her thesis that the primary goal of the school is control. Nor is one obligated to accept the functional explanation relating student behavior to school structure that I put forth in *Inside High School* (Cusick, 1973). That researcher/authors have their own theories and explanations is as it should be. When necessary, they are explained; when appropriate, they are integrated. But there is no obligation to include, argue with, integrate, or accept them as they stand.

A few additional concepts are needed to carry on the discussion. In general, they are not complicated. They are quite common among people who study schools or organizations. Several are integrated into the descriptions. What little explanation those concepts require will be supplied in the text and in the context of the descriptions. For instance, in the chapter on peer groups, it makes sense to explain school structure and so some space is devoted to that end. The elements of a bureaucracy are important and when the term arises, some attention is given to explain the concept. The technology of education is generally considered soft, or indeterminate, and when discussing the problems that technology poses for outsiders who are trying to affect classrooms, a brief explanation of that idea will be included. And in Chapter 6, which describes federal initiatives, some attention will be given to the reasoning that connects education to an improved society. The story is of the separate collectivities who are facing problems and working out solutions, and of the system that their combined efforts create.

Finally, there is one more important assumption—that the participants de- scribed are reasonable men and women, an honest, hard-working, and well- intentioned lot who do what they do for good reasons. On their own terms, their actions make sense. The goal is to understand the educational world as they understand it, their roles as they play them, and the system as their com- bined efforts create it.

2

Students and Students

• Friday Night Lights ~ Sim

INTRODUCTION

The setting is schools and the topic is the system of education. The system is composed of overlapping groups, some from inside, some from outside the formal structure. The most numerous and important collectivity is that of students; the book will therefore begin with them. To focus on students qua students or students as individuals, however, is impossible. America's 38 million students differ widely. Because the descriptive studies show students dividing themselves into smaller subunits or peer groups, even as early as elementary school, this chapter will examine these student groups, show how they are created, how they operate, and how they overlap with other parties both in and out of the school. Students are also described as the school arranges them, but the emphasis will be on students as they group themselves, and as the groups operate in the school and in the system as a whole.

Defined, a peer group is "a number of persons who communicate with one another often over a span of time, and who are few enough so that each person is able to communicate with all the others face to face" (Homans, 1950, p. 1). Along with frequent face-to-face interaction, members share activities, routines, and patterns of communication. Within groups, individuals cooperate, reciprocate, and behave with personal transcendence toward one another. Groups encourage among their members certain values, modes of participation, and ways of decision-making. In them, members take on social roles, share confidences, reciprocate obligations, and develop loyalties. Along with common interests and interactions come orderly patterns of communication and a strong sense of group identity. A peer group is a full-blown social unit. It makes decisions and takes action. The importance of groups to children and adolescents is widely acknowledged.

> In these groups, the child lives. Those who populate these groups are the real people of the earth for him. The activities of these groups are vivid and interesting, and all else is dull by comparison. The loyalties of this world are paramount, and they exclude others. Adults do not enter this world. Most adults are shadowy and unpredictable persons who need only to be reckoned with negatively; other adults are

Note: Much of this chapter has appeared as "Student Groups and School Structure" in the *Handbook of Research on Social Studies Teaching and Learning*, edited by James Shaver, Macmillan Publishing Company, New York, 1991, pp. 276–289. Adapted with permission from Macmillan Publishing Company.

14

able to make themselves useful accessories. No more, for the thing is the game and the people who matter are the members of the little group. (Waller, 1932, p. 181)

Also widely acknowledged is the continuation of these groups in school. Those who study student groups find that they are formed in elementary school and (sometimes the same) groups are continued into high school. Studies indicate that a great deal of what students do in school, they initiate with peers and that a great many problems they face, they solve with peers.

These student groups exist the way teachers would like their classes to exist and the way administrators would like schools to exist, by the willing consent and active participation of the members. The idea of having students think and behave toward school as they do their group, a community with common attitudes, values, and beliefs, and then using the community to bind disparate students together, is very appealing. Its reputed attainment by private schools is frequently cited as a reason for their success. Its nonattainment by public schools is cited for their reputed lack of success. Several reformers would build schools around the characteristics of small groups and would have students behave toward schoolmates and teachers as they do toward group members.

The barrier to this ideal community is put up by the student group itself. The groups are elusive and resilient, very difficult to influence from without, and frequently more strongly normed than the schools in which they operate. Not only are they bound by the members' age, sex, and frequently race, but also by their culture and social class, whose most parochial views the members are likely to reflect. These groups may lend themselves to the schools' goals, but more often they do not. Waller (1932) recognized that "the attempts which members of the faculty have made to organize the primary group life of children and use it for purposes of control have generally been unsuccessful" (p. 185).

As the evidence shows, students' groups are capable of devouring large amounts of student time and energy, influencing teachers, affecting curriculum, and countering legitimate authority. The studies also show that many students will remain within their groups rather than join the school at large and that lower-class students are likely to take refuge in groups where they resist the school's attempts to socialize them. Group notions of appropriate behavior, responsibility, and distributive justice may or may not fit school notions, and student deviance is frequently group-initiated. Particularly for lower-class students, the group may serve as a barrier between the individual and the school, with the members participating in the school at large only to the degree permitted by their group. In sum, these groups are class- and culture-based, operate in school, and are important determiners of student behavior. The overlapping of these groups with the formal and teacher-led classroom is our first and the most important link in the educational system.

This chapter examines the roles students play both within their groups and within the school at large to see how these roles articulate with one another, how and where they conflict, and in general how group roles overlap with school expectations. This and later chapters discuss whether the occasional reluctance of students to leave their groups and enter the school at large may be one of the main reasons schools are structured to deemphasize the normed community and concentrate instead on individual achievement.

THE STUDIES

There are several descriptive studies of student behavior in schools and a few of them were specifically intended to describe group behavior: Cusick (1973), Willis (1977), and Everhart (1983). Everhart's took place in a junior high, Cusick's in a senior high, and Willis's in a working-class high school in England. Each author joined a group of students in order to understand the way the group defined and responded to school situations. Several other studies describe student groups but not as the central focus; instead, each study contains descriptions of student behavior, and particularly group behavior. Additional references will include the Jackson (1968) study of elementary school classrooms and the Lightfoot (1983) examination of "good" schools. They too contain descriptions of student groups along with other aspects of the schools.

The studies span several decades, from the 1920s (Lynd's *Middletown*) to the 1980s (Kidder's *Among Schoolchildren*), and cover the students' ages, from elementary (Johnson, 1985) to junior high (Everhart, 1983) to senior high (Grant, 1988; McNeil, 1986). Of course, there are differences among the schools. The most interesting for our purposes is that the schools described by Lynd and Lynd in 1929 and Hollingshead in 1939, when they did their field work, concentrate on the whole community, and Hollingshead in particular described the school's reinforcement of the community class structure. Later, studies by Grant (1988) and Powell et al. (1985) were done in schools that, in compliance with the government's policy of using education to transfer income to the poor, were consolidated and integrated and had open enrollment and special programs for the disadvantaged. These latter schools were attempting to broaden the concept of equality, break traditional barriers, and provide increased opportunities for all. Peer groups in these schools were presented with different situations and different opportunities for interaction. Using the studies to obtain a long-range, time-lapse perspective, it is argued that despite differences in situations, group behavior in the schools of the 1980s is very similar to group behavior in the schools of the 1920s.

PEER GROUPS: THEIR CLASS AND CULTURE BASE

Among adolescents group life is universal. "Everybody knows that teenagers love being with each other—that they crave conversation with friends in person or on the phone, almost more than they crave food" (Czikszentmihalyi and Larson, 1984, p. 155). The press to have some friends and to have some friends to carry on with is universal, and everyone who examines school life closely finds that students carry on group activities all the time. As Hollingshead (1949) noted:

> This school is full of cliques. You go into the hall, or the commons room [between classes or at noon] and you will find the same kids together day after day. Walk up Freedom Street at noon, or in the evening, you'll see them again. The kids run in bunches just like their parents. This town is full of cliques, and you can't expect the kids to be any different from their parents. (p. 151)

For adolescents, in school with hosts of other adolescents, the importance of these "intimate groups that human beings demand" (Lynd and Lynd, 1929, p. 214) cannot be exaggerated. For students who cannot, or for whatever reason do not, have these primary affiliations, school can be an intimidating and lonely place. Ken summed it up:

> When I first came I hated it. I didn't know anyone. You know, Phil, I skipped fifty-eight days last year because I couldn't stand to come to school because I didn't know anyone, and when I would try to talk to someone, we would just exchange small talk, we never got down to anything. I felt like a real outsider. And it's bad when you don't know anyone. You just walk around by yourself and feel that the other kids are talking about you. (Cusick, 1973, p. 124)

Not only are these peer groups important but they "consume most of the interest, time and activities of the adolescents" (Hollingshead, 1949, p. 152). Cusick (1973) recounted how the groups he studied spent up to two-thirds of their school day carrying on their repertoire of behaviors, which centered around the members' common interests and extended to out-of-school activities. The activities, of course, vary. Willis (1977) and Everhart (1983) reported deviance as their groups' major activities; Cusick (1973) reported sports, music, motorcycles, school activities, and hunting; Grant (1988) reported drugs, sports, extracurricular activities, political activism and added academic achievement as common interests among some groups.

Along with common interests, time, and interaction comes a strong sense of group identity, well-defined roles, acknowledged leadership, and orderly patterns of communication and decision-making. Those who study student groups find that they are formed in early years, and in them, members learn to take on important roles, share confidences, reciprocate obligations, and develop loyalties. These groups also arrange themselves along sex, race, and class lines. "In all the high schools I visited, I was struck by the rigid definition of student groups and their internal homogeneity" (Lightfoot, 1983, p. 352). Sexual lines are understandable. Girls with girls, boys with boys is the way of children and adolescents. Cusick (1973) found that only among the more involved and ambitious students, the ones who controlled the school's extracurricular activities, were females and males together in one group. Otherwise, the groups were sexually segregated, with members being careful to stay away from one another when with their girlfriends or boyfriends.

In biracial schools, in addition to barriers of gender, class, and background, most students are divided along racial lines. Grant (1988), who studied biracial schools in the 1970s, found wariness and hostility between African-Americans and whites, except in well-run classes or adult-supervised activities where students put aside their differences and concentrated on attaining formal goals. Otherwise, more militant African-Americans did not allow other African-Americans to affiliate with whites, who themselves were quite uninterested in affiliating with African-Americans. As Grant's story of Hamilton High progressed into the later 1970s and the 1980s, he reported barriers breaking down, biracial dating, friendships, and groups emerging.

Perhaps those who study biracial schools concentrate too much on racial antagonism and not enough on the diversity of students', particularly male students', perspectives toward school. Johnson (1985) reported in his study of an elementary school that African-American males combined in groups to defy the classrooms' principle norm—that each individual would work quietly and alone. He argued that the referent for these African-American boys was not the school or classroom, but their own peer group:

> Black males continually attempt to dominate the classrooms. These students, however, are not merely being rambunctious; they are rebelling and attacking the value system of the classroom culture. They attack books, literacy, and work, and they consciously interrupt the activities of other students. They attack the social system of the classroom. Autonomy, for example, is a core classroom social norm attacked by those Black males whose orientation and interactional frame of reference are toward their own peer group rather than toward the teacher. (pp. 206–207)

Johnson (1985) went on to compare the behavior of African-American males to the behavior of adolescent Sioux males studied by Wax (1967). She reported that those students' orientation was toward one another and their own culture, not toward the culture of the classroom or toward the majority culture the classroom represents. Johnson suggested that the African-American males in his study behaved as did those Sioux whom Wax reported as behaving in such a way "as to gain status with their peer group rather than with respect to the teacher" (Wax, 1967, p. 46).

The responses of teachers in Johnson's classrooms were to attempt to break up the African-American male groups and enforce the norm of quiet individual work. Johnson (1985) reported that "extensive efforts are made in early and lower grades to break up peer bonding tendencies among children, both Black and White" (pp. 206–207). Failing to break up their groups or to enforce classroom norms onto these students, the teachers defined the African-American males as "slow" and treated them accordingly. But as Johnson stressed, the boys were not slow at all; they were, in their groups, exercising their own culture and rejecting the teacher's and school's alien culture. Such cultural and subsequent class characteristics among groups are not limited to African-American males, but are the major definers of a peer group and are the major sources of the different approaches that students take to school. Class and culture are the major definers of student groups.

They are also the characteristics this chapter will pursue, not only because student groups reflect class and culture differences, but because student groups are the principal vehicle through which society manifests itself in the system. The overlapping of society, as manifested in student groups, with the teacher-led classroom is the most important link in the educational system. All of the system's efforts eventually come down to the meeting between the teacher, who articulates the school's official version of appropriate behavior, and students, who have their own ideas of appropriate behavior and who are holding themselves in their class- and culture-based groups.

There is the matter of what it takes to belong to the more prestigious groups. In some respects, it does not seem to take much. As a young lady told the Lynds (1929), "Being good-looking, a good dancer, and your family owning a car all help" (p. 216). Cusick (1973), who found that it took having a motorcycle to join a motorcycle gang, further pursued "what it took" to be in a prestigious group by asking Debbie, the school's yearbook editor. She replied: "Well, like Alice got in because she's a friend of Dotty's and Barbara is a friend of the twins and they are in with Sally and Kathy, the two leaders." The editor went on to explain that "driving early" and "doing fun things" were important to getting on with the in group (pp. 153-154).

Debbie made these associations appear random, but at a deeper level they usually reflected parents' resources and social standing, particularly because adolescents enter school from class-segregated neighborhoods. As Coleman (1961) noted: "A boy or girl in such a system finds it governed by an elite whose backgrounds exemplify, in the extreme, those of the dominant population group. Hence, a working-class boy or girl will be mostly left out in an upper—middle class school" (p. 217).

Several writers have reported the social embarrassment that school brings to students with poor parents. Agee and Evans (1960), in their study of southern sharecropping families, reported a young girl saying: "My mother made me the prettiest kind of dress, all fresh for school; I wore it the first day, and everyone laughed and poked fun at me; it wasn't like other dresses, neither the cloth nor the way it was cut and I never..." and the mother, "I made her such a pretty dress and she wore it once, and she never wore it away from home again" (p. 74). And Lynd and Lynd (1929) reported a Middletown mother explaining why her son left high school:

> "We couldn't dress him like we ought to and he felt out of it," or "The two boys and the oldest girl all quit because they hated Central High School. They all loved the Junior High School down here, but up there they're so snobbish. If you don't dress right, you haven't any friends." "My two girls and oldest boy have all stopped school," said another mother. "My oldest girl stopped because we couldn't give her no money for the right kind of clothes...now the youngest girl has left 10B this year. She was doing just fine, but she was too proud to go to school unless she could have clothes like the other girls." (1929, p. 186)

The problem is not appearance; it is the class lines that students carry into school. Explaining class as social consciousness accompanied by common traits, Lynd and Lynd (1929) referred to the "adult world upon which the world of the intermediate generation is modeled" (p. 215). And Hollingshead (1949) described students of similar class and background forming groups and "clique ties [that were] strongly associated with an adolescent's position in the [community's] class structure" (p. 156). In Elmtown, where he divided the city into five distinct social classes, Hollingshead found "a corrected coefficient of contingency of .86 for the boys and .90 for the girls . . . when the clique relations of each sex were correlated with class" (p. 156). Class I adolescents in their groups aped the behaviors of their privileged parents. They had the clothes, the cars, the ready money, and access to their parents' possessions, club memberships, and lifestyle. With an easy sense of entitlement, they assumed they would be going on to universities and, furthermore, that they would inherit their parents' privileged place in the community just as they had inherited a privileged place in the school.

Among groups, mobility was limited to moving up or down only one class. Hollingshead (1949) found groups, usually of five students, in which there were three or four Class IIs and one or two Class IIIs, but never a Class II-III group with anyone from Class IV and Class V. In fact, the lowest on the socioeconomic scale, Class V students (those few left in school), maintained primary affiliations with peers outside school whom they expected to soon join.

Divisions by class make sense. To attain membership in an elite group takes a certain level of financial resources. Adolescents are very aware of who does or does not have wealth, certainly as aware as parents. Higher-class adolescents in Elmtown enforced class consciousness rigidly, and students without the necessary resources and background were simply excluded. Hollingshead (1949) recorded the perceptions that accompanied this enforcement:

> The Polish kids live across the tracks and have bad reps. . . . Everything is wrong with the kids May runs with. First, they live down by the old tannery. Their hair isn't fixed right. They're not clean. They don't dress well. Then May can't live her sisters' reps' down. (p. 163)

Not only did students enforce class distinctions, the parents, particularly of more privileged students, expected and pressured teachers and administrators to defer to their children. Expectations of deference went with being upper-class in a small town. In fact, two "community studies" included in this book, *Middletown* and *Elmtown's Youth*, both describe towns with fairly rigid class lines that the school was expected to respect and maintain. As a Class I parent said to Hollingshead (1949) concerning the teachers: "They are such fine teachers. They know the background of each child and teach accordingly" (p. 92). Upper-class parents used their influence to ensure that a girl from the "prominent families" (p. 138) received an academic award she did not deserve, and they demanded privileges, such as to excuse their child from inconvenient school rules. On the other hand, the school's treatment of lower-class students was frankly unpleasant. The principal, after releasing from detention an upper-class boy whose father had complained, was quoted as saying with regard to a lower-class boy:

Now there's a hot one. He's one of our wise guys. He thinks he's a hotshot. His old man is a laborer out at the fertilizer plant, and the kid thinks he's someone, umph. He'll be on relief twenty years from now. There's one guy I'm going to see put in detention. (Hollingshead, 1949, p. 140)

Parents even made personal decisions based on their child's position in the social structure. Lynd and Lynd (1929) described, in the days before car ownership was pervasive, the "persistent rumours of the buying of a car by local families to help their children's social standing in high school" (p. 137). Supported by the parents, class lines among groups and cliques were encouraged and persisted in school.

Although the upper classes expected a great deal from the Elmtown schools, including deference, lower classes expected little. In a discussion of "who influences Elmtown's school?" Hollingshead (1949) reported that "Class IV, as a whole, believed that nothing could be done to challenge the position of the 'inner ring'... [and] Class V people were almost entirely disinterested in the question" (p. 105). Disinterest, sometimes with a sense of resignation, in whatever would occur at school and perhaps in life was reflected by one of Willis's (1977) student's account of his parents' attitude toward his education and future:

I asked the old lady.... "Ain't you...bothered what I become, don't you worry about it like?" Her never said "What do you want to be?" Nor the old man never said anything. But she answered it in a nutshell. She said "What difference would it make if I...said anything?" Her said, "You'll still be what you want to be." So I thought, "Oh well." (p. 75)

The issue is not just parental expectations or influence. Hollingshead (1949) described middle- and lower-class students as frequently obligated to work and thus prevented from having the time to participate in activities. Lower-class students find it difficult to achieve high status in school. They have not been taught to think of themselves as competitors and achievers. The patterns and perspectives that students learn or inherit from their parents are very strong. In fact, class biases and prejudices seem stronger among adolescents than among adults. The school offers a location and time to reinforce their class and culture differences.

The argument is that student groups, even as early as elementary school, are universal, strongly normed, reflect students' social class and culture, and maintain boundaries coterminous with society's class and culture lines. Parents actively encourage this class structure by watching their children to ensure that they are learning and exercising their own (the parents') values. The descriptions indicate that student groups are not as friendly, fluid, and ad hoc as they appear. Groups are serious business, and, from the evidence cited, they provide the locale for teaching, learning, and reinforcing inherited patterns of social awareness, participation, and discrimination. In effect, the students' informal associations carry society's classes and cultures into the school where their varied classes and cultures encounter the school's more limited definition of appropriate behavior. Conflict between the school and the lower-class students is inevitable.

LOWER-CLASS GROUPS AND ACADEMIC EFFORT

The studies describe students as frequently antagonistic or apathetic to the schools' academic demands. The antagonism is particularly evident among lower-class students whose resistance heightens the differences between their own norms and the school's norms. The argument is that students who care little about what the school deems important retreat into their groups for refuge. Willis's (1977) "lads" and Everhart's (1983) "miscreants" not only came from the same lower social classes, but, according to the authors, were recreating their working-class culture while in school and in their groups. As have others who studied working- or lower-class students, these authors noted students' lack of involvement in the academic side of school and their decision to spend school time meeting with friends and carrying on group activities. In response to a question about what school had done for him, one of the British lads replied:

> I don't think school does...anything to you.... It never has had much effect on anybody I don't think [after] you've learnt the basics. I mean school, it's...four hours a day. But it ain't the teachers who mould you, it's the...kids you meet. You'm only with the teachers 30 percent of the time in school, the other two-thirds are just talking,...pickin' an argument, messing about. (Willis, 1977, p. 26)

Furthermore, the school's efforts to break these patterns avail little, partly because the students' perspective toward authority is one of resistance. Like Johnson's (1985) African-American males, Willis (1977) noted that the members of his group had devised a modus operandi toward school.

> [They had] adopted and developed to a fine degree in their school counter-culture specific working class themes: resistance; subversion of authority; informal penetration of the weaknesses and fallibilities of the formal; and an independent ability to create diversion and enjoyment. (p. 84)

Willis (1977) gave examples of resistance combined with diversion and enjoyment.

> Willis: What's the last time you've done some writing?
>
> Fuzz: Oh are, last time was in careers, 'cos I writ "yes" on a piece of paper, that broke me heart.
>
> Willis: Why did it break your heart?
>
> Fuzz: ...'cos I was going to try and go through the term without writing anything. 'Cos since we've cum back, I ain't dun nothing.... [It was halfway through the term.] (p. 27)

Everhart (1983) described similar behavior among his junior high school students who spent their in-school time baiting teachers, picking on weaker students, bantering, smoking, and defying authority at every turn. Following Willis (1977), Everhart related his students' behavior to their social class and to the status they would occupy as adults, a status that, according to both authors, was overtly disavowed but tacitly encouraged by the schools and by the society that sponsored the schools.

A similar view of class antagonism exhibited by adolescents was explained by Stinchcombe (1964), who suggested that among working-class adolescent males, defiance of authority, demand for immediate gratification, and appropriation of adult status are related to those students' inability to articulate in-school activities with their later lives. "High school rebellion, and expressive alienation, occur when future status is not clearly related to present performance" (p. 5). Because these working-class males could not envision themselves as attaining high status through education, they scorned the school's requirements, rules, and regulations. Patterns of rebellion and resistance may be much more visible with the lower-class or "tougher" students, but they are not limited to them. Although less overt, similar patterns show up among working-class adolescents.

Cusick (1973) found his working-class "athletes" at Horatio Gates High to be quite compliant with the rules and friendly with and tolerant of teachers. Unlike Willis's (1977) and Everhart's (1983) students, they were not rebellious, hostile, or teacher-baiting. But like Willis's and Everhart's students, their relation to the intellectual aspects of school was almost nonexistent. They agreed that one "needed an education" and that school had something to do with their life plans. Yet they did not study, did not consider prestigious careers or upward mobility, and did not articulate a relation between attainment of academic excellence and their later lives. Put another way, they understood the market value of a high school education, and were content to stay in school where they could be with their friends and where their size and athletic ability were rewarded. On rare occasions one might do some academic work that reflected, in a small way, his intelligence and ability. However, as a group they did not accept for themselves the idea of academic attainment as useful in a competitive world. They did not transmit notions of ability, merit, and achievement from the football team to their studies. So they did not act as if they understood that "individual differences in ability, motivation, and character define varying degrees of individual worth or merit ... [and] those with the most merit should receive the largest share of social rewards" (Labaree, 1988, p. 23). At the same time, as will be discussed in the next chapter, the teachers did not push the students beyond their limits. Instead, teachers accepted the students' view of academic achievement and allowed them to remain in their groups, where those views prevailed.

These students were quite content to stay in school but primarily as members of their peer groups. While in school, with few exceptions, they entered into academic endeavors only as far as group norms would allow. When and if they turned in their assignments, they copied from one another or had their girlfriends do them. They approached class assignments just as did Johnson's (1985) African-American males, Willis's (1977) lads and Everhart's (1983) miscreants. They kept their group between themselves and their academic requirements, and turned academic assignments into opportunities for group interaction. One of Everhart's students explained the practice:

> We've got this deal, John, me, Mike, and a couple other guys, like when one says something the other guy backs him up, helps him so he doesn't get into a lot of trouble. That's why the rabbit story was so neat. I was able to help John out by asking questions so he could finish his report. He hadn't even started it until we talked about it in class. (p. 175)

Johnson's (1985) African-American males, Wax's (1967) adolescent Sioux, Willis's (1977) working-class lads, Everhart's (1983) junior high friends, Hollingshead's (1949) Class IV's and V's, and Cusick's (1973) "blue collar athletes" were more attuned to the norms of their peer groups, norms which reflected their class and culture origins, than they were to the academic side of the school with its assumption of individual merit and subsequent upward social mobility. Academic requirements were filtered through the group, and the group defined the member's involvement with the school's formal goals.

Such attitudes toward academic achievement were not limited to lower- or working-class students, although they were easier to observe with those students, because their behavior was frequently contrary to school rules and expectations. Both Hollingshead (1949) and Lynd and Lynd (1929) described top groups in which academic efforts were as minimal as among the lower classes. Cusick's (1973) music-drama group, who "ran" Horatio Gates High, included some who bragged about doing almost nothing academic. The "doers" in Grant's (1988) Hamilton High were not noted for academic excellence but for political activism. Some of these groups included academic achievers who believed in the merit value of education or in the value of status attainment within the school. But they made their academic efforts as individuals. Otherwise they, too, stayed within their class- and culture-bound groups and away from students unlike themselves.

On the other hand, some groups center their activities around academic achievement. Cusick and Wheeler (1987) found several such groups: Wheeler in the "magnet" programs of his urban school and Cusick in the "honors" track of his suburban school; Grant (1988) also found them at Hamilton High. Both types of students, those whose groups centered around academic achievement and those whose groups did not, behaved similarly toward the school as a whole. For both academic achievers and academic nonachievers, the groups provide similar opportunities for social training.

RELATIONS AMONG PEER GROUPS

Basic to education in a democratic society is the idea of encouraging students to comingle with others from different backgrounds and thus learn to participate in a democracy. Indeed, Conant, whose *American High School Today* (1959) spurred the continuation and growth of comprehensive secondary schools, argued that in addition to providing increased academic opportunities, such schools would "prepare the...future citizens of a democracy" (p. 15) by "promoting an understanding between students with widely different academic abilities and vocational goals" (p. 20). The goal of promoting democracy has continued as schools have become more comprehensive and as student bodies have become more diversified.

However, promoting understanding among varied students is difficult. Often students, rather than opening themselves to those of different backgrounds and cultures, stay with their like-minded friends and reinforce extant class and cultural lines. Students find it difficult to extend themselves beyond their group norms, and those who do so risk censure by friends. The studies indicate that this is true in both the more homogeneous schools and in schools where the children of several social classes comingle. Lightfoot (1983) noted this Balkanizing in her study of Brookline High School.

> The distinctions of Black, White, and Asian were visible markers of group identification. A more discerning eye could pick out the Irish Catholic kids from High Point, the working-class enclave in Brookline, and distinguish them from the upper middle-class Jewish students. In this case, the divisions of religion, ethnicity, and class seemed to be more harshly drawn than the more obvious categories of race. ...Many students, for example, spoke of the divisions between the "indigenous" upper middle-class Brookline Blacks, and the "interlopers" from inner city Boston. Social class was a powerful divider and close friendships between these two (Black) groups were rare. (pp. 352–353)

Cusick (1983) found a biracial, urban, working-class school, in theory a hothouse for nurturing tolerance and participation, riddled with class and color antagonisms.

> The Blacks disparaged both those whom they called the "rich kikes" and the boys in the auto shop, whom they called "white trash." Some of those called "rich kikes" also referred to the boys in the auto shop as "white trash." The boys in the auto shop talked of the "niggers and spades" while they, along with other whites, were referred to as "honkies" by militant blacks, who reserved a special hatred of those whom they called the "colored," the "toms," and the "white girl lovers." Moderate blacks referred to the militants as "back biting _____" and most of the students scorned the drug users. (p. 22)

In that school one of the "school leaders," a white girl, said with a straight face and totally without guile: "Sure there's a lot of racism here but that's because there's a lot of white trash."

At Grant's (1988) Hamilton High, several designations of differences existed. One of Grant's associates, using terms that the students used, mapped this typology of subcultures based on seating preferences in the cafeteria:

Black
White
Black and white (mixed)

Preps (preppies, senior popular people, haughty people, rich cool seniors)

Druggies (burnouts, outcasts, people of all grades who play guitar or drums, smoke pot, drink and are violent)

Brains (geeks, weirdos, very intelligent seniors, honor society, smart people, ultra intelligent, computer people)

Losers (people without a group, loners and underclass misfits)

Breakers (break dancers)

Homeboys (downtown people, south side, the boys, poor blacks)

Theater people (chorus, dance, artistic types)

ESL (foreign kids, Asians, Koreans, Chinese, Japanese, Latin American, Hispanics, Spanish-speaking)

Poor whites

Special ed (autistic...wheelchairs, handicapped, "slow people—not retarded but not right")

Jocks (athletes) (p. 96)

Such distinctions among groups, often accompanied by suspicion and hostility, are common. Hollingshead's (1949) students were very careful about protecting class lines that were often marked by open antagonism. Willis (1977) recorded the scorn with which his students regarded those who did as the school authorities asked.

> I mean what will they remember of their school life? What will they have to look back on? Sittin in a classroom sweating their bollocks off, you know, while we've been...I mean look at the things we can look back on, fighting on the Pakis, fighting on the JA's [i.e., Jamaicans]. Some of the things we've done on teachers, it'll be a laff when we look back on it. (p. 14)

Although these class and cultural barriers persist among the groups, schools do contain opportunities for social mobility and for awareness of different backgrounds. School activities provide opportunities to those with energy, interest, and intelligence, and for those who can break out of their peer group roles. Cusick's (1973) music-drama group controlled the plays, publications, musical events, and some of the elections, and represented the student body to the administration. Common intellectual and political interests drew them together even while they retained strong affiliations with friends whom they had known for years. The formation of this group and the opportunity to join it had opened and closed quickly in the first year of high school. Once formed, the members maintained rigid lines and when outsiders tried to enter, they were rebuffed. An instance of this occurred when a nonmember auditioned for a part in the senior production, *West Side Story*.

> [She] asked Dick if she could try out for the show. He apparently said it would be all right because she got up and started singing "There's a Place for Us."...she was better than any solo singer I had heard in that school, far better, in fact, than the two popular girls who took the lead parts.... But the other students started giggling and tittering. Joan and Dick were grimacing at each other. Jim and Doug

started burping and the twins started giggling...[and Dick] called to her. "Marion, can you come tomorrow night? We have a lot to do tonight and really can't spare the time." (pp. 170–171)

Athletic activities are a source of mobility across groups. Even in class-conscious Elmtown, an athlete was likely to be valued, but not automatically. Hollingshead (1949) described a lower-class boy who made the football team, but after several in-practice "muggings" by his higher-class teammates, retired from participation. And Lightfoot (1983) noted that the social mobility enjoyed by athletes may be seasonal:

> Students point to the Black "jocks" and their similarity in dress and style to the White jocks. Their preoccupation with athletics becomes more powerful than racial affiliation. This group identification tends to be seasonal and shifts when football fades into basketball season. A different configuration emerges and many athletes may return to their old racial or ethnic groups in the off season. (p. 353)

On the other hand, intramurals are available as a source of mobility. In a study of an integrated suburban school, Cusick and Wheeler (1987) reported an upper-class student, who had already been accepted to Princeton, saying:

> You know what makes this school? It's the [intramural basketball] league.... Everybody plays two nights a week and then we go to someone's house to talk. I meet kids I would never meet. I have four friends from [the projects]. I won't see kids like that when I get to Princeton. (p. 41)

There are additional avenues for social mobility. Grant (1988) described several open to students in the Hamilton High of the 1970s. The drug culture was easily accessible to one who would participate:

> I met this girl. We were sitting down just having a cigarette, because you're allowed to smoke out back, behind the doors. It's not a rule that you can't. You can. And this girl comes out, and we were just sitting by each other, and then she started introducing me to all of her friends, and then we just started partying. It was like I was one of the gang. (p. 90)

Grant (1988) also described the war protesters, a group of eighty students or so, which included both drug-using countercultural freaks and political activists. "They published the underground newspaper; organized a Vietnam moratorium day" (p. 60). They also monitored the staff for violations of students' rights. However, Grant noted that many of these students were encouraged by their university-based, Vietnam war–protesting, rights-advocating, and, sometimes, dope-smoking parents, who backed their children in disputes with the school (p. 61). As one of these students said, "There are only two ways the school can control me—through my parents or through suspending me. My parents agree with me so the school can't use that method" (p. 61).

Another opportunity for social mobility was less voluntary and more coercive, but certainly was a chance to break away from one's background. Grant (1988) described middle-class blacks who, in order to maintain their status with lower class blacks, adopted a militant political perspective and ceased interactions with middle-class whites.

What has been described, with this overlapping of students' class and cultures within school is a difficult situation in which to teach democratic education. Students enter school with formed and/or still forming class and cultural perspectives and behaviors, along with groups of like-minded friends with whom they practice and reinforce these perspectives and behaviors. In school there are opportunities, certainly more than one would normally find in society, for learning about and participating with people from different classes and cultures. The informal groups, supported by neighborhood affiliations, parental expectations, family resources, and a differentiated school organization that places students in tracks with others like themselves, make the school goal of teaching democracy difficult to achieve.

Another factor that decreases opportunities for students to move across groups and increase their social options is work. Many students obtain jobs in their third and fourth year of high school and are unavailable for school-based opportunities. Cusick (1983) reported that half the juniors and two-thirds of the seniors left school after fourth period to go to work. To the dismay of the teachers, students would not come for the extra activities in which they might have developed relations outside their groups. A discouraged teacher explained:

> One time they tried to raise money for a booster club for the school, we went out and sold hot dogs and pop and candy at the games, and when we had money we wanted to have a dinner for the athletes at the end of the year. But so few people came it was embarrassing. OK, so you don't want to have a dinner, we'll have a trip. So more preparation and only a few people came there. Then we tried a canoeing trip up north, and there were more coaches and helpers than kids. Finally, I gave that stuff up. I don't know what they want...these are the less-affluent kids...we can't get them away from working and into school. (p. 69)

From the working- or lower-class student's point of view, not participating in activities is reasonable. After all, it is the student who spends the time in school, foregoes income, and thus bears the major cost of an education. For those who either need the money or do not see the value of increased education, work instead of school makes sense.

Time is a related factor. The years when students might break out of their childhood and early adolescent groups and open themselves to participating with students who are socially and culturally different passes quickly. As the perceptive vice principal of Horatio Gates commented: "High school's only two years long. After that it's a car, a girl, a job, that takes up their life" (Cusick, 1973, p. 25). Given the barriers and the brevity, it is much easier to stay in one's peer group and participate in the school through it.

That is not to deny the opportunities for social mobility and cross-group interaction, but they are mostly open to those who at an early age demonstrate some talent and energy, and who see involvement in school as somehow rewarding. Stereotypically, the good athlete, the attractive girl, the student on his way to Princeton, the talented musician, the curious and energetic, or those who simply understand the merit of individual effort, can either escape their groups or bridge to groups that encorporate school norms. For the less talented or ambitious, the "boys in the auto shop" or the lads, the angry African-American males, or the poor girls with shabby clothes, who see little hope for changing their status with or without the institution, there are few opportunities and little time for social broadening. It is easier for those students to stay in their groups where their status is secure, their attitudes and behaviors (and prejudices) unquestioned, and their social lines drawn and maintained.

Whatever the criticisms one can bring against schools' efforts at fostering democracy, one has to admit that it is an uphill fight against the students' class- and culture-bound groups and against their views of school and those different from themselves. One can understand the accusation by Johnson (1985), Willis (1977), and Everhart (1983) that the schools collude with the extant social structure and encourage and maintain already formed class lines. But the descriptions indicate that class and cultural differences brought in and exercised in school through the peer groups are very formidable. Publicly funded and community-operated schools may little alter these differences.

The descriptions indicate that from Middletown in the 1920s to Hamilton High in the 1980s, schools do not prevent students from carrying on their group life. That is not unreasonable. Students' personal lives, it can be argued, are really not the formal business of the school. Others might contend that the tacit approval of peer groups, and consequently, of continued class lines in school, however unintentional, frustrates rather than encourages the teaching of democratic principles. Still others find that the continuation of these groups, with their class and cultural differences, proves that the schools' overt purpose is to condition children to extant stratified social and cultural relationships, or more bluntly, to keep the lower classes where they are. According to this latter notion, not only do groups preserve and transmit class and cultural differences, they do so with assistance from the school structure.

The school gives the students time and opportunity to carry on their groups. And since groups are important to the way students behave and to what is learned, a description of the school structure is needed. Such a description helps not only with this chapter but also with subsequent chapters.

PEER GROUPS AND SCHOOL STRUCTURE

Schools are large, differentiated organizations. Their size and differentiation stem from two basic mandates—universalism and egalitarianism. Combined, these obligate the school to provide each student with opportunities for social, political, and economic equality. The universalism and egalitarianism have been strengthened in recent years with increased numbers of children in school and the government's policy of using education to transfer income to the poor. Schools of today include all young people, even the unable, the unwilling, and those who in former times might not have come or might not have stayed if they had come.

Universalism has increased student differentiation within the school. The more types of students the schools take and the more functions the schools take on, the more they have to provide separate and different opportunities and categories of specialists. Busing, integration, students' rights, special vocational education, and the recent wave of school reform, which has fostered honors and magnet programs and private-like academies, all serve to further differentiate the schools and further separate students from one another.

That makes organizational sense. As Thompson (1967) pointed out, complex organizations accommodate change by further specializing functions and personnel. Such differentiation serves an additional purpose. It allows the schools to implement high-quality programs, for those (frequently influential) few who desire it for their children, without upsetting the mass of people who are not interested in the effort that high quality requires. As Powell et al. (1985) argue, "the differentiated curriculum made it possible for secondary schools to accommodate demands for improvement at the top while still continuing the older, massive commitment to a weaker curriculum for everyone else" (p. 288). In sum, schools are complex and differentiated and are getting more complex and differentiated. Schools are large and offer specialized experiences with varied curricula for different students. Consequently, they are also very dense and have a great many activities and people crammed into limited amounts of space and time.

A structural element that strongly supports peer groups in the school is ability-grouping, which is based on the assumption that "students learn best in company with others like themselves" (Oakes, 1985, p. 4). As Johnson (1985) describes, it can begin as early as kindergarten:

> At West Haven the garden aspects of this grade are muted by the emergence of a new principle of school and classroom organization: stratification, the division of a social group into internally defined inferior and superior subgroups. Termed "tracking" at West Haven the homogeneous preschool student group is ranked, divided, then placed in different kindergarten rooms. (pp. 55–56)

Such ability-grouping continues all through school, and its use is presently increasing (particularly for the lower-achieving students) with increased use of state-administered graduation tests. In a state where such tests are used, an administrator of one of the school systems explained, "We'll have to segment off large numbers of kids who have trouble passing the tests. The kids at the low ends will have to study for some terms, or maybe years before they can pass them and that separates them out from the rest of the school" (Cusick and Wheeler, 1987, p. 16).

On the other end of the ability scale, that same school had implemented an honors program to assure the remaining upper-class parents that in the increasingly integrated school their children could take classes that would qualify them to enter the best colleges. That program further isolated students by social class and encouraged the continuation of peer groups along those same lines. Cusick and Wheeler (1987) described a remedial English class in that school in which the teacher told the primarily African-American students about some of their schoolmates who had won the academic bowl game on TV the previous Sunday. A girl in the back raised her hand: "I saw that program. I never saw those kids before. Do they go to this school?" (p. 28).

The result of the commitment to universal education and equal opportunity is that schools are severely differentiated and place great emphasis on maintaining their bureaucratic procedures. It is not only, as Callahan (1962) suggested, that schools have to present a business-like efficiency in order to satisfy public expectations. It is that with their size, differentiation, and many more subordinates than superordinates, they have to run smoothly in order to run at all and are, therefore, heavily reliant on a bureaucratic structure. The activities of hundreds of young people engaged in separate activities in separate locations cannot be left to chance, even for a few minutes. The schedule has to be planned and ordered; the routine has to be respected and maintained.

For the purpose of this chapter, this differentiated, bureaucratic structure and the maintenance it demands have two results. First, one of the schools' most important lessons for students is compliance with this demanding organization. Johnson's (1985) West Haven was not characterized by teachers teaching and students learning academic material, but by the constant enforcement and reinforcement of "proper" social behavior. The main lessons even from kindergarten on were "work quietly," "work by yourself," "raise your hand," "line up," "stand still," "control yourself," "obey the teacher . . . the aides . . . the rules." Whatever the content, the instruction was pervaded by an endless series of these directives. It is argued that teaching young children obedience to authority and compliance with organizational directives are major school goals. Those goals combine with and reinforce another organizational characteristic, that the mode of production is to be a single individual working quietly alone. It was to such directives that Johnson's (1985) African-American males refused to adapt, and so were judged "slow" and relegated to the bottom track. In other words, students more likely to stay within class- and culture-based groups that are not aligned with the schools' formal expectations find themselves relegated to slower and lower tracks. For these students, the groups serve as a refuge from the school with its alien demands and expectations.

Several authors, among them McNeil (1986), describe schools where, as she argues, bureaucratic control is the curriculum; content is reduced to worksheets, lists, short-answer tests, "brief, right answers, easily transmitted, easily answered, easily graded" (p. 157). She argues that for both more and less academically inclined students, teachers engage in instructional techniques designed not to instruct but to maintain control. In effect, it is the school's fault that the students stay unengaged with academic matters and seek involvement with one another. Metz (1978) too noted the inordinate amount of class time devoted to maintenance procedures that accompany structured written work and suggested that compliance with procedures was sufficient to ensure one's successful passage through school. She also suggested that it was primarily in the lower-achieving classes where "teachers used structured written work as a device to quiet a class or to keep it calm" (p. 103).

Whatever the interpretation of the descriptions—whether the bureaucracy is logistically necessary, whether control has unintentionally become the curriculum (McNeil, 1986), or whether the schools are engaged in an overt plot to keep the lower classes in their place by denying them knowledge (Willis, 1977; Everhart 1983)—it cannot be denied that the bureaucracy absorbs a great deal of the students' time and that teaching students to operate in a bureaucracy is a major school goal. Compliance with the school's bureaucracy is not very demanding and the dead time created by the routine provides opportunities for group activity.

That brings us to the second result of the bureaucratic structure, that it drives students away from academics and back into their groups. The bureaucracy absorbs students' time, not their energy, and for students in the midst of the differentiated and dense routine, there is a great deal of waiting around with little to do. Schools mass their people just as do armies, stadiums, and prisons, where people spend a lot of time waiting around for others to do something or watching others do something. In schools, the other is a teacher who, in the interest of articulating the school's limited notion of what is appropriate, initiates the activity and maintains the center of the interaction. Of the mass of students, schools demand attendance, passive compliance, and limited attention but not a lot more. Adding up the time spent on announcements or receiving assignments, coming and going, eating, waiting, and watching, and otherwise complying with the procedural demands, students experience a great deal of empty space in the day. As one of Willis's students quoted earlier said, "You'm only with teachers 30 percent of the time in school, the other two-thirds are just talking, ... pickin' an argument, messing about" (1977, p. 26). This phenomenon is not limited to comprehensive secondary schools. It happens in elementary schools. Jackson (1968) referred to the "delay, denial, and interruption" that characterizes life in elementary classrooms:

> Thus in several ways students in elementary classrooms are required to wait their turn and to delay their actions. No one knows for certain how much of the average student's time is spent in neutral, as it were, but for many students in many classrooms it must be a memorable portion. (p. 15)

Left to themselves, students turn to their friends, not to their studies. Most of the authors (Hollingshead, 1949; Willis, 1977; Grant, 1988; Johnson, 1985; Cusick, 1973) described students filling out the day's empty spaces with peer interactions. Indeed, why not? The opportunity is available, and as Czikszentmihalyi and Larson (1984) argued in their study of the internal states of adolescents, "friends can induce psychic negentropy—intrinsic motivation, feelings of freedom, happiness, and excitement—at least in the immediate present" (p. 156). Friends offer intensity and exhilaration that fill the empty spaces and offset the bureaucratic tedium. For students, the dead time magnifies the importance of having a group and helps one understand Ken's statement that he "couldn't stand to come to school because he didn't know anyone" (Cusick, 1973, p. 124).

The fact is that for many students, adult-guided, academic endeavors are not sufficiently attractive to offset the intensity and exhilaration offered by the ever-present groups. The group, or best friend, or simply "friend," is usually present in class and in an idle moment or when the teacher's attention is distracted or an interruption occurs; a glance can bring contact and the whole world of shared perceptions, private jokes, and interests are awakened. Students slide easily from class to group activity. To offset that tendency, teachers deemphasize cooperative projects and encourage instead each student to attend to his or her own learning. In effect there is a reciprocal and dynamic relation between the students' tendency to group and the school's approach to instruction.

Teacher efforts at group learning and cooperative projects frequently fail because as soon as the students come together, there is of necessity some slack time in which the students' group norms and behaviors can usurp the academic endeavors. In my own studies (Cusick, 1973, 1983), I witnessed teachers assigning group projects only to have students shuffle themselves into their extant groups, where group norms prevented anyone from bringing up the assigned topic. Classrooms are always described as busy, but the busyness is, in part, designed to keep the students from sliding into their always present informal associations. The academic material has to compete with groups for students' attention, and the material often lacks sufficient appeal to offset group attractions. Teachers find it more effective to keep the center position, personally direct the activities, and thus discourage the emergence of groups. The result is a strong emphasis on teachers maintaining centrality and a stronger emphasis on working alone by students. Thus emerges the second piece of the system being described. The first piece was the student groups that bring society's classes and cultures into school. The second piece is the overlapping of student groups onto the schools' approaches to instruction.

That students continue their group associations and activities in this free time is seldom regarded as a problem, because peer groups impose behavioral norms on their otherwise uninvolved members. For the most part, the groups support the bureaucracy's need for order. Some groups' interactions may be disruptive, as when Everhart's (1983) miscreants shoot and throw things and punch their friends. More often even these students are not primarily interested in causing trouble, or doing so to the extent of getting sent to the office and perhaps thrown out of school and so out of the group, but in having someone to talk to. Even the worst were careful. "You have to know just how much you can push a teacher if you don't want to get sent to the office" (Everhart, p. 186). Within their groups, students are reasonably orderly, and so the order imposed by group norms and the order imposed by the bureaucracy are intermingled and mutually supportive.

Cusick (1973) reported that the groups he studied monitored their members' compliance with the school's rules. The goal was to stay, not out of trouble, but out of excessive trouble, which would have excluded them from school and hence the group. In fact, for the athletes, a somewhat loose compliance with school rules was a strong norm. When some group members thought that their colleagues were skipping too many classes, they agreed among themselves "those guys are getting too wise" and informed the teacher. That particular group was also a source of information about the school's bureaucratic requirements. The members would keep one another informed about assignments and requirements, where to go and what to do.

In sum, the bureaucracy, with its rules, regulations, and differentiation supports and is supported by a peer group system that is strongly normed along class and cultural lines. Even while individual teachers may be trying to draw students out of their class- and culture-bound attitudes and perspectives, the school structure is inadvertently providing them with space and time to stay within them. The roles required by the strongly normed bureaucracy and by the strongly normed peer groups are supportive and overlapping.

On the other hand, the academic side of the school is much less strongly normed than either the peer groups or the bureaucracy, and it is particularly weak relative to the combined peer groups and bureaucracy. Several of our authors, Lynd and Lynd (1929) and Hollingshead (1949) years ago, and more recently Cusick (1973), Willis (1977), Everhart (1983), Lightfoot (1983), and Grant (1988), describe schools as academically undemanding for those students who did not demand much of themselves. Comparing schools to consumer-oriented shopping malls, Powell et al. (1985) noted:

> The mall works well because it is so exclusively governed by consumer choice. Learning is voluntary: it is one among many things for sale. The mall's central qualities—variety of offerings, choice among them, and neutrality about their value—have succeeded in holding most teenagers on terms they and their teachers can live with. (p. 309)

Lynd and Lynd (1929) found that "even straight-A students in this small Indiana city didn't work hard at their classes, [and]...while most students did very little homework, they got through school quite nicely—even in the top academic courses" (p. 237). Twenty years later it was no different in Elmtown where "the high school load is so light that very few students have to study more than an hour or two a week outside of school hours" (Hollingshead, 1949, p. 199). And fifty years later, Grant (1988) recorded a confirming interview:

Questioner: Describe a typical day for me.

Student: I get up, go downstairs, and eat, at about seven. Watch TV, smoke about half a pack of cigarettes. Go to school. Probably goof around all day.

Questioner: How do you get to school...?

Student: Walk. Probably smoke the other half a pack a day walking to school. Um, I go to school, probably goof off. Skip school, go out and smoke some reefer, and then, go back in school. Goof around a little more.... (p. 91)

One would wonder how such a student managed his classes, but the evidence presented in all the descriptive studies indicates that when a student does not flagrantly abuse the rules, it is possible to survive in school with minimal compliance. It is even possible to "goof around" and "um...goof around a little more" and remain in good standing. Our universal, comprehensive, and bureaucratic schools do not compel learning for those not so inclined. And only a minority are so inclined. As Powell et al. (1985) pointed out, "whatever the reasons most students had for coming to high school, a hunger for academic learning was not high on the list" (p. 237).

Of course schools encourage serious academic effort, but as Powell et al. (1985) also said, "it is voluntary" (p. 309) and therefore limited to those who see the opportunities that accrue to the more educated, or who, early in their lives, articulate the relation between individual academic achievement and their future state. Students with ambitious and successful parents who teach them such things are overwhelmingly advantaged. They enter school open to the opportunities and attuned to "proper" social behavior. As Johnson (1985) pointed out, those students are judged "worthy" even from the earliest grades, and are moved into the higher tracks, where they have greater opportunity for social and emotional interaction with teachers.

The argument is not that all students "goof around" or that a good education is not to be had. The argument is that it is the student's decision whether to participate normatively in school and those who come to school already socialized into achievement norms are most likely to do so. For students not so inclined, the strongest norms operating within the school are those of their own classes and cultures, which they continue and reinforce in their peer groups. The school bureaucracy is not sufficient to offset the power of the peer group.

Instead, the combination of peer group and bureaucracy encourages students to remain in their groups where academic effort, because it is individual, competitive, and merit-oriented, mostly opposes the group norms held by working- or lower-class students. In effect, those students are learning their modes of social participation from their peers. Johnson's (1985) African-American males, Cusick's (1973) blue collar athletes, Willis's (1977) lads, and Everhart's (1983) friends indicated they were quite unwilling to leave their groups and enter that individualistic, competitive, meritocratic world. They preferred to abide by the cultural norms they learned at home and were already socialized into when they entered school. So they participate in the larger school only marginally, resisting the blandishments of learning, intellectual pleasure, affective relations with teachers, and the upward mobility that academic achievement promises those who get on the track early.

The school structure legitimates extant social and cultural patterns that are practiced in peer groups as long as they do not obstruct the schools' bureaucratic processes. The school machine moves smoothly even while it contains and accommodates wide variations in student attitudes and behaviors. And so what students learn in school is that the cultural perspectives they bring— their modes of decision-making and participation and their values and attitudes toward achievement—are quite reasonable as long as they do not interfere with the bureaucracy.

An additional point is that the school's officially sanctioned, bureaucratic culture is extremely narrow. According to the vision, the ideal student operates as an individual who is orderly, organized, optimistic, time-conscious, compliant, and cognizant of the relation between school achievement and life success. For the school the task is to impose this narrow view of acceptable behavior onto students who represent the whole society and who, in groups, exhibit class and culture characteristics that are far outside the school's official vision. There has to be some compromise between the school and the social microcosm. The compromise is that the groups are allowed, even encouraged to continue, as long as their activities do not disrupt the bureaucracy.

There are different possibilities for academic involvement. One may abide by the school's chief norm, that one should work quietly by himself or herself, and as an individual obtain what each wants from the school. That would not deny group involvement, but the group would be kept separate from personal academic goals. Or there is the possibility for students among themselves and for students and teachers to create positive relations around academic content. Those who are selected for special academic programs can even find peer groups centered around academic achievement.

Powell et al. (1985) describe such positive teacher-student relations in what they termed the schools' "speciality tracks," the top academic, special education, and the serious vocational-technical lines. These tracks are selective; they receive increased resources; their classes are smaller; and their teachers give evidence of a certain élan because of their association with special programs and selected students. In such tracks, students and teachers do not "bargain" down the curriculum, make treaties to just endure the endeavor, or slide into informal groups. Instead they cooperate to create a normative society that elicits increased effort and subsequent learning. These speciality shops are for a minority, and except for special education, a self-selected minority. The middle majority, students who lack incentive, whom the school does not incite to academic efforts, and who lack positive relations with teachers, find themselves sorted to classes with students like themselves. For those students, peer groups become increasingly attractive.

In a way, the school's structure teaches all students a powerful lesson, that rewards are available for only a few and though the opportunities come from the school, the impetus comes from the student. Students who come to school without the correct orientation are likely to either remain without the rewards or have to defy their group norms to obtain them. Some do, of course. They form alternative communities with teachers around the academic material and so offset the attractions of group membership.

One might ask, as does Grant (1988), whether schools can do more to extend opportunities for teacher-student alliances and further decrease the influence of group membership. Grant argues that it is possible to develop a school community that would offset the group norms and barriers. Grant contends that the present system with its "corrosive individualism" (p. 1), at best encourages minimal compliance and, at worst, discourages academic effort by leaving each student and each teacher to himself or herself. Grant argues that the present school structure is a "minimalist contractual model lodged in a bureaucratic hierarchy" (p. 1), and is insufficient to either encourage academic effort in those not already inclined or to teach participation in a democracy. It is not enough, he argues, to open the school to individual educational opportunities: too few take advantage of them.

Like many school observers, Grant wants all students to share the opportunity had by students in private schools or in the "special" reaches of the public schools. He wants to see schools develop to be pedagogical entities having strong mores, an ethos, and communal norms in order to teach a responsible social morality, using the school itself as the training ground. Grant advocates a purposive school community to offset peer groups and to call students out of their separate classes and cultures into a learning community.

Grant (1988) buttresses his argument with examples from both private and public schools. Except for the speciality tracks described by Powell et al. (1985), the schools he advocates would be a radical departure from our highly politicized, universal, and publicly supported schools that have to accept and retain everyone. It could be argued that class- and culture-based peer groups with their norms and values may be simply too much for the school to counter effectively. The effort it would take to draw Willis's (1977) lads, Everhart's (1983) miscreants, or Cusick's (1973, 1983) working-class friends away from their groups or Grant's friend from his "um ... goofing off" and into a tightly normed school community where they would be expected to participate might be too much.

Building communities and using them for pedagogical ends is a very difficult task and carries no guarantee of success. It requires an ongoing analysis that borders on self-criticism. Lightfoot's (1983) exclusive Milton Academy is an example of how painful such self-criticism can become:

> the philosophical ideals of humanism invited tough self-criticism, persistent complaints, and nagging disappointments. Among students, faculty, and administrators, there was a clear recognition of the unevenness and weaknesses of their school. Criticism was legitimized, even encouraged. The stark visibility of the institutional vulnerabilities was related ... to a deeply rooted tolerance for conflict, idealism and to feelings of security. (p. 309)

As subsequent chapters show, universal, locally controlled and publicly funded schools generate little feeling of security or "tolerance for conflict." Nor is internal criticism encouraged. The school's mandated universalism and equality already stretch the public's tolerance for debate and the schools' tolerance for disorder, probably about as far as they can go. Public school administrators never feel sufficiently secure to encourage internal criticism. Instead their task is to assure a wary public that "all is well." If such ideals were difficult in the selective Milton Academy, which was attended by such world-class citizens as T. S. Eliot and Robert F. Kennedy, they are probably out of the question for our universal public schools. For the latter, it is easier and politically wiser to leave individual students to select their modes of participation, leave class and cultural differences alone, and informally let the groups serve as training areas for social participation.

The combination of peer group and school structure creates certain problems. It prevents the creation of a school community that might be used to teach broader social values and attitudes, and it discourages students, particularly those without a merit approach to education, from moving beyond their groups. It can actively discourage students from participation in academics, negatively influence the broad goals of democratic education, and encourage the more unpleasant aspects of class and cultural bias. Finally, school staff members can delude themselves into thinking of the students as orderly when in fact the students are perfecting a low-level anarchy, which they will use for the rest of their lives in relations with larger political structures.

On the other hand, perhaps this sometimes uncomfortable and sometimes inconsistent alliance between small groups and the larger school is just what is needed for a successful school and successful society. Perhaps this dual allegiance, to the school and group, is healthy, natural, and needed for a complete education:

> To prosper, man...needs to function on two levels at once. At the small group level, he treasures virtue such as loyalty and selflessness; in the extended order, he depends on narrow self-interest and the profit motive. So be it. The trouble is that man has often made the mistake of finding this apparent inconsistency uncomfortable. Hence his many attempts to stretch small group virtues over society at large. (*The Economist,* January 30, 1989, p. 85)

ON WHAT IS LEARNED IN GROUPS

The argument presented in this chapter is that peer groups, as they operate in school, reflect the social and cultural differences that students bring to school and limit the way their members interact with the school. The school's differentiated bureaucracy has a functional relationship with the groups. It supports them and is supported by them. Just as the bureaucracy creates time for students to interact, so the groups solve a problem of order that might occur if the students were not group-involved during that time.

Student groups not only take up time, they do a considerable amount of teaching. If we take a simple definition of learning as acquiring certain habits and attitudes, we may conclude from the descriptions that in their school groups, students learn certain things. They learn to practice social attitudes and modes of participation, to make judgments, to exercise values, and to refine social practices they will later use in society. They learn the benefits of associating in small primary groups and the opprobrium associated with violating group norms. They learn to express collective judgments about those outside the group, judgments that are frequently class- and culture-based. They learn to limit trust and involvement in formal structures while cultivating a personal affective realm. They learn that groups are difficult to penetrate and often treat outsiders cruelly. They learn that the school, and by extension the world, is competitive; that formal rewards are limited; and that certain students are, early on, advantaged in the competition. They learn that those advantages include not only ability and daring, but inherited social and economic status. They learn that those most favored by circumstances of birth or ability are most likely to identify with the larger formal structure.

Students also practice within their groups a disinterest in affairs outside the group. The less likely they are to succeed in competition for formal rewards, the more they practice that disinterest. In groups, the lower-class and those with few prospects gather to defend themselves against the pejorative judgments expressed by others. They guard themselves, avoid transcending personal interests, and use their groups to limit their at-large involvement in the school. Students also learn about the subtle and not-so-subtle ways that formal authorities select and groom the more talented, able, and advantaged individuals.

Students learn in their groups to differentiate formal from personal associations. They learn also the limits of personal associations, and that they may leave these associations to extend themselves and to expand their interests. Extracurricular activities are replete with such individuals. In clubs and activities students learn about the limits of their groups, and those with talent and energy can move beyond their groups into larger arenas. For school reformers, interested in extending the power of the larger structure relative to the individual, student groups are a problem to be overcome with alternative organizational arrangements. But such efforts might, as Grant (1988) argues, require a more heavy-handed organization than our "'new rules' culture can sustain" (p. 195). Building a community and using it for pedagogical ends are very difficult tasks.

Finally, there is the matter of the place and importance of student groups in the educational system. According to this argument, the school encounters society's classes and cultures among the groups. Students have to adjust to schools, but schools have to adjust to society's classes and cultures as exhibited by students' groups. The two forces compromise. For students, peer groups are a reasonable alternative to school-imposed definitions of appropriate behavior. Just as reasonable is the schools easy tolerance of groups, which give students an outlet for their emotions and energy and which keep them orderly during the bureaucracy's dead time. The compromise between the groups and the school is made by teachers in classrooms, and the next chapter looks closely at that compromise.

SUMMARY

The associations that students form among themselves constitute the first piece of the educational system; not the first piece in a linear sense, because the system is circular; but the first piece described here. Students practice class and cultural behaviors, which they have brought with them to school, in their associations, peer groups, and friendships. The values, beliefs, norms, and attitudes that they exercise in their groups include perspectives toward school, formal learning, authority, society, and the relation between school achievement and later life. Most of the conflicts in school are with students who learned early on that what teachers say is not necessarily true. These students are the most likely to join groups wherein resistance to teachers is itself a norm. All students, not only the lower-class, form groups and bring them into school.

Thus is the argument. Society, with all its class and culture differences, shows up in school where it faces the teacher in the classroom, every day. Onto this microcosm of society the teacher has to impose the school's narrow definition of appropriate behavior. The overlapping of school and society takes place in the classroom as students and teachers meet and work out an accommodation between what the school calls appropriate and what the diverse classes and cultures call appropriate. The first link in the system is students meeting students; the second link, attended to in the next chapter, is students meeting teachers.

3

Students and Teachers

INTRODUCTION

The preceding chapter describes how students, faced with the school's narrow definition of appropriate behavior, bring their class- and culture-based groups into school and intermingle them with the bureaucratic organization. The groups are natural; membership is based on mutual attraction; affinities are freely chosen; leadership and activities are decided by consent. There is some flexibility and movement across groups, but autonomy and isolation limit the ability of events in one group to much affect events in others. The aggregated groups make up a simple system with multiple and discrete parts.

For students and teachers, the situation is different from that of students and students. Classroom membership is assigned—not freely chosen. The teacher's leadership is ascribed, events are fixed and arranged, and coercion, both legal and physical, is possible. Most important, the classroom collectivity overlaps on one end with society's classes and cultures and, on the other, with society's official version of appropriate behavior. The classroom is the place where the society meets the school; it is the most important part of the system being described.

Several excellent studies form the basis of the general description and subsequent discussion of the classroom collectivity. To continue with the dual intent of increasing coherence while decreasing scene-setting, some studies are used from the last chapter, notably Everhart (1983), Johnson (1985), Willis (1977), McNeil (1986), and Lightfoot (1983). Also used are Kidder's *Among Schoolchildren* (1989), which concentrates on a single classroom, and Smith and Geoffrey's *Complexities of an Urban Classroom* (1968), which is a very careful description of successful teaching under difficult circumstances. Moore's *Realities of the Urban Classroom* (1967) is also used.

THE CLASSROOM SETTING

First there is the physical setting. Most of the authors, themselves long acquainted with education, pay little attention to the schools' physical environment. Anthropologists like Johnson (1985), however, look anew at physical and spatial elements that educators take for granted. "The nature and layout of the school campus, the structure and spatial divisions of the school buildings, the very chairs and their array, all these are products of the greater society and its culture—indeed they may at first glance seem so conventional that they fail to register... the significance of their presence" (Johnson, 1985, p. 334).

Johnson (1985) noted that the school appeared to be set apart from the community, constructed of different materials, and more formal and forbidding than other structures in the small town where he did his study. Moore (1967) noted his urban school's size, separation, and isolation from the decaying neighborhoods, and like Johnson, the school's formality and its physical barriers that intimidate visitors. Both noted school distinctions between work areas and play areas and the right-angled corridors and classrooms. Johnson suggests that schools' rectilinear design represents national values such as differentiation, progress, and stratification, and school values such as ranking, self-control, and obedience.

> Classroom sociocultural systems exhibit a core norm and value orientation... [which includes]... emphasis on temporal and spacial coordination, routine housekeeping tasks, ranking, the reinforcement of student self-control, compliance and obedience, regimentation, coming to attention and waiting. (Johnson, 1986, p. 51)

As a contrast, Johnson suggests that societies that emphasize curvilinear spaces, such as Hopi, Zuñi, and Inuit, emphasize community, acceptance, equality, and integration with local environments. Both Johnson (1985) and Moore (1967) noted that schools, even from the earliest grades, emphasize procedure, routine, and control. These core values produce an environment wherein acceptable behavior is defined as autonomous individuals working quietly.

Further, Johnson (1985) and Moore (1967) described the prominence of clocks, clocks denoting national time, which is crucial to the orderly functioning of schools and is itself a subject for classroom study, and the national and state flags, which display symbolically that the nation-state has sovereignty over the school complex and that the school complex is "a nationally rather than... a locally controlled space" (p. 19).

> Students continually are exposed to national socio-cultural orientations and traditions.... Standardized commercially produced classroom maps and globes visually refer to the nation and the world and celebrate and legitimize national events, heroes and leaders, the political structure of the nation and the political relationship of the nation to the rest of the world. No matter at what grade or at what age, then, students are continually exposed to... [symbols]... of American national society and culture. (Johnson, p. 215)

Both authors noted that time and space coordinated events and activities and, as grades progress, that spatial arrangements become more restrictive. Preschool grades encourage movement; later grades have less open space and less movement. This arrangement, argues Johnson (1985), contains the message that students are rational, malleable, and capable of orderly progression toward a more perfect state.

Within these physical environs, teachers and students come together in their rooms. "The task of universal public elementary education is still usually being conducted by a woman alone in a little room, presiding over a youthful distillate of a town or city" (Kidder, 1989, p. 53). A teacher's tasks are to obtain student compliance with and obedience to socially approved behaviors and norms and to teach content. A student's tasks are to comply with and obey the teacher and to learn the approved material and behaviors. These are by nature problematic undertakings.

> The problem is fundamental. Put twenty or more children of roughly the same age in a little room, confine them to desks, make them wait in lines, make them behave. It is as if a secret committee, now lost to history, had made a study of children and, having figured out what the greatest number were least disposed to do, declared that all of them should do it. (Kidder, 1989, p. 115)

One can take the teacher's enforcing of compliance and obedience as a necessary step on the way to instruction, a view conveyed by Edward Netski, the principal who told the author on his first day of teaching, "First, you get them to sit down and be quiet, Philip; then you teach them something." Similar is Chris Zajac's attitude: "She'd say at the end of a bad day, 'It's exhausting being a bitch.' But she never wearied of what discipline brought her. It allowed her to teach" (Kidder, p. 137).

On the other hand, one can take control not as a means, but as an end. Everhart (1983) and Willis (1977) argue that control—that is, socialization, not academic learning—is the "real" curriculum of schools, which are designed to teach the lower classes compliance with an unequal social system. Or one can take McNeil's (1986) view that control is neither a means nor an end, but one of two oppositional forces that dominate the curriculum: "school knowledge is shaped by the tension between the school's goal of educating and of controlling students" (p. 31).

The authors have different ways of viewing control, but they agree that school learning is loaded with institutional definitions. Students must learn not only content, but the approved content in the approved way. For the teacher, the goal is to impose the institution's version of reality on the students. The central issue is control, or "the relationship between teacher direction, usually verbal, and a high probability of pupil compliance" (Smith and Geoffrey, 1968, p. 67).

This chapter includes descriptions from several studies; it begins with more difficult situations. This is not done to argue that poorly controlled classrooms are the norm. They are not. But accounts of disruptions are needed to argue that such disruptions are not accidents or aberrations; they are potentially present in all classrooms and the possibility of their emergence is at the center of teacher-student relations.

THE BASIC ISSUE

Effort and quality may vary, but in working life compliance is not problematic. It is assumed that the secretary will file, the salesman sell, the clerk serve, the manager manage, and so forth. In the adult workplace, one's refusal to accept a legitimate assignment is an aberration, greeted first with disbelief, e.g. "Are you telling me that you refuse?" and followed with a set of disciplinary procedures. On the other hand, although the great majority of classrooms are orderly, pupil compliance with teacher requests can never be assumed; it is always problematic.

> The teacher-pupil relationship is a form of institutionalized dominance and sub-ordination. Teacher and pupil confront each other in the school with an original conflict of desires, and however much that conflict may be reduced in amount or however much it may be hidden, it still remains. (Waller, 1932, p. 195)

To illustrate control as a problem, some illustrations from the studies are extracted. Moore (1967) described a bad eight minutes in a second grade with one child who could not read, but who was extremely well-versed in what Moore calls "scene-stealing."

> Pamela starts looking on a desk for her nickel. She moves over and talks to another girl toward the front of the room. Miss Jorden puts an arm around her and tries to get her back into her seat in a friendly fashion.
>
> "Miss Jorden, somebody took my nickel," she repeats about six times in a loud voice.
>
> She then tells Miss Jorden: "Alvin has my nickel."
>
> Miss Jorden asks Alvin, "Do you have the nickel?"
>
> He says, "I do not."
>
> "He got my nickel," Pamela insists. She now has a red, white and blue scarf in her hand and is playing with it by putting it over her head, bringing it down over her face and wrapping it around her neck.
>
> Miss Jorden takes hold of her and asks Alvin again, "Do you have the nickel?" He says no and Miss Jorden says to Pamela, "OK honey, we'll look for it later."
>
> Pamela goes over to the closet, puts her scarf away and returns to her chair. But rather than sit down, she stands in front of her desk, going through papers, probably looking for the nickel.
>
> 1:50. She is pushing a girl out of her way. Miss Jorden tells her, "Take your seat."
>
> Pamela answers, "I am looking for my nickel, one of the boys wants me."
>
> Miss Jorden tells her, "He doesn't want you. No, he doesn't want you Pamela." She takes Pamela more forcefully this time and sits her down in her chair and addresses the entire class, "Boys and girls, did anybody see Pamela's nickel?"
>
> One boy reports, "It is Anne's nickel."
>
> Somebody else suggests, "Maybe Henry took the nickel."
>
> The teacher asks Henry if he has the nickel, but he denies it. Pamela is up and out of her seat again. The teacher instructs Pamela, "Turn around and sit down."

1:53. Pamela declares, "Henry has the nickel," and she looks at Earnest.

The teacher at this point says, "I am waiting for Pamela." In attempting to get order and quiet in the room, she instructs the class, "Put your heads down on your desk," but none of the children pay any attention to her. Pamela is still turned around looking at Earnest who is sitting behind her, and she starts calling out, "Miss Jorden, I lost my nickel."

Miss Jorden asks, "Do we call out, Pamela?"

This time Pamela raises her hand but still calls out, "I lost my nickel." (pp. 28–30)

In that room, the other students were paying no attention to the teacher, and the web of mutual expectations that constitutes an orderly environment was absent. One daring and troublesome student destroyed the classroom and the teacher's efforts at instruction.

Disorderly classrooms are dangerous, not only for students but for teachers. Moore (1967) describes another classroom where, as the students were fighting, running around, crying, and being roughly disciplined by an older and larger boy, the teacher was quietly writing instructions on the board. Moore suggested the teacher's actions as symptomatic of culture shock. "Putting written work on the board in the midst of all this bedlam is reminiscent of the disaster victims who do trivial things such as sweeping off the steps of a flattened house" (p. 69).

Open defiance is less common than incidents in which students respond to direction with indirection or passive aggression, or in which they steal the scene by dragging the teacher into trivial disputes about who took something or who hit or looked at whom. Johnson (1985) described several classes where students talk out of turn; they refuse to wait, to stay quiet, orderly, and working. In such classes "subtle tensions predominate...as if volatile pressures are being suppressed" (p. 174). And in some "out-of-control" classes, there is order, an order of battle, with students arrayed against the teacher. Opposition to the teacher can unify students with otherwise few common interests. Johnson described such a class in which the teacher "is flustered. She stumbles over her words, repeats herself and contradicts previous statements. Students watch and wait for her errors and when she makes a mistake or contradicts herself, some students...loudly point out her error" (p. 187).

Poor teachers have out-of-control classes but all teachers have difficult students and potentially out-of-control classes. Kidder (1989) chose to study Chris Zajac's classroom because of her excellent reputation, which his descriptions showed she deserved. Even Chris had to manage "an average of thirty disciplinary incidents during each six-hour day" (p. 33). She also had some very difficult students, such as Clarence, who did little work and required an inordinate amount of her time and energy. In one day

Clarence got angry at Alice over a classroom game; kicked Alice in the back of the legs on the way to reading; was rude to Pam, who scolded him; got even by punching Arabella during indoor recess; hit Arabella again right in front of Chris, which was unusual; and when Chris got him out in the hall, called her a bitch. (p. 99)

For Chris, Clarence "was like a physical affliction. Keeping down her anger at his intended manipulations exhausted her, and so did the guilt that followed from letting some of that anger out. He was holding her hostage in her own classroom" (p. 102). Her problems involved not just one student. The previous year, Chris had a gang of five "who whenever she turned her back, threw snots and erasers and made armpit farts at the children who were trying to work" (p. 35).

The disruptive Pamelas and Clarences pose one problem. Equally difficult are students who do nothing. Chris also has Pedro, who has respiratory problems triggered by anxiety. He sits "quietly at his desk, day after day, year after year, learning almost nothing, not even understanding half of what was said and never complaining" (p. 82). Mrs. Zajac worries about Pedro as much as about Clarence. She sees Pedro as a victim of circumstances. His grandmother (female guardian) wants to die, and his uncle (male guardian) wore "a leather vest, a tight white miniskirt and black mesh stockings" to a school conference (p. 84).

So far, the descriptions indicate that control problems pervade studies of elementary classrooms, even the best teachers' classrooms. Children who are difficult, disruptive, slow, and sad are everywhere. Some students oppose what the teacher presents or turn away from teachers who express foreign values or beliefs. Moore (1967) described Mrs. Schiller, who comes to read to a well-behaved set of students. With Mrs. Schiller the children become restless. Not only does she ask questions and then ignore those who are trying to answer, she does not know how to engage them. As she reads aloud from a book, "there is an undercurrent of whispering, Robert balls up a paper... another pupil is talking and makes a little noise..." (p. 105). After she finishes the story, which is about a recluse who lives with animals, she asks how the students feel about the man. "That man is crazy because he is talking to animals like they were people... he treats the animals as though they were people" (p. 105). When Mrs. Schiller admits that she too talks to her pets, the class laughs at her. Moore comments that these lower-class students reject the middle-class romanticization of animals and find the companionship of pets silly.

The argument is not that classrooms are out of control. Instead, the argument is that control is the major issue and always at the center of the student-teacher relations. Orderly behavior can never be expected; it is always problematic and always requires attention. Before describing how teachers handle the matter, some problematic situations in secondary schools are considered.

CONTROL IN SECONDARY SCHOOLS

The student-teacher relation in high school is one of the few authority relations in modern society whose maintenance is constantly problematic. Though authority everywhere frequently meets with lack of enthusiasm by subordinates, it is not often openly flouted and insulted.... It is consistently problematic whether orderly social intercourse will take place in classrooms. (Stinchcombe, 1964, p. 1)

The descriptions of difficult classes in elementary schools are replete with one or a few students like Pamela or Clarence, running around, making noise, stealing the scene, and in general behaving badly. Personal disruption is less common among older students. They know that they can be expelled, and they are commonly bound into group norms that include an accommodation with the school. But their resistance is more entrenched and more difficult to penetrate. Smith and Geoffrey (1968) described a class of seventh-graders, older than their classmates:

> Besides Leonard and Pete (two extremely difficult students) Mr. Geoffrey's class-room contained a number of troublesome children and a number of marginal ones. Two boys were on probation from juvenile court. Several of the boys just sat in class; they would do no classwork and if they did not disturb anyone, the teacher left them alone. One of the girls... was very overweight and each day would present a series of psychosomatic problems; she couldn't see; she felt dizzy; her nose was bleeding and so forth. There were a half dozen boys who were extremely difficult and hard to work with... generally they were engaged in all kinds of nonsense; they were inattentive; they were in trouble on the playground; they missed a lot of school. (pp. 213–214)

With older students there is less open rebellion, running around, and fighting. They understand the curriculum and general social conduct, and sometimes they may engage in the class. Yet if they do not like school and give repeated evidence of it, the teacher has to somehow accommodate them. Mr. Geoffrey found it difficult to deal with Pete:

> a very short boy, the smallest in the class... he does literally no schoolwork or homework. The kind of truce that Geoffrey seems to have made is, "if you sit there and keep your mouth shut and don't bother anyone, I won't bother you either." Second, even though he is the oldest child in the classroom, or at least one of the oldest, he has one of the lowest achievement records in the class. He can't do much above third or fourth grade level. Third, his general attitude is, "I can't, I won't, and you can't make me." (pp. 58–59)

Common among the older, more difficult students is not so much open defiance, but an ennui that can turn to hostility at any time. Cusick (1973) described a class where a teacher was trying to elicit a discussion of language. "Where do we learn to talk? Consider for a minute. Com'on, how do we learn?" Red, who was watching the teacher with disdain, replied, "In school, you have to go and listen to all these stupid people talk all day and that's where you learn" (p. 50). Leonard (1983) described a similar incident in a San Francisco high school.

> "Before we start the next lesson, I would like to say a few words about the last one." "Say a few words," a heavyset Samoan boy in the back row repeated in a loud mindless honking voice. No one paid much attention as Nick went over some common mistakes in the previous day's assignment. Now and then there would be a burst of restless talk or laughter. The Samoan recurrently repeated a phrase in the same loud expressionless voice. (pp. 61–62)

As often, it is not sarcasm or hostility, but students' paying no attention and just drifting into a state of lassitude. Lightfoot (1983) describes a class where "one [student] has her head on her desk and is nodding off to sleep; another girl is chewing gum vigorously and leafing through a magazine; a third student stares ahead with glazed eyes. The three never respond to the teacher's questions and remain glumly silent during the class discussion" (p. 38).

Groups play an important part in classrooms. The groups, representing diverse perspectives toward the endeavor, support a member who expresses their norms in conflict with the teacher. In other words, disruptive students are usually backed by a network of friends who cheer them on as they cause trouble for teachers. Peer groups are also adept at doing what Waller (1932) noted as "laughing off the teacher . . . taking refuge in self-initiated activities that are always just beyond the teacher's reach" (p. 196). Everhart (1983) gave an example of such a group subverting instruction. Mr. Von Hoffman was trying to elicit oral reports. John was unprepared but decided, with the encouragement of his friends, to talk about his rabbits:

"Come on John, give your report or sit down," Von Hoffman directed. John started but began laughing again.

"Great report, Mr. Von Hoffman," said Mike clapping, "give him an A."

"Outstanding," Chris said, "best report of the year."

"OK John, sit down please."

"No No, I'll give it. Tell Chris to stop laughing."

Von Hoffman then walked to the back of the room, stood next to Chris's seat and said to John, "Begin."

"I have some pet rabbits at home and I'd like to tell you about raising them. First you have to feed them and I feed them food that rabbits eat."

Chris raised his hand. "What kind of food do rabbits eat?"

John replied, "They eat rabbit food which I buy at the rabbit food store." (Everyone in the class laughed.) (p. 173)

At the conclusion of the rabbit report, Chris said, "Mr. Von Hoffman, I think he deserves an A." "An A like mad, just sit down and be quiet both of you. I don't know why you can't take anything seriously enough to do a good job on it. I ask you to give one oral report a term and you have to make a big joke out of it" (p. 174).

Students have several ways to resist the teacher. Wax, Wax, and Dumont (1964) describe classes for Sioux students at Pine Ridge, where the major characteristics of the

upper grades are silence and order. Hours may pass without a publicly audible word being uttered by a student. The extraordinary discipline in these upper grades is the creation of the Indian pupils who enforce it upon themselves and upon their teachers.

An Indian observer recorded such a class:

Teacher; "What do we do while we are in line?"

Silence.

"Do we push? Do we try to push somebody?"

Silence.

Teacher: "If you spill something, what do you do? Do you just leave it there?"

Silence.

> She now asked for a volunteer to write the rules on the board and stood there at the front of the room with chalk in hand pleading for one. Half the boys at the rear of the room raised the tops of their desks, some making a pretense of looking for materials, other just plain hiding behind them, while other boys tried to make themselves invisible. (p. 99)

These students surround themselves with a wall of silence, impenetrable by the outsider, and thus exercise control over the teacher. Silence was not the natural state of these young Sioux. "At about 11:00 she gave them a three minute recess. I went and watched them and, boy!—they were really teasing each other, noisy—like other kids....But when they went back into the room, they didn't make no sound" (Wax, Wax, and Dumont, 1964, p. 99). This description illustrates not only the problem of control in the face of group opposition, but the subtle and not so subtle tug-of-war between teacher and students over control of the class. In this class, the Sioux win.

Descriptions indicate that the most resistance occurs in classes where students care little about the teacher. Everhart notes that his students did not like Mr. Von Hoffman and so made systematic efforts to annoy him. They disliked (even more) Mr. Richards, who

> had the most efficiently run classes in the school. Papers were turned in in a uniform manner; books were stacked in a consistent way; he could leave the room for five minutes and rarely would there be a peep from anyone....But Richards was also one of the more disliked teachers in the school and that made students want to goof off far more than they did. (p. 184)

In response to Everhart's (1983) question about their dislike of Mr. Richards, the students responded by saying the class was boring. "You can't get away with doing that much, [he makes us] do the same thing over and over, prepositional phrases, prepositional phrases and we just do it over and over and over every day" (p. 189). "He'll give you detention if you pick your nose" (p. 184). Referring to classes that were boring, Steve told Everhart, "Class is so boring and you wanna have something to do that is fun, so you bug (the teachers) as much as you can" (p. 185).

Mr. Richards was considered "mean" because of "lots of stupid rules that did not make any sense: rules like having to print instead of write your name ...or rules like writing your names and if you didn't you had to do your paper again...or...doing 'stupid exercises' in grammar books" (p. 183). Those same students liked a science teacher because they "did a lot of fun stuff (experiments, played chess, developed computer programs, and the like)" (p. 184) and an art teacher because he permitted them to "sit together, talk while working on projects and he doesn't get uptight if we walk around a little" (p. 184). Consequently, the students did not annoy that teacher as much as they did Mr. Richards.

> There are certain teachers who were bugged almost incessantly, others who were bugged less. Whether a teacher was a target...was at least from the point of view of the students, dependent on two things: whether they thought they could get away with bugging them (or more accurately the degree of bugging they could get away with) and the personal relationship they had with that particular teacher. (p. 183)

A good personal relationship is important, but too much liking can be as much of a problem as too little. The students "liked" Mr. Carnova, but as Grant's (1988) description indicates, liking can defeat instruction.

> Students enter after the bell and constantly interrupt roll call with comments and questions. "Are you telling us our grades yet?" He answers patiently, "Your grades will be on your report cards," to which a student replies, "Report cards are for parents." He completes the roll call and reminds the class that the words on the board are for a spelling test Friday. A student shouts. "Right on! Why don't you give us those work sheets on the words?" Another student, obviously mocking one of the teacher's frequent comments, chimes in: "Take your time on that vocabulary, Mr. Carnova," and a chorus of others join the fun: "Take your time on that spelling, Mr. Carnova...take your time on that teaching, Mr. Carnova." He absorbs this good naturedly, apparently enjoying the ruckus as much as they and calling it to a halt just short of pandemonium. (p. 69)

Amidst this genial banter is the question of whether Mr. Carnova can obtain sufficient compliance to undertake the effort that learning requires. Grant (1988) thinks not. In discussing this, he argued that both Mr. Carnova and his students are victims of the Supreme Court's *Gault* decision of 1967 that students and their schools have the right to rule by law as opposed to rule by personality. This decision and the ensuing "students' rights" movement forced teachers like Mr. Carnova to win the students' friendship in order to obtain a moderate degree of compliance. Grant (1988) argues that a compliance based on friendship and geniality is not sufficient to induce students to do the work it takes to learn.

On the other hand, a lack of affect between teacher and students can ensure that nothing takes place. Cusick (1983) demonstrated the problems in classes taught by substitutes, who had no personal relations with students. In a usually well-behaved black literature class:

> The students started coming in class and after giving [the sub] a quick glance ignored her. Then they started to play cards. There were six of them right in front, others were talking and running around, coming in and going out of the room. She

attempted to get them to stop the card games and watch a movie on prejudice.... When the movie was over she wanted them to engage in a discussion...but...the students went back to talking among themselves, running around the room, playing cards, arm wrestling.... Referring to her plea to discuss prejudice, Mike said, "Lady, I've known that all my life." (she replied) "You're prejudicing me against you right now." "Lady, there's the door. You can leave any time you want to." (pp. 62–63)

Other subs had no more luck. One, after getting nowhere for half the period, was reduced to standing in the middle of room yelling "Quiiiieeeetttt... quiiiieeeetttt...quiiiieeeetttt!" A student looked at him and said, "Don't you yell at us." "Oh, I'm sorry. But I don't know how to get you to be quiet." "It doesn't matter. This is what we do. Just don't yell at us" (Cusick, 1983, p. 62). The sub retreated to the side and was himself quiet for the rest of the period.

One also had to be generally respected as knowing something, and most often something not conflicting with what students already value and know. Earlier, it was recounted how the students ridiculed Mrs. Schiller for talking to her pets. And Agee and Evans (1936) in their study of southern sharecropping families reported a case where instruction conflicted with beliefs:

Fred Ricketts...when his teacher said the earth turned on an axle, he asked her was the axle set in posts, then. She said yes, she reckoned so. He said well, wasn't hell supposed to be under the earth and if it was wouldn't they be all the time trying to chop the axle posts out from under the earth? But here the earth still was so what was all this talk about axles. "Teacher never did bring up nothin 'bout no axles after that. No sir, she never did bring up nothin 'bout no durn axles after that." (p. 304)

And when instruction conflicts with beliefs, students may just turn away from the instruction. Peshkin (1986) in his study of a fundamental Baptist academy, which sought control over its students' behavior and thinking both in and out of school, still had students questioning or sometimes not believing points of doctrine.

They're having this creation/evolution controversy, they're talking about it and they say, "Well, creation is a superior alternative....Creation is right and evolution is wrong." That's all they say and it's supposed to be giving both sides. But then it just cuts out evolution totally. I don't really care how it happened. (pp. 235–236)

In addition to disinterested, bored, troubled, hostile, rebellious, disagreeing, group-oriented, or antagonistic students, classrooms are also prey to irrational and unpredictable outbursts, even from attentive and orderly students. Cusick (1983) witnessed such class-destroying episodes in urban schools of the seventies when racial distrust was just under the surface and could emerge any time. He described one such class in which the teacher was trying to generate a discussion about prejudice. Frank, an avowed black revolutionary, stopped the class cold with a just-off-the-point question: "Mr. H,...how come everybody hates whites? What is wrong with whites? How come Chinese hate them, Africans hate whites, Indians hate whites, Spanish hate whites? How come everybody hates whites?" (p. 50).

For the first time all period, the class was perfectly quiet, but in a few minutes, the students were vigorously debating the point and, in a few more, both whites and blacks were up and yelling at each other about the real issue in that school—racial animosity. At one point, the teacher tried to make a reasoned discussion of the issue and was told by a white boy, "Shut up and let him [Frank] talk" (p. 51). The class further dissolved into threats with both groups talking of guns and calling out older brothers. The bell rang and it ended. The next day the teacher resumed lecturing and said nothing about the previous day's "debate" or about race.

Some of our authors, notably McNeil (1986), argue that teachers avoid substantial issues in class. She contends that the control purposes of school tend to force teachers to transform real world knowledge into school knowledge, "an artificial set of facts and generalizations whose credibility lies (only) in its instrumental value in meeting the obligations...of schooling" (p. 191). Those obligations force teachers to withdraw into the rituals of teaching and to split off what they know and care about from the trivialized knowledge they present to students. But when real issues are brought into classrooms, there is no assurance that they will be discussed peacefully or that the teacher will be in charge at the end of the class. Ideally a class would be a voluntary and free-flowing intellectual discussion with the teacher being the natural leader. Yet classrooms are neither spontaneous nor voluntary. The leadership, decision-making, topics, and even outcomes are bureaucratically prescribed. The teacher has to impose previously determined content, definitions, and behaviors onto students who come from as varied a spectrum of social classes and cultures as exist in society. Control is naturally a problem.

A teacher has to be careful about eliciting too strong a response. In a study of a Detroit Catholic high school, Cusick (1985) described a social studies class into which the teacher invited some Central American leftists who were active in the city's Hispanic community. Along with Hispanic students, that class also contained several children of Polish immigrants who had recently fled their communist homeland. The Poles reacted angrily to the speaker's suggestion that the United States' Central American policy was in error. With the Hispanics calling the Poles "fascists" and the Poles calling the Hispanics "communists," and more talk of older brothers and guns, violence in that classroom was barely avoided.

According to the descriptions of both elementary and secondary schools, several elements are capable of disrupting the relation between teacher direction and student compliance. Jackson (1968) points out that most students like school, their classrooms, and their teachers. Even Clarence, for all the trouble he caused, liked Mrs. Zajac and once told her he loved her. But liking is not enough. That children like their parents does not prevent them from at times behaving badly at home. Emotional attachments do not ensure compliance with authority or learning, nor that the students will stay on the approved topic, nor that if they get off the approved topic, they will get back on in the allotted time.

There can be and frequently are a few students in any class, sometimes more than a few, who do not like school, the teacher, the subject matter, or their enforced presence. Some students may be bored, dislike one another, distrust the teacher and, perhaps, the whole endeavor. Schools take everyone and assume that everyone can learn, wants to learn, and will come to understand that learning, or learning the positive abstract knowledge that schools teach, is both good and useful. However, this stylized set of assumptions encounters resistance when teachers bring it into practice. Many students have not been taught that academic learning, per se, is good or even useful. Okey (1990) pursued the notion of "school worth" with families of dropouts and found no parent with more than a bare instrumental view of education. These parents, their own parents, kinfolks, and children saw schooling as something one had to do in order to obtain an entry-level job—no more.

Even students who agree that knowledge is a good thing may balk at the work it requires to get it. The teacher cannot dismiss students who don't want to learn or send them to the office or to another teacher. Education is a right; schools are bound by egalitarian principles; they have to take, retain, and attempt to educate each student so that each may have an opportunity at social, political, and economic equality. Administrators do not like to shift students around after September. And the most disruptive students know that schools and the teacher have to keep them. They have been to the office enough times. They know that there are limits to administrative authority and that, except in extreme cases, their behavior will not elicit dire results. Expulsions are rare, physical force even rarer. Students know that teachers who send their problems to the office get a reputation as "unable to get along with the kids," a very pejorative judgment, and a frequent basis for dismissal. Students have to adjust to school, but teachers have to adjust to students.

The argument is not that classrooms are out of control or even that difficult situations are common. However, given that classroom doors are usually closed and that teachers are reluctant to admit control problems, no one really knows how common they are. Teachers do not go to the principal and tell him or her that they cannot control the class. Nor do principals go to superintendents or superintendents to boards and report control problems. One is expected to maintain control. And too, teachers have a way of playing down or passing over difficult or potentially difficult situations. Most often, if a subordinate calls his administrative superior "stupid," there would ensue some consequence. But when Red called the teacher "stupid," as in "you have to listen to all these stupid people talk," the teacher ignored the remark and went on. By playing down difficult situations, teachers reduce the impact of these situations on the rest of the class.

One does know that the studies related here were not undertaken with ineffective teachers in out-of-control classes. These incidents, with perhaps the examples from Moore's (1967) study, were taken from well-run classrooms with competent teachers. Indeed none of these studies were undertaken to describe control problems. The administrators who approved these studies and allowed these observers into the classrooms selected the better teachers such as Mrs. Zajac or Mr. Geoffrey. These real examples demonstrate that even in the best teachers' classrooms, control is the primary issue. It is always problematic.

That makes sense. After all, the classroom is not based on natural affinities, freely chosen. Students are placed according to age and chance, and sometimes ability, but not willingness and compatibility. Teachers are assigned according to subspeciality, time in service, and chance. The stylized school and the stylized classroom are constructed, furnished, and organized to permit a much narrower array of behavior than students bring in or are capable of demonstrating. The interaction between the teacher trying to enforce institutional ends and definitions and the students "striving to realize themselves in their own spontaneous manner" (Waller, 1932, p. 196) is always troublesome. Furthermore, given the range of possible disruptions and the myriad ways resistance can be expressed, control is not only problematic, it is only partial: particularly because disruptive students do not risk opprobrium from their peers who, being from the student's class and culture, will support a student in conflict with a teacher. Peer support increases the rewards and decreases the cost of bad behavior. The burden of control is on the teacher; the next section describes how teachers handle this central problem.

In sum, society overlaps into the school in the form of student groups acting out diverse perspectives. The teacher has to channel the students' diversity into school-approved norms and behaviors. The problem for students is diversity; the problem for teachers is control.

TEACHING AND CONTROL

The problem for the classroom group, or any group, is to establish norms. Its participants have to agree on and then submit themselves to some restraints. Ideally, control is self-imposed, as it is in small groups and happy families, where participation is based on mutual affinities, where members share values and understandings and cooperate willingly. They legitimate authority with collective approval and so expend minimal effort on maintenance. A society composed of such freestanding social units is an anarchist's dream.

Our system of universal public education is not an anarchy. It is a bureaucratic endeavor, organized and run with all the authority the state can muster. The school has to impose official definitions of appropriate behavior on students who, unless controlled, will exhibit as wide a range of behavior as exists in society. Teachers take the center position in the class and use their role to absorb, suppress, or iron out the irregularities. What teachers can handle best is their own behavior, and when faced with disruptions, potential disruptions, outbursts, hostility, or irrationality, they add control tactics to their behavior. For teachers, two parallel systems, the instructional system and the corrective-control system, exist at the same time.

Chris turned her eyes to the children solving problems on the board. "Very good, Margaret. Do you understand it now?" There was more whispering behind her. Again, her left hand shot back. "Horace, do your own work." Another flash card for Felipe while she called over her other shoulder. "Henrietta, come on up here." Then she turned her head all the way around, toward the low math scholars at their desks behind her. "Horace, are you all done?"

"No."

"Then, why are you talking to Jorge?"

She turned back around and said to Felipe and Jimmy. "What's the matter with you two? The minute I turn my back, you have to talk? What number do you carry Jimmy?"

"The four."

"Very good. Got it now? Okay Jimmy, you can go back to your desk." (Kidder, 1989, pp. 36–37)

Chris Zajac is thus in charge of herself, the students, and the classroom dialogue. She integrates corrective and disciplinary procedures into the flow of instruction. To say "control is problematic" in Chris's room does not mean that the class is out-of-control, but that Chris attends to it all the time, even as she instructs.

Of course, this may be somewhat easier when the children are termed "bright." Moore (1967) described Ms. Caplan teaching the brightest fourth grade class:

"What number would you try for the problem 5 into 185?" "Suppose there are 96 children and you want to divide them into 4 equal teams?" "Will 4 go into 16 again?" "What is a shorter method of adding?" "How many of you feel this is right?" To the student's correct answers she gives a steady stream of affirmative and complimentary responses. "Some of you are getting very good." "Yes, it (a whole number) can be anything. Can it also be money?" To a student with an almost correct answer, "Think a moment George. Is this correct?" The students are quiet, orderly, wait anxiously to participate. And it is not that she has the best students. Juan was a problem child in earlier years but presents no problem of discipline to Mrs. Caplan. (Moore, 1967, pp. 100–101)

Knowing her students, she evoked their own values when discussing Alaskan statehood. "If you do not belong to groups or to a family, you will feel very lonely and unhappy. This is how Alaska felt" (p. 109). The author describes her gentleness, sensitivity, alertness, and acceptance of the students, and draws the analogy between the class and a family or community. The description does not tell the story. "One cannot put a finger on the success of Ms. Caplan's teaching. The control in the class is so unobtrusive, one hardly knows it exists" (p. 120). If the children were allowed to spontaneously elect a leader, it would be Ms. Caplan.

Moore (1967) demonstrates a different kind of approach by Ms. Rosencranz, who is a terror.

"Take your things and go over and sit where Rose used to sit. For once, I would like to see your own work, not Helen's." To another child.... "Where are the questions? Where are you looking? Will you find it out the window? Turn around and get to work." (p. 125)... "Billy, what are you doing?" "I'm doing it over." "You're not doing anything over." "Close your books and get back to your own seats...Stand. Get into a line in front of the room.... Get quiet, I won't say it a third time.... Aren't you listening? What did I say?".... [to another teacher] "Would you like to throw two of your boys out? Particularly that bigmouth over there" (pp. 126–129). [to a boy who says "I lost my place now."] "You lost it *now*. You lost it *before*. I know you lost it *now*, sit down" (p. 136). "I am warning you Ronald, this is the last time this afternoon" (p. 136). "That's very messy; you will have to do it over for homework" (p. 126). These students are well-behaved, they perform, they learn their lessons. But they, and she, are cowed by the situation. She does not enjoy her time with the class nor her temper tantrums and threats. As she remarked to another teacher "After you've been here for awhile, you won't know who's crazy—you or the kids." (p. 142)

Using one's centrality to intimidate is one way to impose control. Another is to use the central position to socialize students into acceptance of appropriate norms. Smith and Geoffrey's *The Complexities of an Urban Classroom* (1968) illustrates a teacher who stresses group-building along with instruction. Mr. Geoffrey, the teacher, manages the classroom as a "complex pattern of activities, interactions and sentiments" (p. 49). He "grooves" his class into "a kind of interaction in which the teacher issues a series of minor directives and obtains a series of minor complying responses from the children" (p. 265). He molds the class into a coherent social system. To do this, he stresses two beliefs, (1) learning should be going on all the time and (2) learning is work. That means the students are to do things carefully, and they know that if work is incorrect, they will have to do it again. As a pupil raises a question, "Leave that open for anyone who gets his work done." ... (in discussing promotion), "That's not all; the most important thing is doing your work for me. Some of the assignments are difficult. Let's have no nonsense on not doing work...do your best and do it regularly." [On Friday morning, the first full day] "You've had a nice vacation and now it's time to get to work"...[on Friday afternoon] "School is business. Come back on Monday ready to work" (pp. 50–51).

Appropriate norms, equally appropriate roles for himself and his students, and an integrated and productive social system are Geoffrey's goals. He also encourages particular roles such as the "court jester" role for a particular student, and even a "nonparticipant" role for Pete, described earlier in this chapter. The complexity of this classroom results from the combination of these multiple and simultaneous roles, all operating on cues from the teacher.

Like Ms. Rosencranz, Geoffrey is a taskmaster. Unlike Ms. Rosencranz, he varies his behaviors according to the situation. His own role is the variable most under his control, and he uses it all the time, expanding, contracting, or adjusting it in order to keep the class moving. His is a varied mixture of bureaucratic leader softened with humor and drama. He paces lessons and tries for sequential smoothness and continuity. "Ringmanship" is the central concept that Smith, the researcher, uses to describe Geoffrey's approach. It includes elements of "autonomy and aloofness," skirmishing, banter, getting-off-the-hook, and even playing the "ferocious tiger" roaring at the students about their work and behavior (p. 127). With the "court jester," he banters; with Pete, he polices. For each of his students, Geoffrey wants to be the "focal other." He plays to each student's role. Geoffrey's classroom is a social system composed of different role sets, half of them his own.

In addition to taking multiple roles, Geoffrey is constantly evaluating situations and consequences that might flow from decisions. For instance, a decision about assigning homework entails considerations about the benefits to be gained and the students' academic difficulties, the lack of support for school work at home, the unlikeliness that homework will be turned in, the problems caused when assignments are not fulfilled, and so on.

The role of a teacher appears very effective as exercised by Ms. Caplan: interwoven with affective relations that bind the whole class to the teacher. Another way is Mr. Geoffrey's, which keeps the teacher in the center but emphasizes class norms. A third role is Ms. Rosencranz's, which controls the class by intimidation. Situations differ according to the people present, but in each situation, the problem is control and the solution is for the teacher to take the central role and use it to manage everything else.

To illustrate further, a few teachers in Cusick's (1983) Urban High seemed to have little interest in teaching and instead would engage the students in random small talk, which students did not find interesting, as evidenced by the number who put their heads on the desk. One such teacher, Mr. P, seemed to have no agenda except to take up the allotted time. He usually began his classes with some genial banter. "Hey is your hair getting thin?" "No man, it's just that I combed it different. Like it?" "Hey whatsamatter, you look down?" "Bucks lost man, that's my team" (p. 53).

After this exchange, he allowed a student to take a few minutes to sell Christmas candles. The student made his pitch and quickly sat down. Apparently having nothing else in mind, Mr. P then picked up the topic. "George, do these people know about your candles? You gotta tell 'em so they'll buy some. Come here." After demonstrating the way to sell candles, he told a pointless story about the announcer of a Chicago Cubs' game who, while on the air, drank a case of the beer he was advertising (Cusick, 1983, p. 52). Mr. P then assigned some work from the text, walked around the room, and made small talk with different students. His instruction was as aimless as his banter.

> One day he started on railroad mileage. Another teacher walked in. "Hey, I fixed your TV." "Oh. Excuse me," said Mr. P and walked out. Twenty minutes later he returned and he told us that he wanted to talk about the increase in railroad mileage between 1830 and 1940 and while he was reading the graph from the book, not one student was paying a bit of attention. (Cusick, 1983, p. 54)

Mr. P, and others who did as little, had an interesting time-killing control device. He took a potentially complex social situation and diffused it. He would walk around the room and engage this or that individual or group in random bits of small talk, about a piece of apparel, a sporting event, or a common acquaintance. His behavior could not be called teaching, although it kept Mr. P in the center of the room and in a dialogue with the students, a dialogue that he controlled. He selected the other party, he initiated the conversation, and he chose the topic. He also discouraged conversations in which he was not central. He thus prevented the students from either getting out-of-control or gathering among themselves to make a concerted demand, such as that he teach something. Even with non-teaching, Mr. P used his own role to control the situation.

In that school, beset with racial violence and threats of racial violence, where the administrators' only criterion was whether the "lid stayed on," Mr. P's behavior was acceptable. Furthermore, students accepted him uncritically. When asked about Mr. P, students would respond with "he's a good guy" (p. 55). Even though the students did not seem engaged in anything that could be called learning, they did not resent him. In fact, they reacted positively to his geniality, tolerance, and quid pro quo: "I won't bother you; you don't bother me." In that school and at that time, Mr. P was deemed acceptable. He controlled his class and did not have to call the office for assistance or send anyone to the office. His important referents, the students and administrators, were both content with his performance.

People who think hard about classrooms sometimes talk of their potential complexity. They cite the dense web of classroom interactions, numbering up to 200–300 per hour for the teacher (Jackson, 1968, p. 148), and sometimes use complex decision-making models to discuss teacher behavior. The observational studies of classrooms, however, give evidence, not so much of teachers dealing with complexity, as much as reducing complexity to what they can handle within their own role. Even those who don't teach like Mr. P, who banter away their authority like Mr. Carnova, who are disliked as was Mr. Richards, or who inspire fear like Mrs. Rosencranz, keep themselves in the center of attention and define the action through their own role.

Thus teachers solve the control problem: the class stays together, the focus stays on the lessons, and the peer groups with their differing perspectives are kept latent. Simplification of the social situation is the teacher's goal. Jackson (1968) reflected this simplification when he listened to the way teachers talk about their efforts. He noted that they do not use a complicated language. According to Jackson (1968), they "avoid elaborate words" and "shun elaborate ideas" about their efforts (p. 144). Manageability and control are what teachers strive for and what successful teachers attain.

Cusick and Wheeler (1987) described several excellent classes in their study of educational reforms. Both of their districts had, in the interest of retaining the better students, instituted special tracks, called "magnets" in one district, "honors" in another. As part of that study, Cusick followed the honors track in his suburban school and found teachers motivated and working hard to help students on their way to Stanford, Brown, and Yale. Those classes were characterized by enthusiastic and knowledgeable teachers, hard-working and attentive students, and an air of warmth generated by their mutual efforts. Control was exerted by the common understanding that these students were competing for society's preferred positions, and part of the competition was acceptance into prestigious colleges. Those students respected teachers for what they could do for their entrance qualifications. In these content-oriented classes, the teachers had knowledge that the students wanted. The teachers used their knowledge to control the classes.

Powell, Farrar, and Cohen (1985) extended the idea of achievement to vocational classes, where teachers and students place themselves within the discipline to be learned. Those vocational students also valued instruction relative to what it promised later on. But students who do not value knowledge, who do not see themselves as competing for society's higher positions, who do not articulate between school activities and their future status, are less willing to comply with classroom norms and so place additional burdens on the teacher.

CONTROL AND INSTRUCTION

So far, the purpose has been to illustrate how teachers incorporate control, which enables them to continue instruction. However, several authors argue that control is not the means of instruction, but instead is the end of instruction. Chapter 1 covers the notion of bureaucratic control as a means of social control. Here the argument is that students prefer control to the effort required for learning. Powell, Farrar, and Cohen (1985) described classes designed for the "unspecial students" where

> passivity rather than intensity predominates. The lecture method is popular in classes for the unspecial. One teacher said the middle kids were "desirous to have me lead"; they like to "just sit there and listen and take notes." They also like to stay with facts and details. "They'll get edgy when you start in," said one English teacher who encountered resistance to probing questions. "They say that you're destroying the story." ... They often preferred "busy work" such as worksheets because it's "controlled and structured and they can get immediate feedback and build up marks." (p. 186)

In such classes, materials are chosen less for their pedagogical value than for their contribution to classroom control. The mode becomes individual work, segmented material, and short answer quizzes. Metz (1978) described the use of such materials with lower-achieving students.

> The use of much written and individual work in lower level classes was partly a technological response to the constant threat or presence of distracting activity... if students are working individually it is possible for those so inclined to progress with their work despite the colorful or noisy activities of one or more others... teachers used structured written work as a device to quiet a class or keep it calm, partly because most students in Tracks Three and Four actively preferred this kind of work. (pp. 102–103)

Powell, et al. (1985) explained this technique as placing few demands on students unwilling to do much. In effect, the teachers made treaties to "not hassle" students by setting unenforceable standards. As one teacher explained, "We don't hassle them. At least I don't. I don't think anyone else here does." Another agreed, "I think I get along fairly well with most of the kids...but to be perfectly truthful I think I get along because I don't put a lot of pressure on them" (p. 76).

> Baxter's "workshop routine" was standard procedure in many other classes. The motives behind the treaty were clear: "because if you look at kids and say, 'They are out to get me,' and if I keep them busy, if I pass them a worksheet every five minutes,...then you have very busy, very quiet kids." The administrator concluded in frustration that "interpretation, analysis, inference, main ideas are really not part of our educational curriculum." (pp. 69–70)

One problem with that approach, as Johnson (1985) noted, is that the students least likely to put up with control devices are also those most likely to be placed in classes where there is increased control. In his study, students who behaved badly and were thus deemed "slow" were subject to increased doses of control, which elicited their negative reactions in the first place.

This matter of teacher's subverting instruction in order to achieve control was what McNeil (1986) described. Her complaint was not that there was control, but that there was so little else. From her observations she concluded that teachers were primarily interested, not in the topic and not in learning, but in controlling students and the flow of classroom events. She described teachers of both more and less academically inclined students engaging in four instructional techniques that are designed primarily to ensure control.

The first of these, which is prevalent "across differences in teacher ideology" (McNeil, 1986, p. 181), is fragmentation: for example, the "reduction of any topic to fragmented or disjointed pieces of information" (p. 167). The second is mystification: for example, to "surround a controversial topic with mystery in order to close off discussion" (p. 169); the third is "omission" of topics considered important by students. The fourth is defensive simplification: for example, "winning the students' compliance by promising that the topic will not go to any great depth" (p. 174). All of these techniques, in McNeil's words, "trivialize the content" and ensure that the teacher has the central role as well as classroom control.

Cusick (1973) described teachers limiting the dialogue and avoiding comments that fell outside a range in which they felt comfortable. When students asked teachers personal opinions on religion, another time about the (then ongoing) Vietnam war, the teacher told them to ask another teacher who "knew more about the topic." Or teachers might pretend there is a content-related dialogue going on even when there is not. Lightfoot (1983) describes a student telling the teacher, "This is a dumb course. I can't stand it." "Well, why do you say that? Is it because you don't want to do the work?" (p. 143). Teachers refocus student comments that fall outside the realm of acceptable discourse. One can understand why students say that teachers do not listen to them, however, for the teachers to heed them would take away from the central purpose—to control and suppress the elements that can interrupt or distract.

Later chapters will review some attempts to reduce the teacher centrality, which school critics frequently pick out as the element responsible for students' poor performance. Reform efforts frequently focus on reducing the teacher's centrality and creating open classrooms where students are allowed to more freely select material, to pace themselves, to work and talk with others, and to move around more. The assumption is that because students gravitate naturally to learning, a less restrictive environment will assist them.

However, studies cited here show that even otherwise compliant, middle-class students, when left alone, do not direct their energies into their studies. Instead they join with their friends to pursue activities and interests. Teachers then do what Goodlad (1984) asserts they always do . . . "talk and lecture [while] students listen and write." Even though teacher centrality in classrooms is often blamed for educational reforms being, in Goodlad's words, "blunted at the classroom door," he admits that centrality is reasonable given students' natural propensities to drift into their class- and culture-based groups.

> The organization and conduct of the classroom so that individuals work alone may not be conducive to productive team effort and the learning of collaborative values and skills, but at least it can prevent, to a considerable degree, the spillover of group allegiances and rivalries from outside the classroom and the emergence within of cliques and intergroup confrontations. (pp. 110–111)

Hence there is the overlapping between the informal student associations described in Chapter 1 and the teacher-student behavior described here. Because the students, when left alone, drift into their class- and culture-based groups and behaviors, control is always problematic, so teachers have to take the center and direct the class.

This section has broadened the discussion of control by suggesting that it is not only that teachers are obligated to impose control, but that students prefer control over the effort required for learning to take place. Learning is difficult; it is also a much more anarchic, uneven, and unorganized endeavor than teachers, textbooks, lesson plans, and fifty-minute periods portray. Few people, with the exception of Henry Adams (Adams, 1918), who in his middle years reviewed what he knew and how he came to know it, ever review their own learning. If we did, we might find as he did that our education took unpredictable and inexplicable turns, and that although we learned a great deal in school, we did it in our own way and on our own terms. Sometimes learning overlaps classroom organization; sometimes it does not. But even when it does not, the organization has to go on. Students understand and accept that, and some students understand it better than other students.

Control is particularly problematic with students from economically poorer families whose children are more likely to be placed in classes where control aspects are heightened (Johnson, 1985). From the school's view, those students need the most help, yet because of their distance from the school norms and values, they are the most difficult to help. Placing them in situations where control is heightened opens the school to the charge that it oppresses the lower classes.

TEACHING CHILDREN OF POORER PARENTS

Waller (1932) believes that in the larger sense, control problems are natural and occur wherever one party attempts to impose will on another. "Every social situation tends to polarize itself in the relationship of leader and led" (p. 189). Viewed this way, classroom control is not a problem as much as an inconvenient matter, to be handled by competent teachers and administrators.

> It is not clear that anything needs to be done [about rebellion] in a fundamental sense. The rebellion we talk about is basically an inconvenience to teachers and school administrators. Reasonably competent teaching and administration can exercise situational control, so that education may proceed. (Stinchcombe, 1964, p. 178)

On a day-to-day level—that is the way the control issue is viewed—as a fact of life, as something to be handled; no more a problem for competent teachers than is consumer choice for competent salespeople.

Something is missing from this explanation. If bad school behavior were totally natural, it would be more randomly distributed. But it is not. Children of economically poorer parents are the ones most likely to exhibit control problems, and most of the examples given of troubled classrooms were those that contained economically poorer students. That was not intentional. The studies were selected because they are among the best studies, not because they depict schools that teach poorer children. However, children of the economically un-lucky are more likely to steal the scene, drift off, oppose or ridicule the teacher, to display ennui, sarcasm, and otherwise disrupt proceedings.

Why is this the case? Why are children of the economically less-fortunate less likely to accept the school's definition of appropriate behavior? These descriptions were not taken from schools in what Waller (1932) calls the "bad old schools" [when]... "children had to do things they did not like because they did not like to do them" (p. 197). With the exception of Hollingshead's work (1949), they were taken from modern, reward-oriented classrooms with empathetic teachers who value friendly interactions with students and espouse progressive principles of flexibility, cooperation, and participation. These teachers do not start out looking down on poorer children; they believe in the perfectibility of human nature and the possibility of elevating all through education.

One explanation that should be dismissed is that these students are less able. Stupidity exists, certainly, but Frank's "Why does everybody hate whites?" is not a stupid question. Everhart's (1983) group had accurately assessed Mr. Richard's assignment and made a reasonable, even sophisticated, decision to subvert it to their own purposes. Wax, Wax, and Dumont's (1964) Sioux knew perfectly well what the teacher wanted and no doubt a lot more. Cusick's (1973) Red was giving evidence of boredom, not stupidity. Smith and Geoffrey (1968) described Pete as stubborn, not stupid. Mike really does know more about prejudice than the sub, and Agee and Evan's (1936) Fred, more about an axle (and maybe axis) than his teacher. And as Johnson pointed out regarding his rebellious black males, "They are certainly not dumb." Pamela, Joe, Clarence, and Lightfoot's (1983) female students might not have been among the more able, but they had correctly assessed both their teachers' wishes and the situation and were purposely refusing to comply.

Several elements are mixed into the conventional explanation. First among them is the students' parents. As the explanation goes, troubled students have poor parents who are themselves uneducated and have not taught their children basic skills. Therefore the children are unable to move along with their ever-progressing classmates; they become frustrated and behave badly. Teachers express it thusly: "They can't work by themselves." "If I ask them to do homework they don't do it. I gave in-class homework and six of seventeen handed it in. I gave out-of-class homework and two of seventeen handed it in . . . I stopped assigning it." (Why?) "They don't have anyone at home who cares about their education" . . . "They're blue collar" . . . "They're working class" (Cusick, 1983, pp. 47, 64–65).

As it is reasoned, parents of such students, being poor, do not provide them with a home environment that is conducive to learning personal responsibility and orderliness. For example, Kidder (1989) explains Pedro's problem; he lives "on a littered half-demolished street, behind an entry door with busted locks, up four flights of graffiti-covered stairwell that smelled of urine, in an apartment that was as clean as anyone could have made it, but that had unreliable heat and hot water, windowpanes that rattled in the wind, and lots of old woodwork painted dark brown" (p. 83).

And in Mr. Geoffrey's class, Pete's problem is that he

> had unhappy home life resulting both from a more intelligent and obnoxiously arrogant older brother and an apparently cruel father. The father had left. . . . Probably his character has been shaped beyond hope by his environment, especially the family, and the mother is a most unhappy woman in trying to deal with him. (Smith and Geoffrey, 1968, pp. 59–60)

Straitened economic circumstances, poor housing, troubled and troublesome siblings, a mother at her wit's end, and an absent and/or cruel father are stock ingredients of such explanations. So students' problems are attributed to the troubled, bad-behaving, uneducated, and lower-class parents.

Whether parents' economic circumstances and subsequent experiences are the cause is open to question. The juxtaposition and sequence of events make such inference convenient and conceptually appealing. It also places the blame outside the school. Popkewitz, Tabachink, and Wehlage (1982) noted that staff embraced students' economic background as a justification for stressing a basic curriculum and suggested that teachers see the problems of teaching as "uncovering student deficiencies in skills and implementing an instructional system to correct those deficiencies" (p. 127). Staff spoke of poorer students' need for "survival skills" and concomitant lack of need for "the arts." According to the principal:

> The importance of this style of life is that when students do not have enough affluence to appreciate the arts, the school program must limit itself to "survival skills." ...I'm a great supporter of the arts and I believe that those are the things that provide lasting impact upon a civilization...but if [a student] can't go and read a [concert] program, he isn't going to wind up as an adult enjoying those aspects. ...He is going to be too busy trying to survive. (p. 80)

Whereas the principal was talking about cultural inadequacy of children, the students about whom he was talking were not poor. They came from dual-income homes with a high level of affluence. This way of talking about students, as if they were poor and as if they were in need of basic skills, is common among school people who are striving to find a common denominator around which to initiate and continue orderly dialogue.

Another common element in the economic explanation is that poor students resist because the school, and the future it is to prepare them for, are foreign to them. The things they learn and practice at home are not the things the school expects and rewards. As the explanation goes, the school's values, norms, and curriculum present the most difficulties to the economically less-lucky. They are being asked to stop being poor and lower-class; to adopt professional-like work habits; to communicate solely with words, either written or spoken; and to adopt the model of a professional who works quietly by himself or herself. In addition, the school asks students to be time-conscious, orderly, and patient—qualities that one might not find in many poorer people. Classroom verbal patterns include deference to authority, one speaking at a time, and using well-modulated tones. Such verbal patterns are not the way of the African-American males or the adolescent Sioux. They are not the factory culture that Everhart's (1983) miscreants and Willis's (1977) lads learned from their parents, nor are they the way of working classes in general.

School culture extends through the curriculum. In the more advanced social science and humanities classes, criticism, analysis, and general volubility are valued, and students who exhibit them are rewarded and considered intelligent. Students of parents who encourage their children to speak up and out are school-advantaged from the beginning. But there are whole cultures in the United States that do not value criticism and analysis and that distrust people who practice them. There are cultures, which are by no means low-class, but wherein keeping one's mouth closed is a virtue and volubility a vice, wherein one is not asked or expected to volunteer what she or he thinks. Verbal patterns are more culture- than intelligence-based. The school culture favors the students whose verbal patterns match the schools' organizational patterns. Among those most disfavored by the school culture are the lower-class students.

Stinchcombe (1964) echoed an attitudinal difference among rebellious high school males who refused to accept the schools' authority, its constraints on their behavior, or the majority status system that it projected. He termed their behavior "rebellion" and demonstrated that it is consistently related to (1) short-run hedonism, (2) negativism, (3) perception of the status system as unfair, and (4) claims for adult autonomy (p. 116). The students' sense of what they considered acceptable contrasted sharply with the schools' emphasis on long-run goals; namely, a positive approach to what is deemed a fair status system and the doctrine of adolescent inferiority.

Neither were Stinchcombe's (1964) students "slow," but they too were among the lower social and economic classes as evidenced by the future that they projected for themselves. "Expressive alienation appears to be most common among the adolescents of school age who are exposed to more universalistic labor markets, and who will fill the manual working class positions in those markets" (p. 57). He also demonstrated that among the most rebellious males were middle-class youth who were unable to succeed in school and thus were on their way to the same "universalistic" labor market faced by lower-class students.

Stinchcombe (1964) asserted that straitened economic conditions do not "cause" social and emotional problems, which "cause" resistance in classrooms. Nor did he attribute the student deviance to lack of parental support. He argued that students from lower economic levels assess themselves as disadvantaged relative to overall society and equally disadvantaged relative to school. They "know" that what the schools proclaim about their chances for economic equality is false and so they refuse to conform.

Okey's (1990) work supported Stinchcombe's. Okey interviewed families of school dropouts, and reported that the families took the lowest, most instrumental view of education. None expressed any interest in what schools taught or displayed any curiosity that education might satisfy. They saw no relation between what the school offered in terms of content and what might be later required on a job. Entry into the lowest rung of the workforce was all they wanted and, because the required diploma could be gotten in the military or through General Equivalency Diploma (G.E.D.) classes with much less effort, dropping out of school was reasonable. Furthermore, the propensity of these children to run afoul of the rules and regulations confirmed the parents' view that the school did not like them or their children. These students' educational experience was primarily with the punitive underside of the school bureaucracy. In several ways, dropping out was a reasonable solution and, when the student dropped out, the family no longer had to put up with embarrassing scenes in the vice principal's office. Once out of school, the child could return to the good graces of the family. Everyone was happier.

There are several connected elements in the explanation of why poorer students do worse in school. Teachers' personal antipathy toward those students exacerbates the situation. "In most classrooms the behavior that triggers teachers' ire has little to do with wrong answers or other indicators of scholastic failure. Rather it is the violations of institutional expectations that really get under the teacher's skin" (Jackson, 1968 p. 22). Lortie (1975) described an additional element, the importance to teachers of good relations with students; of course, they are also important to students. Teachers treat students who support their efforts better than they treat those who do not.

Some of our authors have described the way teachers treat promising students, even in unpromising classes. Johnson (1985) noted that these were "singled out to be saved" by their teachers (p. 212). "Many teachers override the ideology of perfectibility by intervening to reach in and to help pull out the more 'respectable' students. The other students remain angrily at the bottom of the barrel" (p. 213). Kidder (1989) gave an example of a good student-teacher relation when describing Chris's favorite student, Judith. "Sometimes in the classroom, when Chris was smiling surreptitiously—at one of Claude's homework excuses say—she would look up and notice Judith, turned around in her chair and smiling, too, at Chris's efforts not to smile (p. 85).

Brophy and Good (1974) noted "...there is ample research to show that teachers like high achievers better than other students...students who are attentive, able to work independently, and compliant with teacher rules are especially likely to engender high positive expectations and favorable attitudes in teachers" (p. 336). Similarly students most likely to be rejected or turned off by teachers are those who..."have somewhat higher ability, but have negative attitudes toward school and teachers as well as a tendency to create discipline problems in the classroom through disruptive behavior" (p. 197).

Several of our authors add personal intent to the explanation, arguing that school people, working in places that are designed to reproduce the majority culture, purposely intermingle majority values with content to such an extent that lower-class students who do not espouse majority values are a priori disadvantaged. As Cuban (1984) explains:

> The School is the only public institution in the life of a growing child that stands between the family and the job market. The overriding purposes of the school, not always apparent but nonetheless evident, are to inculcate in children the prevailing social norms, values, and behaviors that will prepare them for participation in the larger culture. The structure of school life, what knowledge is highly valued, and what pedagogical practices occur, mirror the norms of the larger class and economic system. (p. 240)

A corollary of this explanation, according to Cuban, is that teachers personally espouse and embody the majority values of self-improvement, deferred gratification, self-discipline, and personal achievement that they teach.

A final explanation is that the schools and teachers are doing what they have to do in a differentiated and industrial society. Even while offering opportunity to all, they are sorting children along the lines of available opportunities. Top places in school, like top places in society, are limited and competition for them is intense. The school does its best to reduce inequality for individuals, but it is only school and cannot reduce the sum total of inequality. It is unfortunate, but it is a fact that poorer children enter school less-socialized to the norms and values of society and often without work habits needed to compete for society's better positions. Such students are more likely to resist and rebel against the school's efforts and subsequently are more likely to be relegated to the slower classes and eventually to the lower strata of society.

Several of our authors describe wonderful teaching with the lower-achieving. Cusick and Wheeler (1987) described a "law and society" class with one-half white and the rest black, Hispanic, and Asian students. The class was an elective for lower-achievers. The teacher set up a mock trial, and while preparing the students, interjected his humor and opinions constantly.

Explaining "expert witnesses"

"Dr. Verkampen, tell me about your credentials." "Vell, I have 17 PhD's. I've written three books, I've taught at the University of Paris, now the University of California at Berkeley." "See class, he's got the credentials." "May we enter this person as an expert witness?" "Yes, of course." He's entered. "Dr. V. Tell me, do you think John Hinckley is insane?" "Absolutely, he's loonier than a loon." Now you ask some guy on the street. "Do you think Hinckley is crazy? He shot the President." "Hell no, he took his gun out and aimed it." or "Hell no, it's about time somebody shot him." But these people don't have the credentials to be expert witnesses. (pp. 69–70)

When the trial was going on, the teacher continued his central role, standing slightly off to the left, calling back students who were drifting off, correcting mistakes, and looking sharply at a few talking among themselves. He also appointed students whom he could trust to play the key roles in the trial, and with their assistance and cooperation overwhelmed opposition from the less-interested. Even those who were obviously not prepared for their role in the trial were scrambling to do a good job when on the witness stand. It was a wonderful class.

Kidder (1989) illustrated Chris Zajac's creativity with this example from a day when she found herself getting nowhere with the math lesson.

Chris turned and wrote on the board:

$$296$$
$$\times 78$$

"All right, Jimmy, you go to the board."

Jimmy arose slowly, twisting his mouth. He slouched up to the green board and stared at the problem.

Chris sat down in Jimmy's seat. "I want you to pretend you're the teacher, and you're going to show me how to multiply and I don't know how." So saying, and in one abandoned movement, Chris collapsed on Jimmy's desk, one cheek laying flat on the pale brown plastic top and her arms hanging lifelessly over the sides.

A child giggled.

"Gonna get my attention first, Jimmy," called Mrs. Zajac.

Several children giggled. Jorge's eyes opened, and he grinned. All around the little room, heads lifted. Chris's mouth sagged open. Her tongue protruded. Her head lay on the desk top. Up at the board, Jimmy made a low monotonic sound, which was his laugh.

Abruptly, Chris sat up. "Okay Jimmy," she called. "I'm awake now. What do I do first? Seven times six is..."

Jimmy was shaking his head.

"No? Why can't I multiply seven times six first?" she said and she pouted.

There was a lot more light in the room now. It came from smiles. (pp. 42–43)

Excellent teachers can make up for but not eliminate the problems that poorer students exhibit. If and when students enter the classroom enthusiastic about the subject matter, and find a teacher equally enthusiastic, then the social system takes care of itself. If the students are resistant, the teacher has to pick up the elements of orderly discourse that students drop. Children of poorer parents, with their nonacceptance or even rejection of the school's basic assumptions, are more likely to resist and more likely to exhibit just those social characteristics the school is trying to change. With such students, control is more problematic. Control is not a school-fabricated issue. Control problems are the natural result of having to impose a narrow definition of appropriate behavior onto as broad a spectrum of society as exists. The students from the economic and social margins of society are likely to have the most trouble with the school's centrist values.

SUMMARY

The educational system is composed of a set of overlapping collectivities. The first collectivity is society, with all of its differences that it sends into school with its children and that show up in the way children behave. The next collectivity is the students and teachers, the former exhibiting their diversity, the latter charged with channeling the diversity into more narrow lines. The overall society, the student groups, the schools' official version of reality, and the students and teachers working out an acceptable mode are the elements. The overlapping creates the system.

The descriptions present a consistent picture of the classroom as the place where social reality runs into social ideals. Reality is represented by the students and seen most easily in their informal associations. The ideals are represented by the teacher, assigned to create a well-behaved, homogeneous, and purposeful entity from the diverse students, naturally prone to lapse into their class- and culture-based groups. Because much of their group behavior falls outside the school's definitions of appropriateness, control is the central problem. It is the teachers' problem, and they solve it by placing themselves in the center of the class and using their role, liberally mixed with their values, backgrounds, and personalities to manage both the students and the flow of events. For students, the problem is to mesh their class and cultures with the school. For teachers, the problem is to impose the narrow onto the broad. Subsequent chapters pursue this notion of control and describe the gulf that exists between teachers and administrators, who understand that control is the central problem, and groups further away from the schools who do not understand the problem or who misread its importance and centrality.

A criticism of the thesis is that control is overemphasized. But the issue emerged from the descriptive studies without prompting. It was not the author's intent to write an essay on control, rather, only to ferret out what is most common, as seen by knowledgeable people who record classroom events as they naturally occur. The descriptions show that control is the overwhelming issue, even in the best teachers' classrooms. Furthermore, it is not argued that control is not good or cannot be improved, only that it is central. It never goes away. Everything students and teachers do together centers around it.

4

Teachers and Teachers, Teachers and Administrators

Dealing in Symbols?

INTRODUCTION

The second chapter discusses how students, among themselves, use their groups to play out class and cultural differences that are outside the school's definition of acceptable behavior. The third chapter covers students and teachers. Expanding outward, the subject of this chapter concerns teachers with teachers, teachers with administrators, among themselves, working out solutions to problems that the system presents.

There are fewer descriptive studies of staff interactions than there are of student-teacher interactions. As Sarason (1982) says, "teachers are relatively autonomous in their classrooms, and within a school they have surprisingly little to do with each other" (p. 141). They also interact with principals "less frequently than one would think" (p. 142). And too, teacher-administrator interactions often cover personal or personnel matters that are too sensitive to include researchers or that have to be carried out according to contractual agreements stipulating who may or may not be present. However, several good descriptions are folded into studies that focus on larger school events, such as change, reform, curriculum, or discipline. In those studies staff interactions are described in the context of the larger events. Most of the studies have already been referenced: Grant's *Hamilton High,* Smith and Geoffrey's *Complexities of an Urban Classroom,* Smith and Keith's *Anatomy of Educational Innovation,* Lightfoot's *Good High School,* McNeil's *Contradictions of Control,* Cusick's *Inside High School* and *The Egalitarian Ideal and the American High School,* and Peshkin's *God's Choice.* Some of the classroom studies, Everhart's, Willis's, and Kidder's are also used again.

TEACHERS AND TEACHERS

School staff have a dual task: to instruct students in the several areas of knowledge and to manage students' coming and going. These tasks are handled by assigning teacher-specialists to batches of students during fixed periods. In elementary school, students are divided by age and to a lesser extent ability. Secondary students are divided according to subjects studied and to a lesser extent ability. This arrangement requires teachers to spend almost all of their working time apart from one another. Although this separation is frequently decried as a cause of teacher dissatisfaction and a barrier to reform, it is highly functional. Not only does it make pedagogical and organizational sense, it is, according to Kidder (1989), a form of "damage control" in a profession marked by high turnover.

> each teacher to her own room and her own duties...makes teachers conveniently interchangeable...and also gives an institution a ready-made system of damage control....When problems arise, they are isolated from the start in individual rooms. The doors to the rooms of incompetent and inadequately trained teachers can always be closed. (pp. 51–52)

To Lortie (1975), the isolation of teachers is an important characteristic of the profession, just as is their tendency to seek assistance from one another. "Teachers...work largely alone; there is little indication that they share a common technical culture. Yet we have observed that they turn to one another for assistance and consider peer help their most important source of assistance" (p. 76). In this first section, there are two interwoven themes, one is teachers' relations with colleagues, and the other is the way teachers interact as they carry on their duties.

Kidder's (1989) Chris Zajac maintains an ongoing dialogue with colleagues about classroom matters. She calls teacher friends to "discuss ways of handling Clarence" (p. 48). She confers with Debbie, the reading specialist; she works with Pam, her student teacher. She seeks out the principal when she wants something. She sees the vice principal about some students. She lunches in the teachers' room where "banter and complaints were more common than shop talk" (p. 49) and where the teachers talk about "wakes and weddings, sales and husbands" (p. 31).

Such interactions are peripheral to her central concern, her classroom, and she reserves attention for her students. When a minor disagreement arises in the teacher's room, "Chris held her tongue. 'If I worry about what everyone else is doing around here, I'll go out of my mind,' she told herself as she headed back for the lonely but safe and sealed-off domain of her own classroom" (p. 49). She respects the classrooms of other teachers. "The real test of a teacher was her conduct in class, and Chris had never seen most of her colleagues at work in their classrooms" (p 49). The respect extends to teachers even when they take her own students. When the music teacher took over her room and Chris went to the library, another teacher, Mary Ann, called out:

> "Chris, you can't believe what your class sounds like. Are they supposed to be doing that?" "They're having music...and Mary Ann, I don't want to hear about it."...A little later, Mary Ann called down again, "Chris, it's getting worse." "It's not my problem, Mary Ann." (p. 111)

Things happen in Chris's school: decisions are made, resources and assignments allocated. After a conference, Clarence is moved to a special program; Chris confers with school specialists, the psychologist, the reading teacher, the vice principal and principal. These people move into Chris's world, help her attend to one or another particular, then move back, out of her focus. Her classroom consumes her emotions, time, and energy. She does not become involved in others' work unless it affects her own.

Friendly and cordial, but professionally distant relations among teachers were what Cusick (1983) found among the staff in secondary schools. One of the three studies from the book was designed to trace curricular decisions *through* the faculty to see how the teacher network affected what individual teachers did in their classrooms. He found that in neither school did teachers consult with colleagues about classroom matters. Each decided what to teach, how to teach it, how to behave with students, and how to be involved with colleagues outside of class. Each taught selected subject matter deemed appropriate based partly on a personal and untested assessment of the students' "needs." An English teacher taught his "music as expression" elective from the lyrics of current popular music and from the work of black street poets. As he explained, "That's how to relate to these kids." The speech teacher worked on interracial relations and personal adjustment. Down the hall, a social studies teacher insisted that students memorize the preamble to the Constitution and "learn the Pledge of Allegiance even if they can't spell it and study and understand the Bill of Rights and . . . salute the flag" (p. 81).

As far as Cusick could determine, these individual approaches were based on the teacher's own values. The social studies teacher taught the Pledge and the Preamble because, as he explained,

> [the students] don't know anything about their country and they don't have any appreciation; all they know how to do is shout some empty slogan that they heard somewhere and that they don't begin to understand and that passes for knowing something. I won't let that happen in my classes. (p. 81)

An English teacher taught the philosophies of Aristotle and Plato, which he had learned years earlier in a seminary because, as he explained, "the unexamined life isn't worth living." Not only did each teacher have a personal approach, each had a personal justification for the approach and some favored students, who by responding positively, justified the approach.

Each of the three schools also had an approved curriculum and department chairpersons and department meetings; one had an assistant principal for curriculum. None of those people or events, however, could offset the teachers' personal approach to subjects and students. In neither school were the department meetings designed to make decisions about common activities as much as to ensure that one teacher's established fiefdom did not interfere with another's. In the suburban school included in that study, one person was removed from his subject area chairmanship because, as the principal explained, "he wanted to go in classes and check (other teachers') lesson plans." The assistant principal for curriculum at Factory High busied himself with test results, supplies, budgets, and central office relations and when the need arose, as it frequently did, he would join with other administrators to "sweep" the halls of unwanted intruders. In all of Cusick's schools, teachers created their curriculum as each wished. The system was explained succinctly by a teacher who told Cusick, "It's like this Phil, everybody subcontracts" (p. 94).

In her *Contradictions of Control* (1986), McNeil reported similar autonomy and similar distance among faculty in the four high schools she studied, even in Nelson High where

> the staff was organized from the start to consider the content behind course titles and credits; this consideration belonged to principal and teacher alike, in concert with each other. (p. 136)

It was Nelson High's faculty that had adopted a curriculum that "brought together concepts and methods of inquiry from varied social studies disciplines" (p. 139). "Ninth grade focused on world backgrounds up to 1500...tenth grade ...covered the years 1500 to 1870...world conflicts in contemporary history from 1870 formed the eleventh grade course...the senior course was contemporary issues" [with an emphasis on] each individual developing as a thinker, individual, and citizen (p. 139).

General agreement about content was as far as agreement went. "Within the department...all teaching styles are different" (McNeil, 1986, p. 151) and teachers behaved accordingly. "Mr. Lancaster's curiosity knew no limits; his course content...was constantly changing in its particulars. He continually sought new information, read scholarly and news publications, and brought his findings into his classroom" (p. 140). "Mr Hobbs...read widely and gathered material for his classes from many sources. Unlike Mr. Lancaster, he was more organized and demanded more concrete involvement from his students. His course was centered on textbook assignments, with added lectures and films and considerable class discussion based on Socratic-style questions" (p. 143).

Mr. Guthrie, the department chair

> based much of his economic content on his personal experience and on his expectations for the students' future. Since most of them were middle-class and lower middle class, he assumed that their adult lives would follow at least a pattern of trade school or university, steady jobs and modest investments. In his economic units he combined printed handouts, in abundance, with speakers from the community. (p. 146)

Teachers at Nelson were free to select favored material, to develop their own style, and to close the door against intrusion. Like Mr. Guthrie, they were even free to proceed from their own assumptions about the students' future.

In Chapter 1, it was argued that students, when left alone, exhibit in school the class and culture differences that they learn out of school. Teachers have to impose a narrow definition of behavior on this range of classes and cultures. At the teachers' disposal are legal and bureaucratic authority and their own values and personality. They combine these in idiosyncratic ways and keep themselves in the center of the class, thus smoothing out irregularities and irrationalities. In this section, the argument is that teachers not only use idiosyncratic approaches, but behave with colleagues in ways that protect each other's rights to do so. Thus there is an overlap between the way teachers behave with students and the way they behave with colleagues.

There is also the school's need to be rational, and in times of scrutiny and criticism, increasingly rational. School improvement advocates often push for a more collegial school organization wherein teachers interact and work closer with each other. The assumption is that closer cooperation will improve teacher satisfaction, teacher effort, and eventually, student learning. These ideas, which are enjoying a resurgence in the early 1990s, were also part of the early 1970s "open classroom" movement described by Smith and Keith's (1971) *Anatomy of Educational Innovation.*

> The setting was Kensington school, a unique architectural structure with open-space laboratory suites, an instructional materials center, and a theatre.... The program exemplified the new elementary education of team teaching, individualized instruction and multi-aged groups. A broad strategy of innovation... the utilization of temporary systems, and minimal prior commitments was devised and implemented. The intended outcome was pupil development toward maturity—a self directed, internally motivated, and productive competence. (p. v)

Referred to as "open education," the governing idea was to build the organization around student learning, not student learning around the organization. Teachers were told to "individualize," "humanize," "dramatize," "socialize" (p. 23). The program began with a month of group training to prepare faculty for a more flexible and student-centered school. Teachers found group-building interesting and involving, but the business of the group was unfinished when the students entered in September. Throughout the year, it never became clear how group-building efforts crossed over into the work of the school.

Smith and Keith (1971) illustrated the problems of collegial decision-making in a school setting. One day, the first-second grade team, which had four teachers, had decided to go for PE at 10:45. Sue decided things were going so well with her second grade that she did not wish to break. Another teacher took the seventy first-graders while the remaining two took a fifteen-minute break. Smith and Keith spoke to those two

> about the problems attendant to this kind of spur-of-the-moment decision-making. In this discussion, both Jean and Elaine saw very clearly the problems that this brings about. Jean mentioned that this "lack of structure" bound her a great deal. ... In my own self-contained classroom, I had all the freedom in the world. I could extend a learning experience or shorten it or cut it completely if I wished. Here I'm forced into a rigid schedule... the freedom that they wanted was the thing that

inhibited them and made them more rigid. Elaine agreed that 25 children and a self-contained classroom would be far superior for the very objectives that they wish to achieve. (p. 151)

Although the teachers worked hard to avoid the "fate of the self-contained classroom" (p. 152) they had difficulty in reaching consensus about such matters as grouping students, methods, and subject matter. Even maintenance decisions as how to lead the children to different parts of the building and how much noise to tolerate became difficult and time-consuming. Inability to reach consensus and the corresponding inability or unwillingness of the pupils to channel their new-found freedom into learning left the teachers tired and discouraged (p. 157) and David disillusioned and disenchanted (p. 157), and the principal, Eugene, troubled and discontented (p. 158). By December, Eugene gave up on group decision-making and unilaterally issued his own rules about behaviors and procedures.

In discussing the difficulties of implementing open education, Smith and Keith (1971) offer several ideas. They argue that the presence of hundreds of children make it difficult to keep things open and flexible. Large numbers require quick decisions based on few facts. "Frequently in the team, decisions would be made and the results would be forgotten in the press of a later, particular situation" (p. 223). Furthermore, teachers had personal demands that prevented them from giving the time that the endeavor demanded. Kay was sick for the term, Jack had district-wide responsibilities, David was somewhat up and down, Tom was the school's materials coordinator (p. 223). Their various demands prevented teachers from creating a decision base from which they could create some discernible order.

On the other hand, the authors argue that in a self-contained classroom

the teacher has considerable freedom to organize her day and her mode of instruction as she desires. For instance she can be a traditional textbook teacher or a Kilpatrick project teacher. She can integrate science and math or English and social studies into a core curriculum or teach each subject independently. She can proceed abstractly at a verbal level or introduce concrete manipulative materials. She can accentuate objectives such as the learning factual material, abstract integrative concepts or critical and divergent thinking. She can establish relationships with the pupils that go by labels such as democratic or autocratic, learner centered or teacher centered, informal or formal. (p. 218)

The authors argue that large numbers of children and multiple activities require more certainty than "open education" allows. Smith and Keith's story, from the beginning of the year, is of putting that certainty back into the school. There seem to be sound reasons why teachers keep themselves unfettered by colleagues and in sole control of their self-contained classrooms and why the Kensington effort to increase collegiality began to end almost as soon as it started. Kensington was not alone in those years, either in ideas and efforts or in results. Cuban (1984) reported, "by 1975, interest in open education had flagged considerably"

(p. 188) in favor of self-contained classrooms, skill-oriented instruction, and monitoring student progress through tests.

It should be noted, however, that fifteen years later some Kensington teachers remembered the effort as an emotional high. Kleine recorded recollections in that later study when a teacher was asked to describe those years.

> I think a lot of it was successful...it wasn't Utopia, it was nowhere near perfect, but there were so many good things that happened between people of all ages, small ones, big ones, grown ups, kids—but it wasn't self sustaining. It didn't continue...it was something that happened for a year that lingered for a second year and then gradually.... (Smith et al., 1986, p. 268)

Discussing Kensington school, Smith et al. (1986) referred to Thompson's (1967) notion of pooled and sequential interdependence. In schools with a series of self-contained classrooms, certain things are given; that is, numbers of students, minutes, (often) the curriculum, bus schedules, materials, and the measured passage of students through the years. Within this framework, each teacher works to maintain some independence, to avoid interdependence wherein "the moment-to-moment, the day-to-day, and the weekly and monthly activities of one teacher could be contingent on other teachers" (Smith et al., p. 213). Finding reciprocal interdependence unworkable, teachers retreated to a system of pooled and sequential interdependence and limited peer influence. In such a system, faculty interactions are kept at an informal and voluntary level: teachers can both seek advice as they wish and remain unfettered as they wish.

Gold and Miles (1981) studied a similar attempt to implement open education in an elementary school, and their study will be described in the next chapter. For now, it suffices to add that when the teachers who had implemented "open education" came under siege by board and community, they developed an internal support system that would have been the envy of schools trying to build faculty teams. The collegiality, however, was a defensive reaction against hostile outsiders; it did not extend to curriculum building or instruction.

In self-contained classrooms, teachers may not only be better able to handle the exigencies occasioned by crowds of children, but are less likely to generate external criticism occasioned by the visiting parents. The beliefs, biases, opinions, and opposing views that can arise around any educational idea or program are legion and often unresolvable. Opening the school to public scrutiny invites criticism. A system of self-contained classrooms and separated teachers may be less likely to generate criticism and better able to deflect criticism that arises. That is not to say that teachers do not cooperate. These and several more descriptions show they do. But it does say that the problem posed by crowds of students in dense and busy schools is best handled by assigning individual teachers to sets of students and by giving those teachers broad discretion. What teachers do with teachers is a distant second to what they do with students.

TEACHERS AND PRINCIPALS

The next group on the organizational ladder consists of teachers and administrators. These people operate in the same setting, have adjoining duties, and have myriad occasions for formal and informal meetings. Theirs is an organizationally arranged relationship weighed heavily upon by the bureaucracy, by district and state policies, and by contractual agreements. Moreover, the sign that is seen when entering so many schools, VISITORS MUST REPORT TO THE PRINCIPAL'S OFFICE, is not only an admonition to visitors, it is a reminder of the way schools work. The principal is in charge, and what comes into the building to the teachers must pass him or her. This section describes what passes between these parties and how it passes.

Sometimes it is useful to begin an account of what happens with an account of what does not. Classroom studies such as Moore's, Willis's, Smith and Geoffrey's, Johnson's, Jackson's, and Everhart's, all cited earlier, do not report the presence of administrators in classrooms or much direct interaction between teachers and administrators. To the degree the principal is present in these studies, she or he is busy with activities different from those of teachers.

In Moore's (1967) descriptions of seven classrooms, across three schools, there is a single mention of a principal. The author notes that he was described by the teachers as well-liked, but "beset with the problem of faculty recruitment; while the teachers, all new to the school though not necessarily to the neighborhood, are beset by a high turnover of pupils" (p. 51). In his *Life in Classrooms* (1968) Jackson says nothing about administrators, their interactions with teachers, their presence in classrooms, or their influence on classroom events. His singular reference is an account of his own study of good teachers. His procedure in that study was to ask administrators to nominate their "top" teachers whom he then interviewed "to see how they warranted the honor. He found among other things, those so designated (1) were emotionally charged, (2) gave evidence of caring about students and (3) 'did not want their classrooms invaded by administrative superiors bent on evaluation'" (p. 129).

Notions of physical distance between teachers and administrators, of teachers wanting administrators to leave them alone, and of administrators liking teachers whom they can trust and therefore leave alone, recur in Everhart (1983). He described the principal of Harold Spencer Junior High as

> a very direct and imposing individual whose very demeanor created an air of authority and control that often intimidated student, staff member and fieldworker alike. More often than not teachers called him Mr. Edwards, perhaps symbolizing the distance that remained between them and him. (p. 32)

Mr. Edwards said he likes and respects the "traditional" teacher who "did his job, was willing to spend time with students, maintained an orderly classroom and would comply when called upon to serve on district-wide curriculum and policy boards" (p. 36). At the same time, he kept his own role quite clear.

> Edwards liked to make all major decisions himself, and only reluctantly did he delegate decision-making authority to vice principal Pall or teachers. He looked disdainfully at the new breed of principals who were "managers" and who delegated excessive authority to subordinates saying that a principal had to be on top of everything and know exactly what was going on all the time. (p. 32)

Even though for years Mr. Edwards had resisted their desire to "change the schedule from a six to a seven period day...on the basis that it would disrupt the lunch schedule" (Everhart, 1983, p. 34) and even avoided social functions where teachers were present, teachers liked him because he was a well-organized disciplinarian who left them alone.

These studies portray the principal as an authority figure, usually respected, sometimes liked, not sought out except for particular permissions, and depended on to maintain an orderly school. This view is supported by Kidder's (1989) description of Chris's principal, Al, who thought of himself as "responsible for every teacher who walks in this door. Not that I'm in charge of everybody...but I'm responsible. Come in, talk, and I'll decide if we're gonna do it" (p. 44).

> Al was Chris's government, all the government she knew. But Al did not imagine himself expert in instructional theory and practice. Mostly he visited the classrooms of new teachers who needed help in keeping order. This year he'd observed only one lesson taught by each of his veteran teachers. After watching Chris in action, he'd say little more than she was doing a good job. (p. 47)

Chris respects Al because he cares about the school and the staff and because "he wasn't fastidious about every little rule. He wasn't one of those principals who made a hard job harder" (p. 47), because "on really important matters, he usually did what was best for the students" (p. 46) and because "around Kelly school the threat of a trip to the principal's office had weight. When Chris sent a child, Al almost always took some action" (p. 47). In turn, Al respects and values Chris as evidenced by the fact that he left her alone.

Teachers and principals maintaining a respectful distance also comes through in Smith and Geoffrey's *Complexities of an Urban Classroom* (1968). In his study of Mr. Geoffrey's classroom, Smith mentioned the principal, Mr. Inman, only a few times. Two of those times occurred in descriptions of faculty meetings where the limits of mutual interest were revealed.

> The principal spoke at some length about several issues; one of these was the transportee problem, and the fact that the school would have bussed-in pupils and teachers for the first time this year. He made it very clear that his position was that these pupils and their teachers were members of the Washington school and were to be treated as such...the board's position on the administrative difficulties of integrating these children...seemed supported by one of the comments of a transportee teacher who said that they might have difficulty making out their lunch tickets by 9:00 because sometimes the busses didn't run true to schedule....The principal talked a bit about the fact that there had been very little

vandalism during the summer time, in spite of the fact that Geoffrey counted at least seven windows that were cracked or broken wide open in his second floor room (which is not above a playground). The principal commented...that every school has some problems...that children are children everywhere; and... that there were some unique satisfactions in teaching children from less privileged areas. He commented that he was ready and willing to help them with discipline problems...but he expected teachers to tell him what they had already done about the problem before they brought the problem to him personally. (pp. 24–25)

The principal faces the assembled teachers. He speaks, they listen. The topics are the minutiae of the organization: transportation, lunch tickets, bus schedules, tardiness, vandalism, and "other details concerning the building" (Smith and Geoffrey, 1968, p. 25). Important was his admonition that teachers were primarily responsible for discipline.

Smith concluded his account: "The teachers make only a few comments. After forty minutes the teachers filter back to their rooms. The ritual contains one final element: teachers must stay until 3:30" (p. 25). Smith and Geoffrey's only other example of direct interaction between principal and teacher was in a later faculty meeting when Mr. Inman reminded staff of the coming parents' evening. He apologized for asking them to come out in the evening, to that decaying neighborhood, and asked them to be considerate of the few parents that might show up.

Concerning matters originating outside Mr. Inman's building, from the community or central office, principal-teacher communication seems to work like this. Some distant event would foment a situation that demands action. A decision would be made, given to the teachers via the principal, and the teachers would work it out. For instance, in late September it was decided that a room would close and a teacher would be released or transferred. It was unclear who made the decision, or why, and it was particularly bothersome to Mr. Geoffrey and the others who had to receive new students and to start the classroom socializing anew. Teachers took the new students, made the adjustment, and went on.

Mr. Inman did not seek teachers out to explain things, nor did they seek him out, except for permissions. When Geoffrey and another teacher wanted some students scheduled differently, they "consulted" the principal after they had worked out all the details—only his final permission was needed. The way Smith described this was interesting.

These problems prevented Geoffrey and Norton from asking Mr. Inman to allow them to trade classes in areas other than reading. They realized Mr. Inman did not especially like the trading practice and they were reluctant to approach him when he was engrossed in so many other difficult issues. (p. 161)

On a related decision, when Geoffrey and Norton were continuing their discussions of trading students, Smith said that "to the best of my knowledge all of this is being carried out unbeknownst to Mr. Inman" (p. 168), who the teachers know does not like ungraded classrooms (p. 166), and who "would probably be less disturbed if only a few [students] were affected" (p. 167).

Geoffrey and his colleagues know some things about Mr. Inman. He does not like ungraded classrooms. He does not like to have the routine upset. Changes should not disturb the schedule he has worked out. He is concerned about race and integration; he is busy and his time is therefore respected. Teachers are circumspect in their interactions with him. Smith's story is consistent with other studies that describe the principal as a distant presence, who teachers believe is involved in important yet different activities.

The "principal as a distant presence" theme is echoed in Johnson's *West Haven* (1985). There, the principal was involved, at least initially, in curriculum. The impetus for his involvement was the state's recommendation that "each teacher, along with the principal, write(s) a classroom schedule for the manner in which these required subject areas are to be implemented" (p. 89).

In subsequent descriptions, Johnson made no mention of this state recommendation being carried out or of the developed plans. Nor is there any mention of the principal entering classrooms or of having a planned or even a casual interaction with a teacher. In the one case, a teacher referred to a principal not as a person but as "the administration," as in "the administration... feels that if a student is performing (reading) so poorly that he or she must be retained at a grade level, it is the teacher's fault for not working hard enough to bring the student up to 'ability' to pass the test" (p. 177).

Several themes are emerging. One is the echoing of Sarason's (1982) statement that "principals interact with teachers less frequently than one would think." A second is, as Lortie (1975) says, that "teachers do not depend greatly on the school hierarchy for technical assistance..." (p. 76). A third is that although the two parties operate in the same building, each has separate activities and concerns: the principal has the details of the building and the teachers have students in classrooms. The elements that make up the routine of one party are quite different from the elements that make up the routine of the other. Fourth, there is no sense that the parties are working on solutions to mutual problems, except in indirect ways. Principals want teachers to get along with students, to take care of their own problems, and to leave them (the principals) alone. Teachers want principals to manage the organization, to maintain an orderly and supportive atmosphere, and to leave them (the teachers) alone. Principals do not need a lot of interaction with teachers to carry out their duties; nor do teachers need it with them. From these studies, even those from elementary schools with no vice principal or department chairs, one gets the sense that principals and teachers behave as if, in the organizational hierarchy, they were not once but twice removed.

TEACHER-PRINCIPAL IDEOLOGIES

Field studies are good at picking up information that is revealing although not the object of research. One of the interesting things that inadvertently comes through in these studies is some of the ways that teachers and administrators have of talking about each other. Several of the principals see teachers as unsympathetic toward low-achieving and poor students; teachers see principals as too sympathetic toward those same students.

This theme was touched upon by Smith and Geoffrey (1968) when Geoffrey, with his seven broken windows, thought vandalism was a problem. Mr. Inman downplayed vandalism and lectured teachers on the "unique satisfactions in teaching children from less privileged areas" (p. 25). After all, he reasoned, children are children and every school has problems. He also blamed student failure on teachers, an additional element in that theme (p. 25).

Administrators blaming teachers for the treatment of and the attitudes toward poorer children recurs and expands in Johnson's *West Haven* (1985). The newly hired African-American principal explained the teachers' antipathy toward poor students. He believed they

> tend to identify with upper class groups, with their opinions, aspirations and ways of life because many of them long to be accepted in that stratum. The problems of the community and the problems of teacher identity are producing a negative attitude among teachers, as the student body shifts to a black majority...many of our teachers are so busy stating that the students cannot learn that they are overlooking the reasons for behavior problems. They are also getting achievement and intelligence confused and letting achievement in the classroom determine their true attitudes toward the students. (pp. 211–212)

The principal wants the teachers to be more sympathetic toward students with the most personal problems, and he believes that the teachers do not try hard enough. On the other hand, the teachers believe that "low achieving students...do not care much about school. But the school caters to them! The low students exert pressure on the high students not to achieve; low achieving black students bring down the high achieving black students" (p. 212). Johnson believes that the principal is correct, and that the issue does not involve correct perception but instead involves the persistence of the differing perceptions of teachers and administrators.

The theme, principal as champion of the oppressed, was expanded by the principal of a large high school in Cusick and Wheeler's (1987) study of reform efforts. She worried about "the kid nobody sees."

> He's not in sports, not on the honor roll; he's not noticed by anybody. I want the department heads to hear from the parents of a ninth grader who didn't go out one weekend all year...didn't know anyone when he came,...made a few friends but the friends went punk;...didn't make the team or the yearbook. For [that kid] this school is an intimidating place. (p. 54)

An additional variation on the theme casts principals as believing that teachers are overly concerned with "subject matter." In Cusick's (1973) story of students in Horatio Gates High, both the principal and vice principal felt the teachers viewed the students as "pleasant dummies." Mr. Rossi, the vice principal, was worried particularly the school's nonacademic students. "That's what I worry about, the nonacademic kids...how do we get to them. The teachers don't even want to try" (p. 22). He cited what, for him, was a perfect example of the teachers' attitude. "We got one guy, you know what he told me when I asked him to do something one day? He said, 'I'm here to be a scholar in residence, not to supervise the cafeteria." Honest to God, that's what he said, a 'scholar in residence.'" (p. 23-24). The principal shared Mr. Rossi's perceptions of teachers. "They all want to be subject matter specialists; they're not concerned about whether the kids are getting the lecture, it's just the lecture that counts" and he cited "inability to relate to the kids" as the reason for firing a teacher the previous year. "She knew her field, but that's not enough" (p. 21).

The firing was a difficult issue and Mr. Rossi's account is interesting. According to him, the teacher was too interested in the bright students and too inconsiderate of the average.

> A little girl came to see me....She had this paper from Mrs. J's class. It was an essay; it was marked 70. Now I'm no literary scholar but I can read. The sentences were right, the paragraphs were right, the thing made sense, and the words were spelled okay, and she had a 70. So I went to Mrs. J and asked her about the grade. "It lacks depth," she says. Now I'm no literary scholar, but the thing was okay, and the paragraphs were okay, the sentences made sense and the words were spelled all right. What the hell did she want? (Cusick, 1973, p. 34)

In subsequent evaluations, Mr. Rossi found the teacher talking over the heads of the "less sharp kids" and "forcing her sophisticated views on the kids." Mr. Vincent, the principal, said the teacher "knew her material, but couldn't relate to the kids" (Cusick, 1973, p. 34). In subsequent observations she was given poor evaluations and fired. (The irony of the administrators' feeling that the teachers considered students "pleasant dummies" while firing a teacher who was trying to generate some intellectual discourse, was lost on everyone.) Speaking more broadly, Mr. Rossi said that the teachers "are always complaining to me about all the freedom the kids have. They want freedom but you just give some to the kids and watch those teachers bitch" (p. 22).

In order to pursue this theme of principals' championing the less able, poorer, and less popular students, next is a review of secondary schools in the 1960s and 1970s, when equality, particularly in the form of student rights, was interjected between teachers and principals. Grant's (1988) description of the principal of Hamilton High immediately prior to integration reminds us why administrators hark back to the 1950s as an idyllic time. "Once appointed, principals were rarely removed and they expected to run their schools with a free hand. The district had few guidelines and interference was minimal, as long as a school was orderly" (p. 19).

By the mid-1960s, civil and student rights, integration, and African-American awareness had changed all that. The days of the heavy-handed principal,

Mr. Payne, who "when a boy 'got out of line'... might shove him against his office door for an eyeball-to-eyeball talk" were over (p. 19).

> Matters once left to the discretion of principals or teachers were now subject to grievance or courtroom-like review. This...(was) a result...of broad cultural changes redefining relations between children and adult guardians which culminated in the Supreme Court decision in the *Gault* case of 1967 and the *Winship* case of 1970. Little time was lost in applying this reasoning to attack the "paternalism" of the school principal. It was not long before all tests of due process...were applied to schools, namely: notice of charges, right to counsel, right to confrontation and cross examination, privilege against self-incrimination, right to a transcript of the proceedings and right to appellate review. (Grant, 1988, pp. 50–51)

With more students going out for the "student rights" committee than for the football team, no longer could Hamilton High principals physically intimidate students. As control became more problematic, so teacher-administrator relations became more problematic.

Hamilton High's next principal, charged with implementing these changes, generally sided with students against teachers. He stripped the privileges of the older teachers, had phones removed from their rooms, and gave all a mix of the better and worse classes and study halls. In Grant's (1988) words, he "changed the schedule of the entire school to make it student rather than teacher oriented" (p. 41). A teacher who maintained that this principal had "given away the store" recalled him making an announcement.

> "Good people"—he always referred to students that way—"good people," we're going to have an assembly this afternoon and it's going to be fun. After the bell, I want you to get together with your friends and come on down to the auditorium and find any place to sit where you like. I want you to be with your friends and enjoy yourself." Then more routinely, almost brusquely, "teachers, your auditorium assignments are posted in the office." (Grant, p. 63)

Grant's story covers the shift from a 1950s principal with mandates and intimidating ways to the successors, who had no mandates save to satisfy and to keep peace among diverse constituents. The latter not only had to accommodate different and sometimes angry clients, but they had to extend equality to parties previously denied it.

Cusick (1973), who also studied urban schools beset by racial problems in the 1970s, described the tension between the administrators who were charged with creating a more supportive atmosphere for lower-achieving (frequently minority and poorer students) and teachers concerned with achievement and behavior. Teachers blamed the administrators for not setting the right tone:

> When I first came here a few years ago, I raised my hand in the first faculty meeting and asked why ninth graders were coming in from the smoking area late for the first hour and I wanted to know why they had a smoking area, and I was told they smoke

anyway and they might as well have a smoking room, and I knew what to expect in that school, I knew right there...they don't set the tone, there isn't enough getting the kids to respect the place and respect themselves. (p. 32)

Teachers also ridiculed the individual accommodations that administrators made with errant students, and they cited instances in which students bragged about their ability to get around administrators.

Even worse, they believed, some with good reason, that the principal no longer cared about academic standards.

This girl missed 55 days of class, 55 days and she hadn't handed in an assignment since I checked my book, since October 10, and so I flunked her from the class. But the parent came in and talked to the principal, so I got called in and he said, looking right at me, "Mr. _____ is it necessary to fail that student?" and I said "Yes" and showed him what I'm showing you, and then he looked at me and said again, "Is it really necessary to fail that student?" I said "Yes," but the third time he said it I got the message. (p. 39)

The four administrators, on the other hand, felt that the teachers were naïve about the realities of running a public school with dozens of infractions every day, a 20–30 percent truancy rate, and some hard-core criminals among the 2100 students. The administrators had a limited arsenal to deal with all of this. For a given infraction, they could expel, suspend, call a parent conference, or send students back to class. Suspensions and expulsions were monitored by parents who often sided with their children against the school. They were also watched by a community group to make sure "white administrators aren't throwing out the black kids," and by a central office concerned about the per-pupil state funding and voter support for the annual millage. Finally, the districts' Board of Education officially blamed student failure on school structure. Taking terminal action against students was difficult, time-consuming, and except in extreme cases, avoided. Instead, administrators talked to the students and sent them back to teachers who either did not want them or wanted more action taken against them.

Generally, for a teacher faced with a crowd of students, the concerns are a possible dispute acted out in front of a class and an emotional scene. For an administrator faced with one or two students, in his office, the concerns are to follow procedures and to keep minor disputes from turning into major conflicts with racial overtones. In the study, the teachers saw themselves as not getting the help they needed from administrators. The administrators saw themselves as inundated with students sent to the office for trivial reasons. "Honest to God, she sends kids in here because they forget their pencils." Teachers regarded administrators as weak; administrators regarded teachers as naïve.

Metz in her *Classrooms and Corridors* (1978) reported similar findings. She described teachers' anger at deans for not using strong enough measures. But she pointed out, the dean in her school had a limited set of options. His strongest weapon was expulsion and the next strongest, temporary suspension.

These measures were used sparingly. Short of these punishments, "a dean could reprimand a student, keep him after school. . . . But with those children most frequently prone to cause disorder, who were the source of the teacher's serious problems, the punishments available to the dean soon became familiar and thereby lost much of their force" (p. 101).

Further illustrating the difference between the teachers' major problem and the administrators' major problem, note that the teachers' focus is on crowds of students whom they have to both instruct and control. Crowd control is the teacher's major problem. Not so for administrators: as full and busy as their days are, they do not deal with large numbers of students. Instead, they deal with one or a few under conditions in which control is less problematic than the classroom. Of course, the potential for emotional confrontation is present in any disciplinary situation, but the administrator has more latitude. The administrator can focus on the student, hear the student's side of the story, and even empathize. In the classroom the teacher has to correct a deviant student while continuing to control class and subject-matter interaction. The difference between perspectives may be a matter of the different circumstances.

In subsequent chapters, it will be argued that the school routine with its density and busyness absorbs the time that administrators might give to curriculum. Administrators then limit their interest in curriculum to a few elements, such as achievement and test scores, which serve as the medium with which to discuss school matters with superiors and outsiders. Teachers pay little attention to the complexity and routine: they even downplay test and achievement scores, preferring to discuss particular students and their own student relations. As Rossman, Corbett, and Firestone (1988) indicate, teachers prefer discussing students from an understanding rather than from a knowledge perspective.

Control is the common ground on which teachers and administrators meet. This issue appears in the descriptions more frequently than any other. When problems occur, they are most often expressed as an accusation by one party that the other "lacks control." Among teachers themselves and among teachers with administrators, there seems to be little agreement about matters other than control. The best relations occur when both believe that control is good. Principals whom teachers like limit their demands and leave teachers to teach as they wish.

THE POWER OF THE PRINCIPAL

A common belief among school reformers, at least for the past twenty years, is "The principal is (or should be) the instructional leader." Agreed, of course, but what does that mean in the day-to-day operation of the school? How much power do principals have relative to teachers and of what does the power consist? Whom do principals lead and to where? What do teachers do to indicate they are being led? In the previous section, the cited works described teachers and principals having different but related activities: the principal concerned about overall organization and structure, and the teacher with control and instruction.

How do these separate activities intersect, and how does the principal affect the teachers?

First studies are examined that describe efforts to overcome principal-teacher barriers. A very thoughtful account is McNeil's *Contradictions of Control* (1986). She traced the social studies curriculum in four separate high schools and tried to relate teachers' classroom behavior to each school's administrative structure. Her descriptions of the first three schools argue that control is the common denominator. "Forest Hills will be discussed for itself and for its typical arrangement with management-oriented administrators and with teachers fairly autonomous over their course content and instructional methods." (p. 28).

> The teachers at Forest Hills felt little autonomy or authority over procedure. Their school was heavily administered with a principal and four grade-level principals and each had formal authority over some of the subject departments. This authority was rarely actively exercised except in the brief classroom visits to teachers being evaluated. The five principals attended to budgets, discipline, hall order, athletic schedules and other procedural details. They were rarely evident in department meetings, in classrooms, in (non-disciplinary) conversations with students or in instruction." (p. 31)

At her second school, Freeburg High, the principal had a strong role but "was preoccupied with order at the expense of program development, resources, planning and oversight of academic goals." The teachers spoke pleasantly about ...the principal, called him "'nice' and 'gentlemanly' but several stated that he should never have been a principal." They expressed a perception of clear boundaries in the school between teaching responsibilities and administrative functions" (pp. 43–44). A third school, Maizeville, was characterized by "an administration concerned with order keeping and teachers assigned to individual classrooms according to their academic subject" (p. 45). The principal and assistant principal said that "almost half their time was spent 'tracking down truants'" (p. 49) of which there were only 100.

The fourth school, Nelson High, had the most positive description of teacher-principal relations in any of the schools McNeil studied. That school had a traditional structure with the principal holding legal authority over staff, budgets, discipline, and attendance, and the teachers in charge of developing and teaching their courses and evaluating their students. The difference was the principal. Nelson, according to McNeil (1986), was known for its academic principals who "could discuss subject matter and instruction with teachers with involved and informed concern" (pp. 55–56). Nelson's current principal encouraged teachers to adopt the science model of a unified curriculum, supported their efforts to obtain outside grants, and both "staff and students responded to the supportive administrative context" (p. 140).

McNeil (1986) described Nelson High as having excellent relations between the administrators and teachers, and not the antagonistic or unintended relations she found in her other three schools (p. 62). Neither was Nelson's principal obsessed with control. "Nelson High is a place where historical factors, individual and collective commitments and expectations combine to create support for learning" (p. 65) and where "the staff was organized from the start to consider the content behind course titles and credits" (p. 136). The school "had put into place a curriculum in which narrow specializations within broad subject fields were interwoven into courses developed along complex interdisciplinary themes" (p. 56).

A standard assumption, one shared by McNeil at the outset of her study, is that administrators who structure school around learning instead of control can have a positive effect on classroom teaching. At Nelson the effort seemed to pay off.

> [Teachers] . . . felt, and demonstrated less of a wall between their personal knowledge and the "official" knowledge of the classroom. They developed entire courses, used original handouts and continually collected and re-designed materials. They used fewer lists and provided more extended descriptions, more opportunities for student discussion, more varieties of learning experiences (including the willingness to bring speakers in from the community). (p.177)

But at the conclusion of her study McNeil (1986) admits it is unclear whether or how the academic principal and the subsequently improved principal-teacher relations translated into improved classroom interaction or student learning. Nelson High's teachers communicated better among themselves and with the principal, and demonstrated more élan than did teachers in the other three schools. However, McNeil (1986) did not trace this positive relationship to the actual teaching behavior or to the interaction between students and teachers. Just as in less well run schools, the teachers, not the students, were carrying the workload in class (p. 184). Although "the administrative structure generated much teaching effort, it had no means of discerning the impact of the curricula on students" (p. 151). In other words, it is one thing for teachers and principals to like and respect each other. It is quite another for this liking and respect to much affect what goes on in classrooms. Even at Nelson, with its supportive structure and positive climate, and despite the original intention, teachers reduced course content to its most manageable and measurable form (p. 185), just as they did in the other three schools.

Nor could these positive relations much influence elements pressing on the school from without. McNeil (1986) explains several related factors. The students' outside jobs reduced their opportunities for themselves. Declining enrollments posed a threat to stability. Teachers who had "accepted lower beginning salaries in order to participate in a program they could affirm . . . faced layoffs in an era of . . . tight markets for social studies teachers" (p. 153). In other words, good relations between principal and teachers, or as it is stated "a positive climate," although enjoyed and appreciated, did not seem to have much effect on external realities, teachers' behavior, classroom interaction, or student learning. Teacher-administrator interaction was not sufficient to alter teacher or teacher-student behavior.

The issue is the principal's ability to effect change. At the principal's disposal are legitimate authority, personal qualities such as warmth and sensitivity, practiced behaviors such as listening, and management techniques such as shared decision-making. When uttered aloud by management consultants, these are appealing and eagerly embraced by people wanting to change schools through administrative leadership. Yet the descriptions indicate that these techniques do not alter the basic classroom structure, the control issue, teacher centrality, teachers' and administrators' expectations of each other, or student effort. Nor from the studies described in Chapter 2 is there any indication that student associations can be at all affected by teacher-principal relations.

Something is missing between the activities of principals and the activities of teachers. The separate parties are involved in separate realities. The two are related by the control issue and by the pooled and sequential interdependence referred to by Smith, et al., (1986). Beyond that, the activities of each seemed walled up against penetration by the other. Efforts to break the walls and to more directly involve each in the concerns of the other do not seem to work. Each party seems taken up with its own set of different but contiguous activities. Teaching is a personal, involving, and absorbing activity. Teachers give evidence of having little room for anything else. The next chapter shows that for administrators, running a building is similarly absorbing. Principals have little time for anything else.

The distance between what administrators do and what teachers do is measured in Lightfoot's (1983) accounts of what she termed "good" schools. The accounts contain descriptions of classes and interviews with administrators about those classes. George Washington Carver High's principal, Hogans, had been hired, four years before the study, to clean up a trash- and graffiti-ridden, out-of-control, inner city school, known as the "dumping ground of the Atlanta school system" (p. 43). Lightfoot describes him as a man of great energy who "dominates the school." He walks about the campus in perpetual motion, looking severe and determined, always carrying his walkie-talkie"...through which ..."he barks orders and makes inquiries" (p. 33). Hogans "runs a tight ship" (p. 35). He "has a heavy hand and an autocratic style" (p. 43). Strict obedience and absolute conformity of both teachers and students is required. Hogans even docks the pay of a teacher who doesn't use the standard procedure for signing out. "That person is going to be docked. Hit them in the pocketbook.... When teachers are irresponsible, the kids always get the short end of the stick" (p. 44). And like other principals, he expressed most concern about one or another individual student, in this case, a girl with a serious personal and family problem, who tried to reach him and because of his busy schedule could not (p. 42).

Lightfoot reports that his efforts have brought the disorderly and graffiti-ridden school into line. However, the relation between Hogans' energy, dynamism, and organizational skills on one hand and improved instruction on the other was hard to discern.

> In many of the classrooms I visited, very little of substance was happening educationally. Teachers were caught up in procedural directives and students appeared disinterested, turned off or mildly disruptive. The institution has begun to emerge

as stable and secure but attention to the intellectual development and growth of students will require a different kind of focus...." (p. 37)

Lightfoot (1983) describes a class wherein one girl "has her head on her desk and is nodding off to sleep, another girl is chewing gum vigorously and leafing through a magazine and a third student stares straight ahead with glazed eyes....Two boys, Lowry and Richard, sit right under the teacher's nose and spend most of the class period being noisy and disruptive" (p. 38).

Hogans sees himself as fair and concerned. He feeds teachers breakfast, reduces meeting time, and calms the disruption and disorder, but "four years (following his arrival) some faculty are 'dragging their feet' and resisting direction" (p. 44). Older faculty resent his much publicized and frequent absences from the school and his heavy handedness. In their classes and with their students, those teachers behave as if he had never come. Furthermore, the school's best programs antedate the principal by several years. Lightfoot (1983) describes two of these: a work-study program run by Ms. Taylor had been with the school for "several years" (p. 45), and a drycleaning program run by Mr. Ward had been doing good work for thirty years. It seems that the good teachers were good before Hogans came, and several more, by his own admission, Hogans can do nothing with. Both best and worst teachers seem impervious to his efforts.

Highland Park, another of Lightfoot's six schools, is one of a string "of affluent suburbs north of Chicago" (p. 121). The situation is different, but the principal-teacher relation is not. Mr. Benson is described as "calm and affable... has a gift for making people feel comfortable...cool...confident. He is, in his words, 'long on people skills'" (pp. 124–125). When he took over the position the first thing Benson

> did was to visit and talk with every member of the faculty, classified staff and custodial staff. He asked each person what they thought needed changing and refused to get involved in "old stories" and bitter battles from the past....His leadership began subtly, listening for direction from the collective body, working behind the scenes to create alliances, and carefully but willingly delegating responsibility to others....Says one faculty member, "He is the best listener....I can just feel his support and confidence. He is always eager to learn." (Lightfoot, 1983, p. 126)

For all the encomiums that Highland Park teachers and principal pass back and forth, the teachers seem as little affected by Benson's humaneness as Carver's teachers were by Hogans's dynamism. The setting is more favorable; the teacher-administrator relationships auspicious. Yet even after speaking favorably of the "support" and "freedom" they receive from Benson, teachers do not attribute their success to him.

Instead they attribute the high-quality curriculum to "the initiative and hard work of teachers...who are sophisticated about keeping up with the important trends in their field. They go to conferences all over the country to collect new ideas and stay current." When the teachers talk of their classroom efforts, it is themselves and their students, not the administrators, who receive the credit.

"At Highland Park, teachers have to earn the respect of kids. You don't automatically get it because you are a teacher . . . but if you give kids respect, caring and support, it will all come back to you." Many teachers spoke of their first year of harsh scrutiny by students, their determined attempts to gain acceptance and approval from them, and finally their coming together in mutual admiration. (p. 127)

Highland Park's teachers do not seek to please the principal; they seek to please the students. The teachers respect the principal for what he does for them; they respect more their own students and the best among themselves.

Cusick (1983) studied a school in which a principal took a somewhat modest approach to leadership and in doing so revealed an interesting quid pro quo with teachers. By the usual descriptors, this was a good school. Teachers performed their tasks, students were orderly, discipline and attendance problems were few and well-handled, and both graduation rate and SAT/ACT scores were decent. Neither parents nor central office complained. The principal of that school was seldom visible in the halls, never entered classrooms, and dealt with teachers one at a time, usually at their request, and behind closed doors. He communicated mainly with his secretary, the two assistant principals, and a few friends, who were coaches. One would wonder how he ran the school.

Cusick explained the principal's actions in terms of the teachers' actions. Each teacher had a professional life that revolved around a favored class(es), activity, or assignment. And most had integrated their in-school assignments with their out-of-school lives, which frequently included a second job. Good relations with the principal were central to both their in-school assignments and the teachers' ability to handle their jobs outside school. The principal would allocate the favored assignment and the accompanying flexibility to maintain the second job, but in return he wanted teachers to comply with the routine, accommodate students, and help him with what he had to do.

For instance, a teacher might want an honors class, a period off, a double lunch, a free last or first hour, a particular activity, or a department chairmanship. The principal would allot these in exchange for a teacher's extra assistance. His revealing comment about a favored group of male teachers, to whom he gave a double lunch hour and who left school early or came late to accommodate their second jobs was, "I can always count on those guys; they always help me" (p. 98). They in turn considered him "a good guy" (but) were wary of his power to upset the network of interdependent activities that each had created. They understood that when helping with a dance or a project, they were buying his goodwill, which they could exchange for what they wanted. The principal was accused of playing favorites and he did.

"Playing favorites," however, is too crude a term; it connotes a whimsicality that is unfair to the principal. It takes more than what the organizational chart shows or the teachers' contract allows to run a high school. It takes people willing to do extra things, e.g. initiate a class, sponsor a club, chaperon a dance, help with graduation, transport students, keep the clock at athletic events, and talk to parents. That principal could not "order" the tenured and contracted staff to do as many of those things as he needed done. So he "bought" extra effort by supporting the personal accommodations of those who supported him. This exchange system revealed both the principal's power and the limits on his power.

Such a system did not exist at Factory High (Cusick, 1983). Budget cuts and racial problems had eliminated most of the additional elements that teachers wanted and most of the things for which a principal might need help. Factory ran a five-by-five schedule: five periods a day, five days a week, 8:00 A.M. to 1:00 P.M. and then dismissed (no lunch, no teacher duties, no student activities, no sports, no library, only a few meetings). Where there was so little to exchange, there was little ability of the principal to much affect the actions of teachers and little interaction between principal and teachers.

Principals have limited power. They are not the schools' owner/entrepreneurs, but are mid-level bureaucrats in a public service endeavor. Few can hire and fewer can fire. None can pay more or less than the contract allows, or assign more or fewer of the classes and extra duties stipulated in the contract. Teachers seldom choose or evaluate principals; they have little overt power over them. Teachers like principals who are good at control, but except in extreme cases, they cannot do much if the principal does not enforce their idea of control. Even at Nelson High, the elements that controlled the teachers' lives, e.g. the number of students, the community, the glut of social studies teachers, and the teachers' limited prospects for salary increases were not controlled by the principal. Outside events affected him just as they affected the teachers. Teachers and principal liked each other, but good feelings did not extend to mutual influence.

As part of Cusick and Wheeler's (1987) study, Cusick found the principal candid about her limits and attributing the school's successful curriculum to resource teachers.

> I've read all that "principal as leader" stuff and I don't believe it. I think it's five years out of date. There's no way with 105 teachers that I can follow what they're doing. That's why the resource teachers are so good. They're right there. (p. 38)

Resource teachers were a combination of department chair and senior teacher. Each of the larger departments—English, social studies, math, or foreign language—had one. Because they stayed with the teachers' bargaining unit, they were not administrators but were expected to coordinate the curriculum, to observe classes, to hold meetings, and to supervise. In exchange they received a modest stipend, three rather than five classes, and guaranteed summer employment. The system seemed to work well. With the curriculum and supervision thus handled, and the discipline and attendance watched over by three assistants, the principal concentrated on the community, central office relations, legal matters, uncertified staff, and whatever else it took to keep 1735 students warm, dry, orderly, and fed.

The idea of having a principal with power to influence teaching and subsequently learning is appealing. Were principals to have that power, they could more easily influence teachers, motivate students, and reform schools. But the descriptive studies, K–12, tell a rather consistent story of principals and teachers having few interactions, little in common, and few mutual activities. Central to their relations is that each hold up their own end of the control/maintenance agreement. When that system works, the relation goes well. When control is absent, or when one party is not holding up his or her end, the relation deteriorates. The limited interaction and the limited mutual influence does not trouble either party. Just as teachers accept the fact that students comply differentially, so principals accept the fact that teachers comply differentially. Only when the principal tries to stretch his or her authority into what teachers consider their domain do problems occur. To pursue the relationship and their ability to affect each other, some illustrations are drawn from studies of three private schools where one would assume control is less problematic and where the principal has more power relative to the teachers than public schools allow.

PRINCIPALS AND TEACHERS IN PRIVATE SCHOOLS

The first description, of the exclusive Milton Academy, is from Lightfoot's *Good High School* (1983). The principal, Mr. Pieh, wants increased teacher participation in decision-making. He sees himself as the executor of the faculty's collective will, and he wants to be sure he perceives that will correctly. Lightfoot's careful description of a faculty meeting suggests, however, that teachers are not particularly interested in participation. They would prefer to leave organizational business to the principal and get on with their teaching. The meeting proceeds thus:

> Most of the discussion time is devoted to the (issue of final examinations) with faculty offering comments and critiques that refer to procedural issues, pedagogical concerns, motivational questions, and philosophical ruminations. As with most large group discussions the conversation tends to be diffuse and unfocused; the same few people usually dominate the exchange and many grow frustrated by the redundancies. Pieh (the Principal) navigates the meeting with a gentle style and tries to offer summaries and interpretations of what has been said. Several times, he refuses to bring premature closure to a decision despite the prodding of some impatient faculty. At other moments, he decides to cut off a conversation that seems to have reached a dead end. When faculty comments begin to sound like rehearsals of old, worn battles, Pieh says "Many of you are beginning to recollect old discussions, echoes of former conversations." I think this reminder is designed to move people beyond repetition of often discussed issues, but one faculty member views it as an opportunity for seeing new possibilities. "Just because we decide to change our minds and return to an old pattern doesn't mean that we're losing ground...."
>
> He is immediately and hotly contested by a colleague who is less interested in the process of discovery and more interested in the effects of exam scheduling on pedagogical practices. "Having a June exam seduced us into teaching for the mastery of exams...it's not an issue of flexibility. We've run that experiment already." This comment is reinforced by a woman who is admired for her educational leadership. She says forcefully..."April exams can become part of an educational process, a learning experience. A June exam is merely an evaluative procedure. We are sending

that message to children and I lament that message." A more tentative voice provides support for this argument. "In my classes last spring, I saw an increase in student involvement after the April exam and it was very rewarding. The students were released from anxiety and they really blossomed."

With those related comments the exchange breaks down, with faculty offering suggestions and criticisms that sound disjointed. A frustrated voice complains that his earlier motion has been lost in the "irrelevant" conversation and pushes for procedural correctness.... A woman leaps in with a strong concern that seems to be related to the conversation held a half-hour ago: "It is an extremely bad and difficult thing for those who are parents to begin school, or even faculty meetings before Labor Day.... It is totally disruptive. I feel very strongly about this." A young teacher who has now spoken five times offers another contribution. There are some muffled groans when she rises again.... (pp. 275–276)

The meeting goes on with the additional comments just as scattered and random as those cited, and "without reaching a clear resolution and with frustration lingering in the air," Pieh adjourns the meeting (p. 276). The faculty like and admire the principal but consider him indecisive and blame him for failing to be clear "about what is possible or acceptable... the faculty would be happier if he took a more decisive role... they are suspicious of his nonauthoritarian style, claiming it is ineffectual and causes needless frustration and confusion" (p. 276).

This exchange points out just how difficult it is to sustain an educational discussion, replete with the philosophical underpinnings and evidence of faculty disinterest in and difference of opinion about overall school affairs. Teachers seem to know that their disagreements make attempts at consensus futile. What little teachers could agree upon was a desire for a stable environment: only a few, for reasons of their own, wanted more. The teachers in that meeting indicated that they find organizational business neither interesting nor rewarding. Indeed, one might ask, what was to be gained by increased involvement in out-of-class matters? Higher salaries? Unlikely. Better student relations? Equally unlikely. Promotion? Except for those wanting to be administrators, a dead issue. Prestige? More is to be gained from being a competent teacher than from being an administrator.

Two further examples follow, both from schools with strong, visible philosophies, which their principals embody. One is Lightfoot's (1983) St. Paul's School. The second is Peshkin's (1986) Baptist Academy. In both, the administrators have some real power over teachers. Neither school offers teachers tenure. Teachers are on a one-year contract that says, roughly, that they will do what they are told or the principal may fire them.

Lightfoot's (1983) portrayal of St. Paul's Rector is particularly revealing. He makes all the important decisions, e.g. who shall be hired, retained, which students should be admitted, and how discipline should work. He runs admissions with one eye on the students' abilities, the other on the parents' status and income. In the case of a graduation ceremony in which there were to be some student presentations, the "presenters were carefully selected by department heads and the rector. Speeches were written, critiqued by the faculty and rewritten several times. One student exasperated by the close scrutiny, complained of the 'censoring' of her ideas when she tried to speak her mind" (p. 241). Despite the heavy-handed control, Lightfoot reported teachers as working very hard, teaching well, and satisfied with their positions.

But they are intimidated. Lightfoot describes the rector as a person to whom the teachers "leave their fate"...and assume a "child-like role," in submission to his authority. They are totally dominated by him:

> Faculty rarely argue with the rector or even dare to disagree strongly. No one risks being late for meetings with him. People who normally seem strong and sturdy in their role appear strangely submissive and accommodating in his presence. One teacher who challenged the rector with an opposing view in a small planning meeting, told of his [the rector's] restrained but scathing response, her sense of bravery and risk-taking in even raising the issue in his presence, and the buzz around the faculty room when the word leaked out that she had acted irreverently. (p. 237)

Not everyone is so accepting of the naked power the rector wields. Lightfoot describes the split in the faculty between the newer teachers "from less affluent backgrounds (without independent incomes) many of whom were not raised in exclusive schools, more likely to view their role as professional and want some legalistic and contractual safeguards" (p. 238) (against the rector's exercise of power). The advantages of conditions at the school outweigh the inconvenience of being at the weak end of the power relationship. The teachers receive travel grants in the summer, fully paid leaves, and students who pay attention. In turn they obey the rector, work hard, and demonstrate commitment to the school ideals. They see the school as a unit and a strong principal (rector) as central to the unit. The school offers teachers several advantages, and the rector, working from the authority that they and others allow him, protects their advantages.

The headmaster of Peshkin's (1986) Christian Bethany Academy had similar authority. In a brief section entitled "Teacher behavior with Administrators." Peshkin (1986) paraphrased what teachers said about their relations with administrators.

> Guided by scriptural injunctions about authority, we are to be submissive to our administrators. When we work for somebody, we do things his way. All orders come from the top, administrators have the final authority, and, therefore, teacher obedience is appropriate and expected. Of course, you won't always agree with your leader's policies, but you must accept them with a good attitude. The relationship is reciprocal: if you are obedient, dependable, prompt in your work and willing to go that extra mile, administrators should be supportive and responsive to your concerns. Don't be afraid to bring up any problem to them; above all don't take your problems with them or the academy outside the academy. They expect your loyalty and you should give it. (pp. 82–83)

It should be noted that these teachers give approximately 65 percent of their waking hours to the school for $6,000 to $9,000 (1980 dollars) per year. Their duties, in addition to teaching, include driving the school bus, teaching the classes at the Sunday school, attending services and coming back at 5:30 for choir practice, coaching on Monday, attending after school activities on Tuesday, attending and helping with evening prayer sessions on Wednesday, making "soul-winning" visitations to adults on Thursday, attending evening sports activities on Friday and, for male teachers, attending the church prayer breakfast on Saturday. Female teachers cook the breakfast for the men who attend the Saturday breakfast. All of that is expected in addition to teaching.

At both St. Paul's and the Baptist Academy the teachers are clearly subordinate to the administrators. In both cases, more is asked of teachers and principals than is asked in public schools. Both submit themselves to an abstract ideal and agree on the way that ideal is interpreted in reality. Both schools are, in Goffman's (1961) terms, "total institutions" in which teachers and principal submit themselves to some larger authority, in one case, the school's, in the second, the church. Both schools were free to reject students and teachers who did not accept the boundaries. The power of the principal in these schools was evident. But the power consisted of his ability to drive a few simple ideas through the faculty into the classrooms. The ideas were the basis of the school. In St. Paul's the ideas were class and quality; in the Baptist Academy the ideas were the Church doctrine. But even these principals, with all their power, did not go too far into instruction, student-teacher relations, and classroom behavior. They limited their power to broad school matters in which it was agreed that they were the experts. From the studies, there is no evidence that they tried to tell teachers how to teach.

In the public schools cited throughout the chapters, staff generally agree on education's broad goals of learning, equality, universality, and democracy and they agree well enough on the basic structure of schools. Attempts to establish collegial working agreements that exceeded those broad goals resulted more often in conflict than consensus. Private schools have more narrow ranges of acceptable behavior for everyone. But there too, administrators do not interfere in the way teachers run their classes. A final point about the way teachers and administrators see each other is that each tends to render simple explanations for the other's behavior. Hogans docks a teacher's pay for being late: "When the teachers mess up, it's the kids who suffer." Rossi believes kids should not have sophisticated views forced on them. Johnson's principal attributes low student achievement to teacher's "envy of the middle class." Powell et al.'s principal likes teachers who "don't hassle kids."

Teachers do the same thing to principals. Pieh's teachers say he "needs" interaction. Teachers say Payne has a "Queeg-like streak." The studies are littered with simple and random bits of psychologizing that each party uses to explain the behavior of the other. There does not seem to be much room for analysis, discussion, or exploration of issues. Teachers' and principals' brief interactions and limited mutual interests encourage them to make quick judgments about each other. It may be that schools are too busy, that children demand immediate attention, or that events press too quickly in succession, leaving little time for discussion and reflection. It may be that issues are too complex or that teachers are too absorbed in classrooms and administrators too absorbed in students' coming and going. It may be that teachers accurately perceive that too little is to be gained from involvement in matters beyond the classroom. Whatever the reason, teachers and administrators limit their common ground to the smooth running of the endeavor.

SUMMARY

Teachers work together, share materials and advice, are frequently friends, and work out their professional lives adjacent to one another—adjacent, but not together. The studies are consistent. However supportive and friendly teachers are, they avoid intruding too far into one another's classrooms. A professional distance is maintained. Each has the problem of imposing the school's definition of reality onto students. This is a personal problem and teachers solve it personally.

Teachers and principals are important to each other. They work in the same setting; their duties adjoin; the success of each is contingent on the other. They are frequently friends as well as colleagues. They respect and in many instances give evidence that they like each other. The principals need teachers who can instruct and enforce the school's narrow definition of acceptable behavior. Teachers need principals who support them and manage the school outside the classroom so they can get on with their business inside the classroom. Each judges the other according to how well the arrangement is handled. When things are smooth and coordinated, differences of personality and style are overlooked. When things are not smooth, matters of personality and style emerge. For orderliness, the teachers rely on the principal and they judge him on whether he provides it. If he does, they like him, even when they don't like him; if he doesn't, they don't like him, even when they do.

The parties interact around the logistics. The common issue is control, which may be an unsatisfying term; it is not meant to imply a heavy handedness or severity. Instead, I mean an acceptance of common norms, graceful relations, and easy coordination of myriad overlapping events. This is by nature problematic in schools that are crowded, dense, and busy, particularly those that contain many students who resist the school's definitions of appropriate behavior.

The system's pieces are beginning to overlap. The initial group is the students, divided as they are by class and culture and having a tendency to drift into groups where they practice behaviors they brought with them rather than those the school condones. The task of imposing the schools' limited version of reality lies with the classroom teacher. The immediacy of the task demands that teachers take a central position in the classroom and a personal and personalized approach. The interdependence of school activities requires an orderly atmosphere outside the classroom. That is the administrator's job. The next chapter describes how they do it and how they integrate their in-school and out-of-school duties.

Also to be explored is an emerging characteristic of the system: the freedom of individuals to set their own levels of participation and compliance. Students decide how and to what degree they will participate in class. Teachers decide how and to what degree they will comply with administrators. Each reserves the right to alter the definition of the situation and to make judgments from his or her own perspective. This right of individuals to behave as they wish is an important characteristic of the system, one that we will pursue in subsequent chapters.

* Profiles — Symbolic representations of core values (self) because of risk?

5

Administrators, Administrators and Outside Parties

INTRODUCTION

Lodged as they are on the schools' periphery, administrators deal with people inside and outside the schools. This chapter describes administrators, first in the schools, and second with parties outside the schools and outside the formal organization. Examining administrators' interactions with people outside the school opens the way to subsequent chapters, which describe collectivities that surround the schools, and the actions of those groups relative to schools.

This chapter begins with observational studies that sum up the behaviors of several building and mid-level administrators. It then moves into a more detailed description, provided in Wolcott's (1978) *Man in the Principal's Office*. Added to that are accounts drawn from school and classroom studies cited in earlier chapters. Also included are several interesting stories of conflicts between school staff and outside groups. Among these are Gold and Miles's *Whose School Is this Anyway?* (1981), Hentoff's *Our Children Are Dying* (1966), and Cuban's "*Hobson* vs. *Hanson*" (1975). Finally, there are community studies, among them Hollingshead's *Elmtown's Youth* (1949) and Vidich and Bensman's *Small Town in Mass Society* (1956), both of which place the school in communities and describe administrators as they smooth out school-community conflicts.

THE PRINCIPAL AND THE ROUTINE

In schools, hundreds and sometimes thousands of people are housed together and grouped into a series of activities. To handle the coming and going entailed by the large numbers and varied activities, schools have to have a routine. That routine has to be both carefully planned and sufficiently flexible to handle the people and events. The effort required to plan, maintain, and adjust the routine is considerable, and studies of building administrators indicate that is how they spend their time. They move from activity to activity, person to person, making dozens of minor but needed adjustments in the routine.

Kmetz and Willower (1982) reported that the elementary principals they studied "averaged 40 unscheduled meetings a day . . . with a mean duration of 4.4 minutes" (p. 68). Eighty-six percent of these principals' activities (70 percent of their time) was spent in personal contact with one or more persons, and another 8 percent was spent on the telephone. The remainder was spent writing notes, completing reports, and processing correspondence, or doing similar chores (p. 66). Those authors concluded that the job of building administrator is characterized by a "high volume of work completed at an unrelenting pace." The work is characterized by "variety, brevity and fragmentation of tasks, and preferences for verbal media and live action" (p. 72).

Martin and Willower (1981) reported secondary principals as exhibiting the same "busy person" syndrome as elementary principals, just described. These people spent 16 percent of their time on desk work. An additional 45 percent was spent on meetings, scheduled and unscheduled (and exchanges, sometimes on the phone, sometimes in person, amounted to 19 percent). The remainder of the time was spent being in charge and being available; that is, touring, observing, monitoring, announcing, and supervising. In these latter situations, principals positioned themselves visibly so as to invite further interaction.

Martin and Willower found that secondary principals' routine, too, was marked by multiple, verbal interactions with the same variety of people that interacted with the elementary principals. The principals' encounters usually lasted at most a few minutes and, even these were interrupted; for example, "407 separate activities . . . (were) interrupted by 1457 other tasks" (p. 74). Fifty percent of all observed activities in that study were interrupted or were interruptions of other activities. Interruptions proliferated to the point that much of the principals' day is spent in what the authors call, "polychronics," doing two things at once.

Crowson and Porter-Gehrie (1980) reported a similarly large number of interactions, up to thirty per hour, for the urban principals they studied. According to them:

> [A typical urban principal is] approached throughout each day by teachers and by pupils; is at the beck and call of central office personnel; is in frequent consultation with janitors, clerks, assistant principals and counselors; is often on the telephone with fellow principals; and is additionally available to social workers, teacher aides, attendance and security officers, cafeteria workers, reading consultants, nurses, psychologists and many others who add to the institutional fabric of the urban school. (p. 50)

Those authors also describe administrators' interactions as brief, conducted on the run, one-to-one, and usually initiated by the other person. Their principals are not authority/leader figures, but street-level bureaucrats, who represent government to the people (p. 46) and who, like most street-level bureaucrats, develop shortcuts to alleviate the tensions produced by too many activities crammed into too little space and time. Principals make decisions on the spot by concentrating on elements of a problem they can solve, by ignoring elements they cannot, and by preventing the emergence of problems by being present and accessible.

The behavior of these building administrators is quite similar to a group of educational program managers that Sproull (1981) studied. She characterized her subjects' routine as (1) "choppy...with many episodes of brief duration," (2) "oral...spent talking to people," (3) "unpredictable...without visible pattern,"...and (4) "as much other directed as self directed" (pp. 116–118). Her administrators were always busy and active. They engaged in approximately sixty interactions a day with a mean duration of 5.6 minutes, most always inside, not outside the building, and always with other people, with those others setting the agenda. "Even when the manager...is the initiator of interaction, it is usually to attend a topic raised by someone else" (p. 116).

These managers were not experts in a technical sense; rather they were facilitators and their specialty was managing the coming and going of people and events. From the summary studies, one could conclude that the task of school administration is to manage multiple and simultaneous issues through a series of personal interactions. One could also conclude that the principal's central concern is with the routine that meshes people and events into predictable patterns.

Sproull (1981), who concentrated on communication patterns of her managers, described administrative activities as "short range, casual, familiar, idiosyncratic and not highly redundant" (p. 117). She found that they paid relatively "little attention to issues directly related to teaching and learning. Teachers do not come to him or her for advice about difficult or interesting teaching situations" (p. 117). The administrators she studied spent their time scheduling people and events, attending meetings at which scheduling events was a major topic, and processing the flow of activity through the organization. They also "grease" their interactions with a great deal of informal socializing. Her estimate of the time spent on "last night's football game or next week's motorcycle trip" (p. 117) was 11 percent of the entire day and 35 percent of the nonstructured part of the day. Both Sproull (1981) and Crowson and Porter-Gehrie (1980) cite Mintzberg (1971), and support his characterization of managerial work as unrelenting, varied, brief, ad hoc, verbal, and personal (pp. 436–437).

For more detail, in *The Man in the Principal's Office* (1978), Wolcott describes the annual work cycle of Ed Bell, principal of Freedom Elementary School. Ed does just what the summary studies said principals do: engages in a series of activities, many originating in chance encounters. He also attends meetings, calls people, seeks or gives information, and walks around opening himself to further interactions and inquiries from staff and students.

For example, the following occurred in the first half-hour of one day. (1) Ed was greeted before he took off his coat by the cook who first asked if she could talk to him and then without waiting for a reply launched into the problem of milk deliveries being short seven or eight bottles. (2) Ed accompanied the cook to the cafeteria to examine the issue in more detail. (3) He returned to the office, began his first tour, and stopped to chat with a beginning teacher. (4) He checked the aquarium in which he became interested during a science fair. (5) He entered a conversation between a teacher and counselor about one boy who had bitten another. He greeted another teacher and a few children and chatted with another teacher in her room. (6) He went to talk to another staff member about the disappearing milk. That person agreed to monitor the milk distribution. (7) He led a class while waiting for a sub. (8) He greeted the sub and answered some of her questions. (9) He picked up a broken chair to take to the office. (10) He checked on another staff member who had been ill. (11) He returned to the office with the broken chair, and greeted a new student (pp. 124–125). A broken chair, some missing milk, an aquarium, an inquiry into a staff member's health, greeting a sub, and a bitten child are the minutiae that initiate this principal's full and busy day.

Not all of Ed Bell's activities are so unconnected. Sometimes a set of interactions revolves around a particular problem. For instance:

1. A first grade child had been sent to the office by the substitute teacher to get a "different" record player. Her pupils were already gathered in the multi-purpose room and waiting to use it.
2. The secretary asked Ed (the principal) what to do. Ed said he would go see what was wrong.
3. Ed accompanied the child to the multi-purpose room. The substitute teacher showed him a broken stylus on the record player she had taken from the classroom to the multi-purpose room. She had been assured earlier in the day that a machine was always available there, although that had not been the case. She had returned to the classroom to get a player but had been unable to use it because of the broken stylus.
4. Ed said he would get a record player for her.
5. Ed went to the intermediate wing to check with the teacher who supervised the upper grade lunchroom (Mr. Adam) to ask why the record player that was supposed to remain in the multi-purpose room was not there and to learn who had taken it. Adam told him which teacher had borrowed it.
6. Ed went to the primary wing to get the player that belonged in the multi-purpose room. He had to interrupt another class to do this. As he closed up the machine in order to carry it, he reminded the teacher (Mrs. Skirmish) that the player in the multi-purpose room was not to be removed. She, in turn, explained that she had needed to borrow it this one time because the other players were all spoken for that afternoon.
7. Ed took the player to the multi-purpose room, set it up and waited to see if it operated properly before leaving.
8. Returning to the office with the broken player, he told the secretary to "type out a work order" for his signature so the player could be repaired in the audio-visual department at the central office.
9. Ed glanced at the clock and realized he should already have been on his way to pick up Bill St. Claire en route to a meeting at another school. He grabbed his coat and hat, hurriedly informing the secretary where he would be and that he would return around 4:00 P.M. (Wolcott, 1978, p. 128)

A broken stylus may seem trivial, but placed in the context of the classroom, with its crowds, activity, and motion and inside a school, where hundreds of people and events are crammed into a small amount of space and time, it is not trivial. The player that worked was essential to the plan that the regular teacher developed, whereas the player that did not work disrupted the other teacher's plans. Ed is the logical choice to solve problems. He has freedom of movement; he knows where things are and where they are supposed to be; he knows whom to see, about what. And he carries the authority needed to get the record player, and whatever is broken, working. He is the staff member least specialized, least role-bound, least confined by space, and most open to going wherever there is a problem.

Wolcott (1978) said of Ed Bell, he was "caught up with problems and problems caught up with him" (p. 123). The term "problem" deserves explanation. It appears that a problem is anything that upsets or is capable of upsetting the routine. In Freedom Elementary, the problems were a broken stylus, missing milk, a broken chair, and a bitten or wandering child. Other studies describe administrators involved with somewhat more difficult issues, e.g., persistent skipping, discipline, fights, and unhappy parents. By themselves and except in rare cases, these are minor issues, which administrators attend among their ongoing duties. In any school, packed with people and events, one can depend on incurring several of these minor disturbances each day. The trick is to address them quickly and effectively, and prevent them from rippling through and upsetting contiguous events. Just as the school routine is essential to making sense of the coming and going, so a problem is anything that can upset the coming and going. The principal's job is to serially attend to those and thus preserve the routine.

Evidence of the routine's importance to administrators is given in Smith and Keith's (1971) study of why open education was discontinued at Kensington elementary. Extracted from their December 9th field notes are some observations of visitors who comment

> about the noise level that existed in the perception core.... The kids were rather wild and much more like the first two weeks of school over at the junior high building. Part of this is because...several teachers are out today. Irma and Liz are ill, and Jack is at some kind of meeting. David's kids are roaming quite freely, and he lets them come and go as they please. One teacher told me that on Monday David's kids were wandering all over the building (Smith and Keith, 1971, p. 165)

Smith and Keith (1971) continue: "Most school personnel, in their franker moments, will speak of rules and control of pupils as a necessity. In its simplest form, control means that pupils comply with school rules and the directives of teachers" (p. 165). Pupil control is the issue. The elements that confound the issue for the administrators are crowdedness, busyness, and a narrow definition of appropriate behavior.

Kensington Elementary's story is one of the staff trying to broaden the definition of appropriate behavior. However, they could not agree on what constituted appropriate behavior. Their inability to agree meant that pupil behavior in that school, though certainly not bad, was not coordinated into a discernible routine, and was therefore deemed unacceptable. After only three months of open education, Eugene, the principal, could no longer tolerate students' wandering randomly, the staff's inability to agree on standards, and parents' complaints. In December he unilaterally issued three single-spaced pages of rules and regulations. Covered in detail were lunch behavior, waste disposal, student grouping, safety, noise, fighting, running, promptness, assorted do's and don't's, and the dictum that teachers enforce all of the above. The routine was back and the principal was in charge.

Several authors speak of the principal's commitment to the routine. Smith and Geoffrey's (1968) Mr. Inman does not like the routine upset. Kidder (1989) described how the principal prevented trouble.

> Al would lean slightly backward, arms folded on his chest, and bark at the first signs of mischief. "Hey you! Yeah, you! Excuse me! Stay in line with your mouth shut." (Kidder, 1989, p. 45)

In the urban schools studied in the 1970s, maintaining the routine was particularly important because it was believed central to racial peace and safety. Disruptions and possible disruptions were legion. Mr. D, the administrative assistant at Urban High, described a morning thus.

> What a day...we started out with 20 dogs in the building this morning. We chased them all over the building but when we got back to the office there were 25 kids waiting. Halfway through them, the junior high called and they had food poisoning and dismissed 600 kids and 300 of them came over here. I'm running around all morning trying to get them out. (Cusick, 1983, pp. 26–27)

It was in that and similar schools that, in the interest of safety and racial peace, the routine was minimized to "five by five," five periods a day, five days a week; no homeroom, no study halls, no cafeteria, no activities, no sports. The administrators believed that unstructured situations were dangerous and so reduced the routine to what was manageable, given the situation.

Problems with the routine fill up administrators' days. Cusick and Peters (1979, field notes) interviewed thirty small-town principals regarding their role and found them spending their time settling minor issues. On the day of Mr. Benson's interview, Peters found him weary to the point of resigning, which he did a few months later. At 1:00 P.M., on the day Peters came to interview,

> [Mr. Benson had] spent from 7:40 filling out slips, checking notes. I've a stack of notes here calling parents to make sure they are legitimate, doing assistant principal work basically and I've not yet done anything to this point that a principal would do...except answer the phone on a few inquiries. But the rest of my time is spent entirely on attendance. I've got 7–8 kids now I've caught skipping out of the group, an hour here, an hour there type thing, one student all day...this is where I've spent my time. (Cusick and Peters, 1979, field notes)

Sometimes "problems" are mere misunderstanding, but sometimes they involve the inevitable disputes that occur when people with separate interests bump into each other. Cusick and Peters's principals were usually in the center of one or another minor dispute.

> Well...cheerleaders and pom pom girls have been fighting like cats and dogs...if they would get me in on some of these things a little earlier, it would be much easier because at the time I got into it, it was at the point where everybody would just as soon kill everybody as look at them. So then you are in there trying to play peacemaker and father confessor...all at the same time. (Cusick and Peters, 1979, field notes)

Another explained how she had to iron out a dispute with a territorial custodian who guards the

> keys to all the closets and the brooms and when we put on a performance, here we are to clean it up and we have to find a custodian to find the brooms and when I said something about it, he said "Do you have a key to your office?" and I said "Yes." And he said "Do you have a key to the building?" and I said "Yes." and he said "Then, that's all you need." (Cusick and Peters, 1979, field notes)

So far the descriptions show building administrators as busy, active, and involved. They spend their days turned from one matter to another, usually with other people setting the agenda. The topics are the minutiae of the routine and frequently involve some question over behavior, space, supplies and resources. Most often, administrators enter into these issues with the responsibility to alter, adjust, or otherwise solve these matters so that the established routine can continue.

It appears that school administration requires two specialized skills. First, one has to get along with people. When students, teachers, or parents head for the principal's office, it is often because they are upset. The principal cannot become upset because to do so would exacerbate an already emotional situation. The principal has to factor out the emotions, including her or his own, before dealing with the parties.

Administrators may demonstrate a severity bordering on anger, for example, Kidder's (1989) Al: "Hey, you! Yeah, you! Excuse me! Stay in line with your mouth shut!" One has the feeling, however, that the anger is feigned to impress potential offenders in the audience. Nor can the administrator be inflexible. As one of Peters's interviewees said of his superintendent who would have liked a more strictly run school,

> [the superintendent] realizes that if he walked into the building and tried to take it over, he'd have chaos in no time at all. He'd like to see things run on a very strict program. It doesn't work and he knows it doesn't work and he knows if he sat down in this seat and tried to take that approach, they'd have him out of here in a week. (Cusick and Peters, 1979, field notes)

In addition to an even temper and good personal skills, the principal has to have some abstract sense of the school as an entity. The many adjustments principals make have to fit into a coherent plan that combines people and events. The plan has to include the way people and events coalesce. It probably includes a definition of education, an idea about the place of education in life, and a connecting of what goes on with what should or could go on. That abstract coherence existing in the mind of the administrator is the center of the school as an organization. If the principal has no abstraction of how things coordinate, contiguous events will collide with one another, disorder will spread, and routine will fall apart. Being able to get along serially with a great many people and having an overall idea of the school as an organization are the essentials of school administration.

ADMINISTRATORS AND DISCIPLINE

The summarizing studies cited earlier show that administrators spend approximately 25 percent of their time in activities related to discipline, either with offending students or with teachers and parents talking about offending students. This major concern, in large and small, urban and rural, public and private schools deserves particular attention. Attendance and discipline have to be discussed directly in relation to the school routine, because, except in rare cases, they are violations of the routine. This section describes these issues and the way principals handle them.

Sometimes it is not the principal, but the assistant principal(s) who handles discipline. The principal avoids an unwanted image. Lightfoot (1983) reported that in her large schools, vice principals and assistants attended to student infractions. At JFK a vice principal was assigned to exert toughness, to be the "head chopper" (p. 70), because (according to one observer) the principal "could not be seen as good if [the vice principal] wasn't seen as bad" (p. 70).

When control is problematic, all administrators work on it. At Carver High in Atlanta, even with a vice principal, the principal was still out in the halls with his walkie-talkie through which he maintained surveillance of corridors and grounds, students, and teachers (Lightfoot, 1983). Grant (1988) reported that at Hamilton High in the 1970s, the issue consumed 90 percent of the principal's time. In Cusick's (1983) Factory High and Urban High, all administrators were assigned to it, and periodically they would gather and "sweep" the corridors, lavatories, and open spaces to get the students into class and the nonstudents out of the building.

The particulars vary with the situation. At Freedom Elementary, a serious issue involved defacing of school property or roughhousing by some second grade boys (Wolcott, 1978, pp. 141–142). The issue was more serious at Hamilton High where in one race riot, the principal himself was hit with a chair and suffered a concussion; and after another, the members of one side were "all on one knee" and 14 or 15 members of the other were "laid out all over the place" (Grant, 1988, p. 44).

A prevailing attitude among administrators is that good discipline and good attendance go together. If the students will show up in school and attend class, they will behave and learn. Monitoring attendance also casts administrators as instructors, teaching one of life's all-important lessons, to show up on time. As Mr. D of Urban High said:

> You know what the biggest problem we have here?...It's attendance. We can't get the kids to school and if we do then we have to get them to class. You really have to believe that what you're doing is right. I couldn't do it otherwise. Like...you know what's the worst thing kids can do, not knifing, not talking back to teachers, but skipping, because one thing we can't do is let kids come to class, walk in, look around and decide, 'Well, I don't want to be here, I think I'll go home.' Someday those kids will be in places where they have to show up and we have to teach them that. (Cusick, 1983, p. 27)

What was important to the routine was also important in life. If one learned to abide by school rules, he or she would learn how to behave correctly in society. A vision of the larger society and correct behavior in that society was thus integrated in Mr. D's abstract coherence.

Several interesting sides emerge regarding the principals' involvement with attendance and discipline. One is the solicitousness they show to errant pupils. Discipline is not absolute, nor is it handled absolutely. Administrators enforce the rules with a combination of caring about the school and caring about the students. They might bark when out in the hall, but with a troubled or errant student, more often they display personal concern. Rossman, Corbett, and Firestone (1988) describe a scene at Somerville High:

> Shouts are heard outside the discipline room. Five or six students come in with one girl, holding her arms. The dean walks in, takes the girl over to a bench, asks her to sit down, while telling her friends to go back to their classes. He turns to the girl and asks softly, "What happened? Do you know the other girl [the one who started the fight]?...Do you live near her? Have classes with her?"
> The girl is pretty upset but can tell her side of the story. The dean asks her, "Do you want to go home? Do you want to see the nurse?"
> The other girl is brought in by one of the disciplinarians. The dean talks to both, trying to find out what went on. He turns to me and says "It was a 'he say, I say' or a 'she say, I say' type of dispute." He shrugs his shoulders. The girls are suspended but with some TLC. (p. 104)

At Suburban High Cusick and Wheeler (1987) described a vice principal worried about a troublesome student, to the point of going over to the boy's house in the evening to check on him. As he explained, "It's Christmas and his mother's having trouble. He hasn't been in school and I was worried about him" (p. 22). Solicitousness is not an end in itself. However much the administrators may like and care about students, the purpose of their actions and of their personal concern is to bring the offending students back into the school's definition of appropriate behavior. Solicitousness and civility are among the means they use.

Factory High studied by Cusick (1983) had four administrators, a principal, and three grade principals assigned to discipline and attendance. Student infractions ranged from tardiness to skipping, verbal exchanges to assaults, forgetting a pencil to threatening a teacher. Even the serious matters, accompanied by emotional outbursts, calm down by the time the parties reach the office where the principal takes over the matter.

The movements in the office were almost ritualized. The offender approaches the counter, hears the charge, gives a predictable excuse, and enters into an exchange with the administrator: "I didn't do nothing." "Well, it says here you failed to hand in your work five days in a row." "That old teacher doesn't like me. Like all I do is walk in and she starts yelling" (p. 29). The administrator listens, but having heard it all several times, does not take the excuse too seriously. Neither does he take the student's infraction too seriously. The administrator cites previous incidents, imposes the penalty, issues a warning, adds a homily on citizenship, perhaps adds an inquiry about a sibling or a comment on the student's good behavior in other classes or performance on a school team, and the matter is finished. The student leaves, another approaches the desk and the scene is repeated. Infractions and penalities are as much a part of routine as is the schedule.

Just as teachers care a great deal about their personal relations with students, so administrators care about the students they encounter, even the frequent offenders. In most cases, these have been to the office several times and know what to expect. The administrators have seen these students before, and are not emotionally involved in the infraction, as might be the teacher back in the classroom. The emotions accompanying the interactions reflect some reciprocated liking on the part of the administrators for the offending students.

Solicitousness ends, however, when the offending behavior threatens the school routine. Wheeler (Cusick and Wheeler, 1987) studied Urban High in 1986 and found the vice principal for attendance so besieged with students requesting late slips that he refused to pass them out (p. 23) and just sent the students away rather than have them enter and upset others.

> The bell ended the second period.... A steady stream of students started walking in, eight of them asking for late slips. (The attendance officer) started telling them: "You've got to get it the best way you can. Go home." "Look, I'm going to miss a test." "Well, I'm sorry. You'll have to get in there the best way you can. Go Home." He turned to me and said: "If I gave them a late slip, I would be giving out 200 a day." (Cusick and Wheeler, 1987, field notes)

Students who could neither show up nor show up on time were simply not welcome in that school. The attendance office appeared out of control, but classes were protected from a steady stream of tardy students. The school's routine was thus preserved. Along with its preservation went an absence of personal concern for students who threatened the routine. In that office, faced with literally hundreds of offending students, solicitousness was abandoned. Excuses were not heeded; it wasn't clear where the ejected students were to go. No attention was paid as to how they might get home, what they might do the rest of the day, or what the suspension meant for their academic program. They were just thrown out. Administrators are tolerant of errant students, up to the point where their behavior threatens to undermine the routine. At that point either the situation for them is redefined and they are sent to alternative schools, which Wheeler also described, or they are simply thrown out. Either way, they are no longer present and no longer disturbing the flow of events.

To further illustrate the limited place of personal concern in preserving the coherence, consider Peshkin's (1986) Baptist Academy, where the principal and teachers did everything they could to bring students into their version of Christian reality. Peshkin described the principal making disciplinary decisions

> within the framework of an extensive structure designed to control students' time, thought, movement and social relations. He and his fellow educators hope students will develop self-discipline that is securely rooted in the Word, so that their love of Christ, not a signed pledge or a demerit system, will constrain their behavior. (p. 109)

In practice, this severe-sounding policy was administered in a personal and caring way. Peshkin described one of Headmaster McGraw's disciplinary sessions.

> "How are you Jon? I like your belt buckle. 'Talking after being warned'." [He reads from the demerit slip.] "I didn't say a word." "OK. You're forgiven."
>
> "Hi Rita. Moved your seat to talk to Perry." "Yes, but I didn't talk. Just moved my hands." "That's communicating and it disrupts the study hall. Five demerits."
>
> "Jenny, come right in and join the fellowship. 'Talking with Sue after being warned.'" "The second time Sue and I just looked at each other." "No Talking at all?" "No Sir." "OK."
>
> "Hello Dick. What a mass of these [demerit slips] you have . . . . It's a good thing I don't have arthritis or I couldn't lift the pile." (pp. 108–109)

Enforcement was thus placed within a context of personal concern and warm relations, but concern and warmth did not extend to students who rejected the school's vision of Christian reality. The academy could not tolerate students who did not accept the world as the school presented it. Just as students who threatened the administrator's notion of abstract coherence were rejected from Urban High, so they were rejected by Mr. McGraw.

The administrator's task is to protect and propagate the school's coherence and to align students' behavior with that coherence. The coherence includes both the school's internal routine and a notion of the world outside the school, for which students are being prepared. School rules protect the routine, reflect the school's notion of the outside world, and prepare students for the outside world.

Students who refuse to conform to school rules mark themselves as opposed to everything the school stands for and thus mark themselves as aliens.

An additional example of limited solicitousness is from Lightfoot's (1983) account of the upper-class St. Paul's school. The rector did everything he could to make sure no student "fell through the cracks" (p. 234). His influence extended to every aspect of the program; for example, mandatory chapel, communal and formal dinners, small classes, Sunday evenings at his home, and even psychologists to put the "mind, body and soul together" (p. 234) so that each student would develop the character and habits of the ideal upper-class adult. St Paul's wanted to imbue in these most privileged students, trustworthiness, responsibility, and morality on and off campus. But when some students were caught drinking off campus, an offense that would be ignored in most high schools, they were denied graduation. The rector's concern for the boys ended at his definition of what was appropriate.

Administrators' primary concern is the school, or more accurately, the abstract coherence by which the school makes sense of both itself and its larger world. They spend their days making minor adjustments in the coming and going, correcting discrepancies and conflicts, prodding, admonishing, encouraging, always in accord with that abstraction. They care about students in a very humane way. However, they are administrators, and their solicitousness ends when the students' actions fall outside what the school's abstract notion can tolerate. Preservation of the school, or more accurately, of the abstract coherence within which the school's myriad events make sense, is the administrators' chief concern.

CONTROL VERSUS EDUCATION

It is rarely the case that young people, if left alone in school, do bad things. But it is unlikely that when left alone they will do what the school calls "good things." Left to themselves, students rarely choose to sit quietly, open math, history, English, and science books and read. On the contrary, they slide easily into peer interactions and carry on behaviors reflective of their class, culture, and youthful interests. There is a great difference between the behavior students freely choose and the behavior schools have to enforce. That air of quiet industry that school visitors like so much to find is not the result of students being left alone to pursue their inclinations, but the result of constant planning, vigilance, and monitoring by staff. Because the schools' definition of appropriate behavior is so much more restricted than what students would freely choose, control is always problematic.

Crowdedness exacerbates the problem. Had the blacks and whites in Hamilton High in the early 1970s been left alone, they would have avoided one another, rather than fought. Only when the school pushed them together into a small space did their animosities erupt into violence. The busyness occasioned by the specialized curriculum exacerbates crowdedness. In the suburban school studied by Cusick and Wheeler in 1987, every 50 minutes, nine times a day, 1735 students and 105 teachers got up, moved into the narrow halls, went somewhere else, and began a different activity. Policemen, firemen, and theater managers know that crowds are dangerous, and nine times a day those halls were extremely crowded. Density, busyness, and narrowly defined appropriateness demand constant monitoring of student behavior. It is with good reason that administrators are obsessed with control.

Consider McNeil's (1986) account of administrators and order. At her Forest Hills school, "routine was the key" (p. 67) and "administrative purposes dealt mostly with processing students through the credentialing system" (p. 68). In that school, which was orderly, she explained that "disciplinary controls were less overtly a part of administrative concern...than the maintenance of general order in programs as well as of behavior" (p. 68). At Freeburg High there was a "preoccupation with control" and "attention to academics...was lost in the pressure to keep students physically corralled and correctly behaved." Administrative policies treated students in the aggregate, announcing policies that affected the movement or activities of all, though most caused no problems (p. 91).

At Maizeville High, "lack of administrative expertise or active interest in academics; administrative absorption in disciplining a small number of chronic offenders...administrative attention to truancy and minor but frequent infractions such as littering or occasionally skipping class grew into a full time exercise which left little time or staff for supporting...educational purposes" (p. 120). McNeil was careful to say that none of the schools she studied were "out-of-control." In fact, save for Grant's Hamilton High in 1969, none of the schools described was ever out of control. Still, control was the administrator's central concern.

The issue is not whether administrators are obsessed with control—they are. The issue is whether their obsession is justified and whether it overrides their concern with education. To address the issue one would have to consider learning apart from control. But the studies do not show administrators doing that: they do not regard learning as an activity separate from their abstract coherence. Instead, they fold the elements together into a single notion with several parts, learning, only one of them. Outsiders may dichotomize control and learning. But for administrators they are not dichotomized; they are bound together.

Definitions of learning change according to school, class, and even staff member. The importance of showing up on time was the basis of Mr. D's comments in Urban High (Cusick, 1983). "One thing the kids have to learn is to show up on time...." At Hamilton High, learning was noninterfering behavior, and a student could "goof around" as long as he did not interfere. In West Haven, learning was working quietly by oneself. "Minding one's own business" was the referent that Powell, et al. (1985) found in large secondary schools with their libertarian requirement that a student not prevent another from doing what the other wanted. At St. Paul's learning was acquiring the characteristics of the elite; at the Baptist Academy, it was acceptance of the school's version of Christian reality. More precise notions of learning exist, certainly, but they belong to teachers and students. For administrators assigned to make sense of the whole endeavor, learning occurs as students give evidence of accepting the school's abstract coherence. As the guardians of that coherence, the administrators become teachers, and what they teach is one of life's important lessons, compliance with the institution. Good control is visible evidence that the administrator(s) has successfully blended people and events, teaching and administration.

And as argued in Chapter 9, control—the imposition of collective norms onto a social microcosm—is also an equity issue. First, it is visible proof that all students, those more and less economically advantaged, are bound by the same rules, regulations, and requirements. All have to show up, dress and behave in an acceptable manner, and take the required courses in English, math, social studies, and science. Second, when the teacher and the principal are in control, all students are equal. Class and culture differences, so visible and important in the students' informal associations, are neutralized. Finally, the schools' bureaucracy sets a learning agenda for students who come to school without one. The emphasis on control not only contains the students and enables orderly processes to go on, it is visible evidence of the school's commitment to egalitarian ideals.

A related issue, touched on in earlier chapters, is whether the principal is the instructional leader. The descriptive studies give a few instances of administrators actually working on instruction. Some reflect on what they would do if they had time to work on curriculum. Mr. Benson, who shortly after Peters's interview resigned, had some ideas:

> I could concentrate on having these teachers sit down and rewrite course descriptions, meeting a couple nights a week. But right now I have detention every night after school. The teachers go at 3:00; the kids leave at 2:30. But in order to get anything done, you have to meet within the department, right after school. They don't like to start a meeting at 3:00 or 3:30 when they are supposed to be out. (Cusick and Peters, 1979, field notes)

Not only does Mr. Benson not have the time, it is questionable whether, if he did have the time, instruction would improve. The few descriptions of principals working on instruction show that their ability to improve it is limited. McNeil's (1986) Nelson High was a place known for hiring "academic principals" whose "beginnings as teachers had not been rationalized into bureaucratic modes"... who "could discuss subject matter and instruction with teachers" (p. 55), who did not let "administrative attention to discipline...intrude into teacher's time" (p. 59), and who "provided supports for curriculum building" (p. 56). Nelson's principal was himself "with the teachers [working] on long range goals of better articulation with the junior highs and of more attempts...to cross subject field lines for curriculum development" (p. 58). He narrowed the distance between himself and teachers, joined with them in collegial decision-making, limited his authority while enlarging theirs, and de-emphasized his role in maintaining the organization. But even in Nelson High, where the principal did all the right things, classrooms were still characterized by the emphasis on control described in the preceding chapter. The principal's efforts did not penetrate the classroom.

Another example was from Lightfoot's (1983) John F. Kennedy High, where the vice principal was assigned the "head chopping" while the principal worked on curriculum. The latter's efforts included implementing a curriculum around the quarter system, encouraging new courses, and allowing students to have increased choice. By his own admission, the

> individual freedom soon turned to chaos. There was utter confusion, greater inef-
> ficiency, and unbelievable administrative hassle."...After two years of experimen-
> tation, [the principal] decided to streamline the curriculum and return to the tra-
> ditional arrangement of semesters. He wanted to develop a core curriculum that
> reflected the essential building blocks of learning, "basic, substantive, no frills, all
> real." (p. 65)

Unlike McNeil's (1986) principal who would have made "working on cur-
riculum" a collegial endeavor, JFK's principal acted alone, and as he explained about his second restructuring, "I didn't care about the outcry of teachers, parents, or kids...." (Lightfoot, 1983, p. 65).

To "work on curriculum" then, appears to mean, sometimes broadening and in others cases narrowing the range of offerings and the degree of teacher autonomy. It can also mean encouraging teachers to do some revising of their courses. In some schools, it means giving up some decision-making and taking a more collegial role. In others, it means the principal making decisions alone. The principal of JFK was apparently free to reorganize the school's curriculum and reorganize it again when his first efforts failed. Working on curriculum does not seem to mean anything very different from either working on the routine or working with discipline. The administrator's attention is still on the arrangement of people and events. One has the sense that curriculum work is similar to the principal's other activities: busy, verbal, interacting serially with a great many people, and concerned primarily with the abstract coherence by which the many activities make sense. The interest and the focus change, but the activity remains constant.

THE PRINCIPAL OUTSIDE THE SCHOOL

Standing at the intersection of the school and external groups, administrators have to make sense of events and parties outside their school. Described next is how they mesh, or overlap, activities inside the school with groups outside, who are also part of the overall system.

Ideally, the descriptions from here on should progress in an orderly fash-
ion: from the school to the central office, board, community, and state department. However, the descriptions do not portray so tidy a world. They show the

educational system beyond the school as crowded, messy, and unpredictable, with numerous interest and advocacy groups exerting influence. Iannaccone (1967) explains the confusion as a result of educational governance, a

> holdover from the eighteenth and nineteenth century in the United States. It has been superceded in many other areas of governmental affairs by more centralized state agencies, but school districts remain the governmental operation most like a midwestern adaptation of the New England Town Meeting. (pp. 8–9)

The public forum, however, is somewhat more contentious than the peaceful vision elicited by a New England town meeting. Cuban (1975) in his study of school politics in Washington, D.C., referred to

> the gross number of part-time participants in school-system decision making.... Beyond board members, superintendent and central administration, there are principal, teacher and student organizations, municipal officials, parental and civic groups, as well as cranky and fired up individuals. Many of these participants enter, make noise and exit at different points in time, with varying volume and energy invested. ...(p. 27)

Participants shift but issues persist. One is student control, which is as much an issue between schools and outside groups as between administrators and teachers. In Cusick's (1983) Factory High, the teachers wanted the principal to throw out some of the more difficult students. However, several groups were watching and counting to see that the school was not too hard on those same students. Expulsions had to be acted on by a central staff that did not like to lose the money each student brought under the state's system of per-pupil funding. The Black Ministers' Association did not like white administrators expelling African-American students. The Board of Education had adopted a policy that blamed staff for student problems; for example, children do not fail to learn, the schools...fail to educate (p. 36). Expulsions cost financial support. As the superintendent of a neighboring district put it: "You don't get parents to vote (financial support) by throwing their kids out of school" (p. 37).

In Grant's (1988) Hamilton High, rights-conscious parents watched to see how the school treated rights-demanding children. A community organizer urged parents to "Get the facts on the teacher. Take a friend with you to observe the teacher, three or four times" (p. 55). Other studies portray parents as feeling that their own job is finished if they send their children to school. Any trouble is the school's fault. In response to being told her boy would not graduate, a mother told the principal in Hennigh's (1979) study of South Umpqua, Oregon, "I did my part. I sent my boy to high school in clean underwear and clean socks for four years and I expect him to graduate on time" (p. 86).

School-community interactions are further complicated by the propensity of people to exaggerate events in which their children are involved. The high school principal in South Umpqua gave an example. A mother phoned saying that her daughter had been threatened by a girl with a knife. The principal asked the daughter, "Did [you] see the knife?" "No." "Did the other girl have a knife in her purse?" She did not remember if the girl had a purse. "Why did you say she threatened you with a knife?" "Well, she talked to me in a way I thought she was going to attack me with a knife" (Hennigh, 1979, p. 148).

Disputes between the school and the community can foment dissension between principals and superintendents. Hollingshead (1949) described the Elmtown principal's detention policy, which inconvenienced children of influential parents, who took their complaints to the superintendent, who in turn overrode the principal's policy. The superintendent reflected on the pressures.

> I used to be a reformer and stood for strict ideals, but I've grown older and I've learned that you have to give a lot and take a lot in this business. I don't mean to say I have abandoned all principles, but you have to work with people, and so at times you just have to wink at things. It's a hard thing to meet all the criticisms that are brought to bear on a person in a position like this. It used to make me mad and I'd really blow up; but now I just keep still and let things take their course. (p. 135)

Principals need an abstract coherence to make sense of the schools' myriad and disparate events, but they have to negotiate that abstract coherence with several parties and individuals, outside of school, each of which has its own notions. In such a situation, administrative authority is limited. The building, the mostly tenured and contracted staff, the students, the curriculum created by the district, state accrediting agencies, and colleges to which students aspire, are independent of principals. Contracts tell teachers when to come and go; transportation schedules tell students when to come and go.

Most schools run smoothly, but whatever authority principals manage to achieve is dependent on their ability to accommodate several parties. Energetic principals take their openings where they can find them. In difficult situations, principals have more freedom. The principal of Carver was brought in to "turn the school around" (Lightfoot, 1983). Hamilton High appointed a new principal with the expectation that he would "do something dramatic" to improve the situation. Sometimes in larger cities principals can push their educational agenda, even in opposition to the formal system.

Elliott Shapiro, principal of P.S. no. 119 in Manhattan's Harlem, was so incensed at conditions in his school and inaction on the part of the central office that he placed this notice in a New York City newspaper.

HELP!
HELP US TO GET A NEW SCHOOL
TO SAVE OUR CHILDREN
GIVE US A BUILDING WITHOUT

1. Rats and Roaches on Every Floor.
2. A Leaking Roof.
3. Broken Door Frames.
4. Split Sessions (1/2 an Education).

5. Refrigerator Temperatures in the Winter and Oven-like Sweltering during Summer.
6. Irreparable Plumbing Resulting in: Backups, Leaks, Flooded Yards and Corridors and Lunchrooms.
7. Sagging, Dangerous Walls.
8. Overcrowding in Lunchrooms and Classrooms.
9. Unsanitary Children's Toilets.
10. Wasteful Temporary Patching of Obsolete and Intrinsically Inadequate Scrap Pile Facilities Without Shoving the Taxpayers' Money Down the Drain.
11. Condemnation of Nine Classrooms in Our Old (1899) School Where Our Entire Building Is Wrought with Fire and Health Hazards.

OUR CHILDREN DESERVE
A NEW SCHOOL
NOW!!

The Teaching, Clerical and Administrative staff of Public School no. 119. (In *World Telegram,* May 22, 1961, and Hentoff, 1966, p. 36).

Shapiro and his school received the desired attention, first, predictably enough, from an associate superintendent: "Ellie, you're disgracing us! This should have been kept a family affair" (p. 37). He also received visits from the board of education—"a Rolls Royce stopped at the door of P.S. no. 119. A member of the Board of Education stepped out" (p. 40). Even the Mayor made a visit, during which a rat was sighted: "A teacher and several students suddenly pointed vigorously at a corner of the room and yelled 'Rat'" (p. 37). Even the superintendent called: "Hello, Elliott, this is John...." "John who?" (p. 36).

Naturally embarrassed, the superintendent accused Shapiro of faking the appearance of the rat during the Mayor's visit; Shapiro in turn accused the superintendent of allowing himself to be misled about actual conditions in schools that serve poor children.

Shapiro told the superintendent that all the way up the chain of command in the school system were people with a vested interest in keeping the truth away from the person on the next rung up. By the time anything came to the top...conditions were reported as being fine. (p. 39)

Hentoff's book, which helped foment the disaggregation of the New York City school system, portrayed Shapiro as having a coherent view of his obligations. Shapiro believed children deserved more money, food, attention, and respect. He formed an alliance with the community and used the media to get what he wanted. He got exterminators in the building and some needed repairs, although he later had to organize a parent demonstration to prevent repairs from interfering with instruction. Although not reported in the book, Hentoff told this author in winter 1989, that at the time of the events Shapiro's immediate superiors at the central office respected and protected him, and he was never disciplined for insubordination nor moved from his preferred P.S. no. 119.

The idea of a principal's going outside the chain of command to pressure his superiors seems unusual. But in this case, where the parties inside the organization were not responding to what Elliott wanted, he did what he had to do, or what he felt he had to do. He allied himself with outside parties—in this case, the parents and newspapers. As a player in the system, a principal may form alliances with others, inside and outside the organization to achieve his goals.

Principals create their support groups from several sources. Shapiro turned to the community and the press. Chris Zajac's principal, Al, supported the teachers in disputes with the students (Kidder, 1989). A principal at Hamilton High allied himself with the students against teachers (Grant, 1988). St. Paul's Rector allied himself with parents as evidenced by the care he exhibited in arranging a graduation ceremony attended by them. "The presenters were carefully selected by department heads and the Rector. Speeches were written, critiqued by faculty and rewritten several times." (Lightfoot, 1983, p. 241). Mr. McGraw, the principal at Peshkin's (1986) Baptist Academy, allied himself with the Minister and the Church.

For a principal to go outside the formal organization was rare in the small towns that Cusick and Peters (1979) studied where principals were restricted by their superintendents. The principal in Atlanta, Michigan described the superintendent

> coming...upstairs where most of the high school classes are and (he) walks in the teachers' lounge and it is 10 minutes before classes start...and I guess he interrogated the lot to see why they were there. Then he came to me and wanted to know why they were there and I said I wanted them in class five minutes before classes start. He wanted them in class 10 minutes before class so we changed it. (Cusick and Peters, 1979, field notes)

What was not rare was for elements from the town to show up and make their wishes known. Even Boards of Education intrude on the principal's decisions. From several interviews,

> "the junior high principal...painted the doors of the old junior high some pretty loud colors and that wasn't taken too well by a couple of members."

> "The board is concerned with kids in the halls. The parents call the school board members and they call me."

> "The parents downtown want the kids off the streets and they call the board members and they pressure me." (Cusick and Peters, 1979, field notes)

Peters's principals were most happy when left alone.

> "Most weeks I don't even see the [superintendent]."

> "He and I talk about business and there is a good feeling there."

> "He lets me run the school program. I don't think he's ever told me to do something; it rests on my decision."

> "He backs me all the way; it's my high school and I run it." "His attitude is...'here it is, you run it. You make too many mistakes we'll find someone else'" (Cusick and Peters, 1979, field notes)

One would think that one's administrative colleagues would be an important referent but the descriptions are mixed. Wolcott's (1978) Ed Bell was one of several elementary administrators supervised by a coordinator of elementary education and a superintendent. Little joint action or collegiality went on within the group. Ed admitted "I haven't seemed to have much in common with them ..." (p. 85). Even though formal interactions with his peers and subsequent influence were limited, Ed was part of a larger network of community educators. Wolcott attributed more influence to these kinship and communication networks that linked schools and staff and set the school apart from the community.

> Both male classroom teachers had wives who taught at other elementary schools within the district. Four of the women teachers had husbands who were teachers, two who taught at high schools within the district, two who taught in neighboring districts. The sister of another teacher taught at the school where Ed's colleague, Bill St. Claire, was principal. The secretary's husband taught in a junior high school nearby. The husband of another teacher worked for the district's maintenance department. (Wolcott, 1978, p. 86)

Community-school ties became important when school financial support was being sought, but Wolcott believed that this "educator subculture" exerted more influence. Comparing educators' ties to the community with their ties to one another, he noted that

> school people tend in their professional lives to serve one community—the geographical one of the attendance area—but to participate more fully in ... the cultural subsystem comprised of their fellow educators. This is especially true for administrators because of the ease with which they can circulate throughout a school district in person and by telephone.... Although educators like to think of themselves as working closely with the community they serve, the anthropologist finds it equally useful to look at the educator subculture as a relatively closed one, and to link school and community as instances of culture contact. (Wolcott, 1978, p. 87)

So far, the principal has been described as being at the conflux of several, sometimes conflicting, elements. The number of elements and the mix of participants change according to the school. Some of the elements come from inside, some from outside. The principal's task is to make sense of events outside school relative to events inside school and to create alliances with some parties in order to lever others. Both inside and outside forces are part of the principal's abstract coherence.

THE SCHOOL AND THE COMMUNITY

It is axiomatic in our federated system that the school maintain good relations with its community, not the community, per se, but community elements that interest themselves in the school. There are several points of potential conflict between school and community, most generated by the emotional ties between parents and the children they are sending to the school. Parents want their children to reflect themselves, and what schools teach may not reflect what some community members believe. Waller (1932) suggested that the separate subculture of the school is at odds with the community just because it is charged with passing an idealized culture on to the children. Agee and Evans (1936) describe schools as teaching students the locally conventional and acceptable range of knowledge. Lynd and Lynd (1929) speak of the curriculum as laced with civics, history, social studies, and government reflecting the parents' expectation that the school instill a sense of patriotism in students. In the 1950s the parents did not interfere with Hamilton High as long as the school enforced "middle class standards of courtesy and respect" (p. 19). Elmtown High (Hollingshead, 1949) was tied to the town's status system, and not-so-subtle messages clued teachers to parents' social status.

> Teachers...act judiciously in their relations with the children of the powerful; on appropriate occasions they look the other way. Teachers experienced in the system warn newcomers about this boy or that girl. Narratives, gossip, a hint here, a warning there, remarks in faculty meetings give the teacher some understanding of the situation. (p. 132)

Another matter is safety. A safe atmosphere is an orderly atmosphere and the principal's obsession with order is in part a response to the demand for safety. Urban High's principal put it succinctly. "People have to know their kids are safe. That's what we work on, all the time." (Cusick, 1983, p. 67) The worst thing that could happen in that school, which happened both in that and the previous year, was a racial conflict that spilled into the streets and so invited participation by police, by TV reporters with cameras, and by anxious parents, some carrying guns, coming to protect their children. Suburban High's vice principal said the same thing: "Parents have to know that if they send their kids here, no one is going to be patting them on the backside, holding them up in the bathroom or stealing their stuff" (Cusick and Wheeler, 1987, p. 22).

And too many parents have particular expectations for their children, and they expect the school to reflect their wishes. They have their own ideas of education, of the education they want for their children, and of what the school should do. The successful professionals who sent their children to that suburban school bluntly told the principal they would take their children to private schools if they did not get the honors curriculum they wanted. Many teachers believed that parents' expectations were unrealistic and resented the ones who in their opinion wanted to go to cocktail parties and brag that their children were in honors classes. Wolcott's (1978) Ed Bell felt that many parents had unrealistic expectations and blamed the school for their children's inability to live up to the expectations.

> We don't meet the needs of children because parents don't want them to be what they are. They want them to be doctors and lawyers.... The farther up the social ladder the parents have come, the harder it is for them. (p. 79)

Separating school from community can be difficult. Community people may not regard school people as "experts" and may, in fact, think they know little. Part of that is the familiarity of the school people in the community. Many grow up and go to school in the region where they work and so bind a school to local norms and values. School-community kinship can be surprisingly deep. Furthermore, what happens in the school is the community's business. News, gossip, and rumors are carried out of school every day by teachers, bus drivers, cafeteria workers, and substitute teachers. These people not only work in the school, they are related to other people who work in the school. The ties are not only kinship, social and cultural; they are economic. A school is a major business; in many towns it may be the biggest business, too important to be left to outside experts. People in such communities have a personal interest in the school and enter school debates freely. Ed Bell felt that the parents should respect the staff's expertise and leave decisions to them.

> I get pretty annoyed by the idea... that because a person has a child in school he is an expert about education. The learning process is so complex that parents should leave it up to school people and have confidence in them. (Wolcott, 1978, p. 79)

If Ed Bell had ruminated on, he might have admitted that the learning process is so complex that professionals do not understand it any better than parents. There is no hard technology of teaching and learning that experts know and that nonexperts do not know, and that experts inside the organization can use to keep those outside at bay. Or perhaps, I am wrong. Perhaps there is a hard technology, but if there is, experts have not convinced the nonexperts of its existence and worth. Teachers have experience, common sense, authority, and a monopoly on the endeavor. But these are not sufficient to protect them from parents who feel free, as indeed they are free, to participate in the system. The system is constructed to account for their active participation; moreover, the studies show that part of the principal's job is to accommodate their participation and the increased uncertainty that it causes, in order to keep the school on an even keel.

The downtown merchants in Caseville wanted an open lunch hour, the residents wanted a closed lunch hour. Vidich and Bensman (1958) described the high school principal at Springdale letting the high school students sell ice cream to raise money for a senior trip. This meant the local tradesmen were deprived of the students' ice-cream business. One such tradesman came to the board meeting and reported

> the guy who drives the [ice cream] truck told him that he delivers enough ice cream at the school for them all to swim in. He added with feeling that his business has been going to pot since the "kids started selling ice cream." (p. 186)

Those comments generated a larger argument between tradesmen and the poorer farmers who were in favor of children raising money. For administrators, frequently caught in such situations, caution becomes an "art form."

Many of the mentioned studies were done in schools where the term "community" made some sense. When the community makes no sense, or worse, when it is ridden with conflicts, the conflicts are likely to get played out in the school. Hamilton High's violence reflected the real divisiveness among classes and cultures in that area. During the school's worst days, the principal was in an impossible situation. One day he just quit.

> That day I went home to my wife and said, "Look, that's it. I can't deal with this anymore." I realized that whatever the problems were, they were bigger than me ... I really realized that the community had a big problem and somebody better help these people do something about it. It was beyond my ability. (Grant, 1988, p. 40)

Although that principal and his school were in an unusual situation, examples of communities intruding into schools and causing problems are common. When it happens, the results often include discharges or resignations. The trick for administrators is to run the school so that the community, or at least the elements in the community that are most influential and most likely to cause trouble, support what goes on inside. However, as some of the descriptions indicate, it is difficult to predict where controversy will arise. Gold and Miles (1981) illustrated the problems that happen when community elements enter the school and make its running their business.

Their *Whose School Is this Anyway?* (Gold and Miles, 1981) contains several elements. The setting was a newly developed community that was building a new school. The parents were reasonably well educated and affluent. There, a progressive superintendent advocated the latest ideas: open space, team teaching, individualization, and building autonomy.

> We need a high degree of trust, competency, planning skills, imagination and creativity.... We will organize in teams, each responsible for a group of kids. It would be a multi-age group, the focus would be on the developmental aspects of the kids etc. (Gold and Miles, 1981, p. 50)

The new school's beginning was inauspicious. The principal-selection committee, composed of community and school people, interviewed and presented the superintendent with a list of candidates. The superintendent altered the order of candidates before presenting the list to the board. The selection committee in turn went to the board and forced the acceptance of their candidate over the superintendent's. The superintendent went along with the re-revised list but began rethinking the lines between amateurs and professionals.

> I believe ideally and theoretically in the involvement of parents, teachers, and educators on the committee level, but I'll never use it again because I do not find, unless people are trained as observers and in group process that it works. Next time I will do it myself. (Gold and Miles, p. 61)

As the open school was being built and teachers hired, dissatisfaction accelerated. The principal and teachers had been hired on the basis of their support for openness, but several community people were suspicious of allowing students freedom of movement and choice of activity. They equated openness with disorganization and permissiveness and then formed a school-surveillance association that was joined by other citizens who wanted lower taxes. Initial suspicion of "openness" prompted the principal to encourage visitors; the hope being that when people came in and saw how well things were going, concerns would diminish. But when they came in, they did not like what they saw. They wanted to see students working quietly, teachers holding forth from the center and lecturing, students doing seatwork, and so on. The citizenry had their own notions of what is appropriate student behavior, and not finding it, they used their access to examine students' papers to question staff about "discipline, attention span, motivation, curriculum, evaluation, noise" (p. 107), and in general to decide that they knew more about schooling than did the teachers. They also spread stories about students wandering around. One hundred fifty-three parents then petitioned for a closed alternative at each grade level (p. 101).

Lincoln teachers did not like the parents' using the principal's invitation into school to question them or snoop around for evidence that students were not learning. Nor did they like the principal trying to soothe parents and so appearing to vacillate on openness. The superintendent was distancing himself from the issue. He wanted the principal to resolve the conflicts and blamed the principal for an incorrect understanding of the concept. That was the same accusation teachers were using against interfering parents. The board wanted to be responsive to parents, particularly after the surveillance group elected two of their members to the school board.

School-community relations deteriorated. One PTA goal, among seventeen others, was to "find out what's going on in the school" (Gold and Miles, 1981, p. 200). The decision to allow parents into the school and the tendency of some of them to use the opportunity to criticize everything did not help, nor did the intrusion of one parent, who was also an educator and the director of the state's "Right to Read" program. Combining his professional and parental positions, and using the concerns of other parents as a power base, he made opposition to openness his personal project—thus the book's title—*Whose School Is this Anyway?*

By November of the school's first year, 27 percent of the parents considered transferring their children and several were doing it. By December, PTA attendance was running at 175; PTA members were actually running for PTA office and several parents were requesting that their children be transferred to a school with self-contained classrooms. There ensued a teacher firing, a superintendent seeing his vision destroyed by the increasing belligerence and so withdrawing himself, and the principal interviewing for jobs out of state.

The experiment with openness was over. A new supervisor came from the central office; basic subjects began to be taught in basic ways; floor to ceiling partitions were added; one teacher was assigned to 25 students; visitors were restricted. Some teachers continued to team but they did so within the confines of a traditional structure. Most interestingly, in the middle of the controversy the students took the state tests and scored the highest of all the district's elementary schools.

For our purposes, the lesson from Lincoln Acres elementary is less about open education than about what can happen when individuals and groups are allowed to make school business their business, or more accurately, when the school's internal business is conducted in such a way as to arouse the latent wariness among groups outside the school. Reading Gold and Miles's (1981) account one can understand the wariness voiced by the Elmtown superintendent, and Ed Bell at Freedom Elementary. Many people would like to be involved in schools, but when they become involved, no one can guarantee that they will like what they see. The idea of citizens dissatisfied with foreign policy taking over the United States State Department is laughable. But the idea of disgruntled citizens taking over a school is not laughable. It can happen. It does happen. Administrators know that, and they treat their communities carefully.

Not only small-town schools are subject to community influences that disrupt schools. Cuban's (1975) "Hobson v. Hanson" is an account of what happened when Julian Hobson, a civil rights activist in Washington, D.C., brought suit against the Washington school system for racial and economic discrimination. The judge ruled in favor of Hobson and called for

> the abolition of the track system... busing from overcrowded black schools to near-empty white schools, teacher integration and an end to particular pupil assignment policies. (p. 17)

The board refused the request by then superintendent Carl Hanson to appeal the decision, and he resigned. An interim superintendent was appointed, but the president of the board took over the implementation of the court order. She drafted position papers, directed top school executives, and monitored administrative decisions. She and the originator of the suit, Julian Hobson, who had since been elected to the board, then vied for control of that board.

> Hobson drew his support from black and white activists [mostly affluent] and the teacher's union. [The president's] support came from PTAs, civic organizations and black ministerial associations.... Board meetings... were chaotic. Yelling out from the audience. Popcorn thrown at the chair, bongo drummers noisily interrupting, heated clashes between board members, hours spent arguing over trivial agenda items... while the board president gaveled for order, but with little success. (Cuban, 1975, p. 18)

Counting Carl Hanson, the Washington schools had three superintendents in the next two years, but none of them could make any sense of the situation. The acting superintendent filled in, but felt he too was trapped by a dissension-filled board and by the administrators who, knowing he was only temporary, refused to commit themselves to his policies.

The notion of principals wary of their community came through the interviews conducted by Wayne Peters (Cusick and Peters, 1979). Every one of the thirty-four principals, when asked to describe his or her community, used the term "conservative." The indicants of the term varied, but there was no mistaking the message. The principal was to keep the school free of controversy.

"They don't let the girls wear slacks." "They want the school clean, quiet, no trouble." "They don't want to change, they're Catholic and Polish, you know." "They're Dutch. They want the kids in school." "It's a German town; they don't want new things." "They want a good program that doesn't conflict with their value system." (Cusick and Peters, 1979, field notes)

These principals kept themselves closely attuned to community dialogue about schools and regarded the dialogue they did not control as dangerous and ill-informed. They also kept their personal lives free of controversy. Always under communal scrutiny, they were expected to be responsible, active, church-going, family people.

"(the parents) like to see you at all school functions." "There is someone in and out of the house all the time, either some kid or some parent calling here in the evening or sometime during the day." "It's a small town and I work here. I live at my home and I walk a straight line between the school and home. I don't go downtown or into a local bar. You just don't do that and survive in a small town." "People look at me and say, you are everything a person ought to be." (Cusick and Peters, 1979, p. 26)

The trust that the principal engendered through his personal life transferred to positive relations for the school. If the principal remained above reproach, the school could be trusted and the citizens would keep a respectful distance. Principals then may be said to use their personal lives to buffer the school against unwanted intrusion by the community. So the principals' private lives were a public matter.

Being expected to personify the community's ideal can be burdensome as noted by Richardson (1981) in her recollections of life as a small-town principal. She recalled that one day, she had

erred by mowing my lawn in shorts and a tee-shirt instead of a snowsuit and my exhibitionist tendencies were the topic of conversation for a week. (p. 23)

She was also expected to shop in town and watch what she purchased.

It is expected that I shop at each of the five local grocery stores weekly, that I eat only health foods (no chips, beer, cigarettes, or TV dinners) and that anyone may stop me in the middle of the store to discuss any...school happening. (p. 23)

Gary Kamminga, another small-town principal, wrote about the tendency of community people to engage him in school-related matters anytime they saw him, anywhere (Kamminga, 1981). Just as he was expected to respond to conversations initiated by others anytime in school, he was expected to do the same outside school. He recalled walking in a restaurant on Sunday morning with his date and seeing the several diners almost break their necks to see who he was with and then check their watches to see if the lady, not a resident, had had time to come in that morning from another town. Of course, they assumed he was on duty.

> From two booths back . . . "Mr. Kamminga, could I see you a second? . . . Hey what's going on down at that school?" "Do you mean last week?" "Ya, I mean this past week?" "Do you mean with your son or your daughter?" "With Jim." "Do you mean the problem Jim is having with the English instructor?" "Ya, what's the deal?"

In small towns, school business is public business and the principal's private life is a public matter. Judicial use of that publicness can engender trust for the school. It can also protect the school from unwanted intrusion from the community. In larger cities, the administrators are much less bound by such scrutiny, but the wariness with which they regard the public and the care they take to assure the public that all is well, is similar. The public has to be assuaged and the principal is the person to do it.

As in Lincoln Acres, when circumstances allow the community into the school, several try to make school business their personal business. Why not? Schools are interesting places. Many would like the power and prestige associated with making decisions and having their views on education sought. People inside the school have yet to convince the people outside the school that what insiders know is based on much more than authority, experience, and common sense. The principal has to make sense, not only of events inside, but of the combination of events inside and outside. If she or he is successful, the school can run smoothly and that is what everyone wants.

Summary

Schools are complex organizations and thus have to make sense of several parts. The state has a curriculum that the district may modify; communities and parents have ideals and expectations; students have abilities, aspirations, interests, and personalities. They also have their class and culture differences and their propensity to drift into informal associations. Teachers have all those things and unions too. Colleges and occupations, to which students aspire, have entrance requirements. The federal government has programs designed to make society more equal. Combined into a limited time and space, the sense of all these things is not natural; it is highly contrived; it exists as an abstraction, primarily in the mind of the building administrator.

The problem for administrators is to make the abstract sense work. Each has to have some idea of the school as a single, purposive entity. Operationalized, school administration is the taking of one of the innumerable elements that is or threatens to be out of kilter with the others and putting it back into the routine, or even fitting something new into the routine. An errant child, an irate parent, a board-initiated change, a citizens group, a superintendent's idea, a heating or lighting problem, a federal initiative or state program—the possibilities are endless.

"Obsession with control" is a charge often leveled at administrators. The question is not whether administrators are obsessed with control—they are. The question is whether the obsession is justified. Put another way, if administrators eased off on maintenance and control, would the school still make sense? Would the adolescent energy, crowdedness, and constant shifting of activities and events come together in some natural manner? Referring to Chapter 2, where it is argued that students left alone drift into class- and culture-based associations, and to this chapter, where the fragility of school-community consensus is explored, the answer is no. The school would no longer make sense, events would begin to back into one another, rumors of "lack of control at school" would spread and the administrator would be fired. A new administrator would be brought in and told that she or he was to "get things under control."

Another question is, does the administrator's abstract coherence make sense? The answer is yes, it does to her or him. But because it contains value judgments, experience, inferences, and personal beliefs, it may not make sense to outsiders. It is a personal and stylized entity, to be protected from too much scrutiny and analysis. The principal of Lincoln Elementary had thought all was well, so he invited the parents to see for themselves. They concluded that all was not well despite high student achievement, and so they organized the opposition. The trick for administrators is to keep the school in such a way that outsiders, with different notions, do not come in and upset what has been created. Control is the one element all parties agree upon. A controlled school will not be interfered with by outsiders, even those who want to make school business their business. Thus despite their ostensible friendliness and public spiritedness, administrators keep schools difficult to penetrate and, as described in the ensuing chapters, equally difficult to change.

6

The System beyond the Schools

INTRODUCTION

Our educational system includes all sorts of people who want something and who think education, usually someone else's, is the way to get it. The system is the sum of these people and their efforts. The formal organization is the set of compromises they work out. Just as preceding chapters described how class and culture affect classrooms and how communities affect administrators, this chapter describes how events at national and state levels affect national and state educational policy. Subsequent chapters describe how events recounted here wend their way into schools and what teachers, administrators, and students make of them.

A central topic in this chapter is how and to what degree federal and state efforts affect schools and classrooms. In general, the argument is that federal and state efforts make the system busier and more dense, fill it with more options and opportunities—but do not restrict the actions of people at other levels. The descriptions presented in this and the next chapters support Cohen's (1982) argument that the growth of educational activity at the federal and state levels has opened rather than restricted options for individuals and groups in communities and schools.

> The expansion of state and federal policy has stimulated growth in the organization and often in the power of education agencies at all levels of government...the growth of public policy has enhanced power and expanded organization for many private agencies concerned with education governance...power and organization often have grown in tandem, rather than growing in one place at the expense of another. (p. 476)

Further, while centers of power and influence grow at state and federal levels, they grow correspondingly at local levels.

> In the education of disadvantaged children, for example, diverse specialities developed in teaching, administration, testing, and research. Specialized agencies were

126

drawn into educational curriculum development, evaluation and the provision of services. New parent and child advocate groups sprang up. Few of these interests were organized twenty years ago, but now each had distinctive issues of special concern, and distinctive perspectives on the issues.... Each new policy increases the organized interests, and these interests open up new facets of issues.... (Cohen, 1982, p. 485)

Cohen (1982) supports the notion of the system, not as a hierarchy, but as a broad flat plain whereon multiple interests exercise influence over select aspects of the enterprise. Control is spread among the system's myriad and competing parties. The sheer number of interests "restrains the unbalanced concentration of power in any particular agency." There is a hierarchy but it is not a centralized hierarchy; there is coordination but it runs through vertically integrated channels within which people and groups from different levels coalesce around particular interests. There are continually more people, parties, and interests. There are also more resources to be divided up.

The proliferation of policy and organization has slowed the decision process, made it more contentious, and introduced new complexities. One source of these changes in decision making is a simple increase in the density of organizations concerned with educational governance. A political world that was rather sparsely inhabited seven or eight decades ago is more crowded.... A school's decision about vocational education ... once might have been a sovereign local affair. Now it involves state and federal bureaus, and private agencies as well. (p. 484)

This chapter describes federal and state roles, and also federal and state efforts to push their agendas into local schools. It describes a rich and expanding, more dense and busy system. But it will not describe a more controlled or centralized system.

EDUCATION AS SOCIAL POLICY

At the center of national and state efforts is a tradition that connects education to an improved social order. According to Tyack and Hansot (1982), early nineteenth-century common schools were founded by Protestant ministers who believed in education as preparation for the millenium, prophesied by John as a time when the Lord would cast Satan "into the bottomless pit, and shut him up, and set a seal upon him that he should deceive the nations no more, till the thousand years should be fulfilled" (Revelations, 20:3). Education, it was reasoned, could help individuals and the whole society both prepare for the millenium and hasten its arrival. Tyack and Hansot argue that millenial notions of salvation, morality, and fulfillment were incorporated into public schools by latter nineteenth-century school managers with strong religious backgrounds; and they argue further that millenial notions of social reform and personal renewal continue to underlie the educational system.

Education has long been connected with political and economic renewal. Article 3 of the Northwest Territories Act (1787) states, "Religion, morality and knowledge being necessary to good government and the happiness of mankind, the means of education shall forever be encouraged" (1787).

Education is particularly important to good democratic government with its tenet that ... "everyone deserve[s] a chance if human dignity [is] to mean anything and ... the polity [will] benefit from the maximum development of human potential" (Cremin, 1977, p. 124). Education is even more important in a liberal democracy with its general belief that "ignorance ... is ... the only obstacle to the good society ... and ignorance can be dispelled by ... education" (Burnham, 1964, p. 137). Finally is the capitalistic notion that education is a commodity, capable of paying its investors high returns. Thus undergirded by a quartet of religious, democratic, liberal, and capitalistic values, education is frequently posed as an answer to social problems.

To describe federal efforts to use education for solving social problems and to describe the system at the national level, there are three studies. The first, by Bailey and Mosher (1968), describes the founding and early years of the Elementary and Secondary Education Act (ESEA) of 1965. It was an effort begun by President John Kennedy (1960–1963) and brought to fruition by President Lyndon Johnson (1963–1968), who was personally committed both to education and to providing direct educational assistance to disadvantaged students. This is a very fitting issue because, according to Bailey and Mosher (1968), ESEA signaled "a massive shift in the locus of policy-making power in American Education" (p. 3) from states to national government.

A second study is Sproull, Weiner, and Wolf's (1978) account of the founding and first few years of the National Institute of Education. Their book, *Organizing an Anarchy* (1978), describes President Richard Nixon's efforts, based on a reassessment of ESEA, to find a different educational role for the federal government, one based on generating knowledge that could be used to improve teaching and learning.

The third study is Terrell Bell's *The Thirteenth Man* (1988), a personal account of his years (1981–1985) as U.S. Secretary of Education. Bell gives particular attention to how education became important to President Reagan, despite his original intent to reduce the federal role and eliminate the Department of Education. These three separate but sequentially connected accounts provide a rough chronology of the federal government's education efforts from the mid-1960s to the 1990s.

Esea: THE FEDERAL GOVERNMENT ADMINISTERS A LAW

Bailey and Mosher's (1968) story on the Elementary and Secondary Education Act (P.L. 89-10) of 1965 is, in the authors' terms, a story of "the slow and intermittent increase of broad, just, humane and national perspectives over parochialism" (p. xi). In the early 1960s, there was a great deal of national concern with racial and economic inequality. Much of the concern was generated by African-Americans disillusioned by snail-paced school integration. In the ten years following the 1954 Supreme Court decision, *Brown v. The Board of Education*, which required school districts to desegregate "with all deliberate speed," only 2.5 percent of African-American children in the South attended integrated schools.

Additional concern was generated through Harrington's widely read book *The Other America* (1963), in which he argued that up to 40 percent of the population was not only poor, but trapped in a "cycle of poverty." Harrington argued that poverty was an inherited condition and not a result of personal deficiencies. It was related to structural inequalities, constituted a serious threat to a democratic society, and could be remediated through social action. Harrington's thesis was picked up by President Kennedy, a change-seeking democrat committed to helping the poor.

Alongside broad social issues were specific school problems. The school-age population was growing faster than local school districts could handle. In addition, teachers were dissatisfied with salaries, which had lagged behind postwar prosperity. Urban school districts were at a loss on how to accommodate the large influx of African-American children from the rural South, whose families had been displaced by changing social and agricultural conditions. Many of these children were the first in their families to attend formal schools.

These problems were reflected and paralleled by the negative views of schools being put forth by the national press. In benevolent terms, it was argued that local control, local politics and interests, and local and middle-class values made schools unresponsive to poorer students. In less benevolent terms, schools were depicted as oppressive, unproductive, and racist. Not untypical was *Fortune Magazine* editor Charles Silberman's (1970) description of schools as "grim, joyless places... oppressive and petty... intellectually sterile and esthetically barren" preoccupied above all with "order and control" demanding "docility and conformity" (pp. 28–29). Such widely propagated and popularly accepted views convinced influential non-educators that schools were unable to respond to the needs of the economically disadvantaged. Schools had to be changed, and change would only take place with federal assistance. Implied in the criticisms of schools was the notion that local districts, having local governance, administration, and funding, were not adequate to solve problems associated with education. A more rational bureaucracy and better people (smarter, better educated, more cosmopolitan) were needed in order to develop and administer more enlightened policies.

Tying educational solutions to social problems requires a connecting logic, a paradigm, around which policies can be formulated and support mobilized. Paradigms reduce and simplify reality. They explain the connection between activities and desired outcomes. They connect events that are otherwise unconnected and allow broad movements to be spoken of intelligibly.

For the ESEA, the paradigm went like this. A great many people are living in poverty and their children are inheriting that poverty. These people are poor because they have no jobs and they have no jobs because, being uneducated, they have nothing to offer employers. If educated, that is, given skills, their employment opportunities would improve; they could obtain jobs and could break from the "cycle of poverty" Harrington (1963) described. Because many of the poor are also minorities, schooling, which improves economic status, would subsequently improve their social status and thus decrease racism. By reducing racism to economics, education to job skills, and poverty to joblessness, the paradigm is complete. Improving schools can be offered as a solution to the triad of poverty, inequality, and racism.

The ESEA solution was not only plausible as a tactic for transferring wealth from the rich to the poor, it was politically feasible, more so than either revising the tax structure in favor of the poor or giving them a guaranteed annual income. The presidents from 1960 to 1975, Kennedy, Johnson, and Nixon, considered those options, but rejected them as too radical. Finally, blaming schools for social problems had few negative political consequences. School people themselves can be the schools' most vocal critics and most eager to join reform efforts. Whatever blame educational reformers cast is usually depersonalized, and proposed solutions always contain increased resources for schools. For educators, much is to be gained and little lost from joining their critics.

According to Bailey and Mosher (1968), some elements had frustrated President Kennedy's earlier attempts to provide schools with federal aid. First there was the matter of enacting general aid to education without extending it to Catholic schools. Urban Catholics who had supported Mr. Kennedy opposed federal aid that did not include them; but to include them would blur the lines between church and state. A second barrier was the fear of Southern congressmen that federal aid would accelerate integration, which they had been fighting forever, particularly since the *Brown v. The Board of Education* decision. Third was the traditional fear of big government best expressed by President Eisenhower who opposed

> any grant by the federal government to all states in the Union for educational purposes...unless we are careful even the great and necessary educational processes in our country will become yet another vehicle by which the believers in paternalism, if not outright socialism, will gain still additional power for the central government. (Bailey and Mosher, 1968, p. 21)

According to Bailey and Mosher (1968), the attractiveness and feasibility of education as a solution to poverty was sufficiently strong that the fears of communism, religion, and race could be overcome if federal aid were not accompanied by control, if Catholic and other private schools could benefit, and if fear of further integration were allayed. The strategy was to provide direct federal assistance with a minimum of federal control.

Of course, there would be fights. Fiscal experts in the U.S. Bureau of the Budget were critical of fragmented federal aid and the absence of performance standards for ensuring that funds were well expended. "The avant-garde professional and academic educational reformers agreed with fiscal experts that traditional school practices had been uncritically perpetuated" (Bailey and Mosher, 1968, p. 47). Many also believed that locally run school systems could not be trusted with funds obtained, ostensibly, for egalitarian ends. If subject only to local control, federal funds could be folded into general funds and schools would continue their unequal practices.

The ESEA of 1965, finally arrived at by a coalition of professionals, legislators, presidential aides, and educational insiders, was the most broad-based and far reaching federal education program ever. As Bailey and Mosher (1968) wrote, it "involved a massive shift in the locus of policy making power in American Education" (Bailey and Mosher, 1968, p. 3) from the local to the federal level. No longer would the government be a "distant financial patron" (p. 3), but a direct participant in education.

The most important provision was Title I, which enabled the federal government to provide funds directly to school districts that served disadvantaged students, as indeed most districts did. Additional beneficiaries included private schools, which would receive resources under Title II; educational centers, which would receive money under Title III; universities, which would receive money under Title IV; and state departments, which would receive flow-through funds for administration as well as direct aid under Title V.

President Johnson was committed to this centerpiece in his "war on poverty." Also committed were Wayne Morse, chair of the Senate Committee on Labor and Public Welfare (of which education was a subcommittee) and Congressman Adam Clayton Powell, chair of the Education Subcommittee in the House of Representatives. The bill moved quickly through the legislative and appropriations processes, and President Johnson signed the $1.34 billion P.L. 89-10 on April 11, 1965, three months after it was proposed. Four and one-half million dollars was added to assist the USOE (U.S. Office of Education) with administration. In its first fifteen months, the ESEA distributed an average of $40,000 to 25,000 school districts to be spent on the educationally disadvantaged.

Several problems accompanied the influx of federal money to the system. The USOE was more geared to President Eisenhower's time, when the organizing principle had been "assistance" (Bailey and Mosher, 1968, p. 74). Implementing the ESEA required a move from assistance to surveillance, and the Office of Education had to develop standards, guidelines, and reporting procedures for the flood of requests coming from local districts. Major reorganizations of personnel and financial administration, planning and evaluation, reporting and information, and contracting and evaluation systems followed quickly. Seventeen of the agency's top administrators were assigned new responsibilities, and outsiders filled twenty new super-grade jobs.

Bailey and Mosher (1968) detailed the problems between administrators brought in to execute the ESEA and administrators already in the USOE. Typical of new administrators was William Gorhman, the "young and talented protégé" (p. 91) of the Secretary of Defense, with his "rich background in...science, defense, and foreign policy, and with national recognition for public service accomplishments" (p. 77). According to the authors, the new administrators were prepared for their position with everything "except a sympathetic understanding of the slow speech and sometimes muddled behavior of the non-ivy, midwestern types who peopled the halls and cubicles of the USOE" (p. 77). The younger people considered the USOE administrators "too much a part of the older establishment to provide the tough leadership needed to remake the agency" (p. 76). And as one would expect, the new administrators were regarded as "alien, cold, domineering and ruthless" (p. 77) by the non-ivy, midwestern, older bureaucrats.

Another issue was how to dispense federal monies for particular purposes without undercutting "the traditional and decentralized responsibilities of state and local officials" (Bailey and Mosher, 1968, p. 116). The ESEA emerged from a coalition of politicians, USOE staff, and interest groups who would not allow the USOE to execute the bill in an arbitrary or heavy-handed manner. But the USOE was obligated by law and conviction to see that federal aid was used for specific, not general, purposes. The conflict was between states and local districts trying to broaden their control over federal funds and the USOE, which was committed to making an impact on behalf of disadvantaged students. USOE Commissioner Harold Howe and ESEA supporters believed that a mandated reporting system was essential for review and supervision. He reasoned, "We have not asked for good intentions but specific things, done with specific children in specific places" (p. 123).

Disagreement centered around the authority of the USOE to demand progress and evaluation reports on local initiatives. There is no question that the USOE had authority to ask how its funds were being spent.

> In the case of ESEA... the legislative mandate for formal reports and evaluations of programs was loud and clear, and unprecedented in scope. Each of the operating titles of the act provided either for the establishment of procedures for making continuing and periodic evaluations of the effectiveness of the programs; or for annual or other reports; or for both (Bailey and Mosher, 1968, p. 163)

Political feasibility demanded that the USOE engage in sensitive negotiations with states and districts to see that required reports included data, but were not treated as evaluations. During fiscal year 1966, 17,481 districts had submitted 22,173 projects (p. 121). The initial reports did not include any baseline data that could be used to evaluate effectiveness. USOE efforts to obtain such data met with complaints from states and local districts, articulated through congressmen, about federal red tape. The USOE considered that complaints were designed to mask the fact that districts and states did not have social, financial, or baseline achievement data needed to measure their current progress, regardless of the effects of new ESEA programs. People in local districts did not know answers to questions being asked, but rather than admit it, they complained about federal bureaucrats and red tape.

Finally, the USOE eased back from forcing states to allocate the money to districts with the most disadvantaged children. Force was not part of the original agenda. The care given to this matter and the concession made by the USOE to the states and local districts are shown in the revision of Section 116.17 (ESEA, 1965), which defined acceptable project areas: "target areas [were defined] as those in which the percentage of children from poor families had to be as large as the district or area average, approval was given to fund projects in"

> other areas with high concentrations of children from low-income families may be approved as project areas but only if the State agency determines that projects to meet the most pressing needs of educationally deprived children in areas of higher than average concentration have been approved and adequately funded. (p. 119)

Put simply, the USOE gave states the right to use the money on projects as they saw fit as long as they could argue that they were also doing something for areas most severely hurt by poverty. According to one USOE official, "that is when we gave away the ball game" (Bailey and Mosher, 1968, p. 119). However, Bailey and Mosher argue that this was not a "giving away." Instead, the ESEA had made real both federal aid to the disadvantaged through education and federal surveillance of funded projects; their expedient retreat from an untenable position was necessary.

ESEA AND THE CIVIL RIGHTS ACT

Bailey and Mosher (1968) tell how federal policy is initiated, adapted to political realities, and carried into practice via the bureaucracy. They tell how problems and solutions evolve as new agendas are added. The initial intent of the ESEA was to use education to improve opportunities for the disadvantaged. It overlapped with Title VI of the Civil Rights Act of 1964, which stated that

> No person...shall, on the ground of race, color, or national origin, be excluded from participation in, be denied the benefits of, or be subjected to discrimination under any program or activity receiving Federal financial assistance.
> Compliance...may be effectuated (1) by the termination of or refusal to grant or continue assistance...or (2) by any other means authorized by law. (p. 142)

In effect, the Civil Rights Act obligated the ESEA to withhold funds from districts that refused to desegregate or refused to plan desegregation. So in order to pursue its own ends, the USOE had to "induce instant desegregation and to end programmatic discrimination in every school district slated for the award of federal aid" (Bailey and Mosher, 1968, p. 144). Initially, Title VI had been passed without guidelines, so the USOE, along with the Justice Department and White House staff, had to develop them. In the summer of 1965, round-the-clock efforts by two teams of reviewers in the USOE processed 900 school desegregation plans from districts requesting federal funds.

Tension in the USOE continued between those anxious to get on with the business of education and those who believed desegregation to be the first and most important task. As usual, tensions centered on procedural confusion. Title

I called for the money to be spent in school districts that served large numbers of poor children, and many districts were directing the aid to those schools. But many plans from the South were centered around "choice"; that is, parents choosing their schools rather than being assigned them by neighborhood. Poor African-American parents who chose an integrated school for their child might forego ESEA funds allocated to their area school and thus not receive benefits the child deserved. In March 1968, the U.S. Department of Health, Education, and Welfare's Office for Civil Rights issued a new provision designed to correct this problem.

> For the first time, districts which had not formerly been legally segregated were required to provide detailed information on practices in their schools. Practices which may be considered denials of equal educational opportunity may include: overcrowded classes and activities; assigning less qualified teachers to schools attended largely by minority children, poorer facilities and instructional equipment at such schools; and high pupil teacher ratios or lower per pupil expenditures. The new policies also hold all local districts responsible for: planning the location of new schools in a way that does not segregate students on the ground of race, color or national origin; and hiring and assigning teachers and other professional staff on a non-racial basis. (pp. 156–157)

In other words, local districts that contained minority children and that wanted federal aid for those children, now had to consider USOE guidelines when building and staffing schools, buying equipment, hiring and assigning teachers, and even placing children. The resentment to this expansion of federal power was evidenced by the epithets applied to Harold Howe, Commissioner of Education, who was variously called the "education commissar," "socialist quack," and "commissioner of integration" (Bailey and Mosher, 1968, p. 151). One Southern legislator even called for his impeachment.

The purpose here is not to dwell on the problems, but to outline the role of the federal government in education and the impact of the ESEA on that role. In addition to providing more money to schools, the ESEA had several other effects. State departments grew because of the funds provided through Title V and flow-through funds provided to states for project administration. In the ESEA's first year, over 1000 new professional positions were created for state departments, which were also given funds for upgrading and training staff.

The ESEA placed the federal government in the middle of almost every school district and established the government's role as education's "guardian of equality." And although the original paradigm of education as the answer to poverty later lost credibility, the federal operation was sufficiently important to maintain the ESEA bureaucracy—even through successive presidents less sanguine with the idea of federal aid to education solving social problems. In addition, the ESEA expanded the educational system, first with groups aligning themselves with and competing for federal funds, and second with a network of specialists assigned to transfer and monitor particular programs. Within this latter group are the vertically integrated coalitions that include program staff from federal, state, and local levels who monitor particular programs.

Finally, as the ESEA shifted the locus of educational policy from state capitals to Washington, interest groups grew up around the federal operation. Years after the ESEA, groups with staff assigned to monitor Title I included the National Advisory Council for the Education of Disadvantaged Children, the National Welfare Rights Organization, The Legal Standards and Education Project of the National Association for the Advancement of Colored People, The Lawyers Committee for Civil Rights under Law, the National Association of Administrators of State and Federally Assisted Education Programs...the Education Commission of the States...the Ford Foundation, and the Harvard Center for Law and Education (Bailey and Mosher, 1968, p. 130). The ESEA left the educational system more crowded, more busy, and with more groups, more interests, and more efforts.

Central to our description of the system is the question of whether the expansion of the federal role left education more centralized and controlled. Initially and ostensibly, the ESEA was designed for a school system that worked, but needed help with poorer students. Less ostensible was the agenda of groups who believed the educational system needed more centralization and were using "the disadvantaged child" as a symbol to press for more federal influence over state and local efforts. The question about whether education would benefit from increased centralization and subsequent control is asked perennially in a system that contains so much of what priests and politicians hold dear.

To address the question, it is necessary to differentiate between centralization and control. As illustrated by Bailey and Mosher's (1968) history of the ESEA, federally initiated reform increased the number of important players at the federal level. With more resources coming from federal agencies, more people in the Capitol agitating for and dividing up resources, and more state and local groups looking to Washington for money and guidance, events were more centralized. Were they also more controlled? In the sense that federal agendas were forced into state and local districts, the answer is yes. But as the history of the ESEA illustrates, initiatives that begin at the federal level tend to attract other groups and other agendas and get retranslated as they move along. The joining of the ESEA with the Office of Civil Rights (OCR) is an example. Funding events is one thing; controlling events after they start to move through the system is another.

Furthermore, federal intervention does not increase control as much as it changes the locus of control. Hamilton High as described by Grant (1988) was much less controlled after the actions of the ESEA and the OCR than it was in the 1950s when the principal, who was supported by the elite families, ran everything. And no school described in the studies was more controlled than Elmtown High in the late 1930s, where the local plutocrats ran everything and got away with it. They controlled the board, the superintendent, and the teachers; they told the principal who he could keep after school, and they allocated merit (supposed) scholarships to their own children rather than to the students who earned them (Hollingshead, 1949). Comparing pre-ESEA Elmtown High to post-ESEA Hamilton High is the best illustration of our argument that the system is bigger and busier than it was previously, but is not more controlled.

THE NATIONAL INSTITUTE OF EDUCATION

The second story of this federal trilogy is Sproull, Weiner, and Wolf's (1978) account of the founding and early years of the National Institute of Education. *Organizing an Anarchy: The National Institute of Education* connects sequentially to Bailey and Mosher (1968). It is also useful for its illustration of the way groups are created and the way federal funding processes operate within the system.

In the early 1970s, when President Nixon was in the White House, federal policymakers had become disillusioned about former President Johnson's efforts to reduce poverty via education. The urban riots of the late 1960s convinced many that minority problems were more intractable than earlier envisioned and perhaps beyond the power of the schools to cure. Federal aid had not only failed at solving social problems; people were wondering whether it could even succeed at solving educational problems. The Coleman et al. study of 1966, the Westinghouse (1969) study on the impact of Head Start preschool programs, and evaluations of Title I programs all argued that school differences were not sufficient to explain students' success. "The effects of family background, ethnic heritage, social class and peer groups seemed to leave little margin for the possible effectiveness of compensatory schooling" (Sproull et al., 1978, p. 33).

Many of Mr. Nixon's domestic aides, and specifically the head of the White House Domestic Council, Daniel Moynihan, believed that the ESEA had not worked. Disillusion with the power of schools to reduce inequality and a need to provide President Nixon with a coherent educational policy, required a new paradigm. President Nixon expressed the paradigm on March 3, 1970, when he proposed the National Institute of Education (NIE).

> We must stop pretending that we understand the mystery of the learning process or that we are significantly applying science and technology to the techniques of teaching when we spend less than one-half of one percent of our educational budget on research, compared with 5 percent of our health budget and 10 percent on defense.
>
> We must stop congratulating ourselves for spending nearly as much money on education as does the entire rest of the world—65 billion a year on all levels—when we are not getting as much as we should out of the dollars we spend. . . .
>
> Therefore I propose that the Congress create a National Institute of Education as a focus for educational research and experimentation in the United States. When fully developed, the Institute would be an important element in the nation's educational system, overseeing the annual expenditure of as much as a quarter of a billion dollars. (Sproull et al., p. 35)

The implication was that the USOE would stop dispensing money to schools until research did its work. But the principle of federal aid to poor students was entrenched, and, though some of his supporters did not like it, Mr. Nixon made little attempt to cease ongoing ESEA programs. In fact, educational aid to states and districts actually increased throughout Mr. Nixon's era.

Initially Roger Levien of the Rand Corporation was engaged to lead the NIE effort. Levien contacted 137 people inside and outside education for their suggestions for the new agency and their ideas about improving research. His February 1971 report targeted three important areas the new agency should work on: equality, quality, and effective use of resources. After the Levien report was issued, the new Commissioner of Education, who was personally more interested in career education than in educational research, moved the NIE planning effort into the Office of Education, right where many thought it should not go. In the opinion of NIE planners, the best minds were not in education, but in the sciences and social sciences. NIE planners believed further that the problem with educational research was that it was conducted by educationists. Federal planners associated with Mr. Nixon were suspicious of educationists and particularly of educationists in the U.S. Office of Education. Federal policymakers who started the NIE spoke of the people in the USOE just as had USOE people appointed by President Johnson spoke of their predecessors. Each new group regarded the old group as parochial, unscientific, bureaucratic, nonrational, and undynamic. In turn, each old group regarded newcomers as arrogant, ignorant about education, inexperienced, and overly optimistic about their ability to achieve desired change.

When the move came, Levien was not asked by the commissioner to continue his planning, and he resigned. Several of the newcomers to USOE were then assigned to work on NIE planning. By December 1972, with the help of White House staff, they had synthesized their thinking into a final report that called for a new set of priorities: higher education, technology, choice, community resources, financial inequities, preschool, and school board selection.

Among the hopes expressed during the planning period was that the NIE would obtain the $250 million that President Nixon originally envisioned, that it would be independent of the Office of Education, and that it would be free from having to produce immediate results. Several problems impeded these hopes. One was how to move personnel and research units from the USOE into the NIE. If the NIE were to start over with new efforts, its backers did not want it burdened with USOE people and efforts, which they viewed as unproductive.

> One powerful theme recurring throughout the NIE planning period was that NIE must not be another [U.S. Office of Education]. It was imperative that NIE attract "better people" than OE had done. OE personnel were perceived to be uninterested in the substance of research, to be paper pushers and not even competent paper pushers at that. (Sproull et al., 1978, p. 112)

The American Federation of Government Employees, however, insisted that if projects were transferred to the NIE from the USOE, project personnel had to go with the projects. The Civil Service Commission reviewed the matter and agreed. The compromise proposal was to take those units from the USOE who were working on new knowledge, and leave in the USOE units assigned to teach "consumers" to use what was already known (p. 49). In August 1972, the NIE took eighty-four research people from the Office of Education.

A second barrier was the departure from the White House of Daniel P. Moynihan, and the ensuing lack of interest in education by top people in the White House. Mr. Nixon considered foreign affairs his major interest, and education was not a high priority for his top domestic advisors. The fate of the NIE was then left to the Department of Health, Education, and Welfare, where it was only a small part of a much larger budget. The NIE was not even supported by the American Educational Research Association, which suspected that the NIE was Mr. Nixon's way to avoid increased spending on education.

A third barrier to tying together a coalition of NIE supporters was the paradigm connecting research to planning to school problems or social problems that show up in school. Stripped to essentials, the ESEA offered a three-step paradigm: (1) improved schools would (2) improve people and so (3) improve society. The NIE added two steps so that all together: (1) improved research would (2) improve practice, which would (3) improve schools and (4) improve people, who would (5) improve society. This latter paradigm did not excite people outside the immediate circle of believers, particularly because the ESEA's three-step paradigm was already suspect. A paradigm has to condense several overlapping interests, and there were not enough groups convinced of its worth. NIE's paradigm was thus exposed to more initial skepticism than was the ESEA's. John Brademas, chair of the House Select Subcommittee on Education, and according to Sproull et al., (1978) a "friend" of education, expressed suspicion.

> My own perception is that educational research does not stand very well on Capitol Hill for several reasons, one of which is, we don't know what it is. Another is that, whatever it is, we don't think it makes much difference. And another . . . is that we have the apprehension that the fruits of investment in educational research are not really translated into the system. (p. 68)

This skepticism of research and the somewhat related feeling that the real work of education is carried on in classrooms and everything else is superfluous, was aired on the House floor during NIE's appropriations discussion. Congresswoman Edith Green, chair of the Special House Subcommittee on Education, who had long opposed educational research on the grounds of its inability to improve what goes on in classrooms, referred to the research "nonsense" that

> we are financing and that taxpayers in the Members' districts are paying for and that my taxpayers are paying for, when our schools and our classrooms do not have enough money for basic essentials, but we can pay out millions and millions [for research] . . . some of it esoteric research and some of it just plain nonsense and we ought to stop it. (p. 82)

The suspicion, even by education backers, that research was unhelpful and the belief that the ESEA's research had not done any ostensible good undermined the NIE's assertion that "better" people would get "better" results. Perhaps also the logic was perceived as arrogant, as promising centralized decision-making, and as allowing teachers to use only researcher-approved practices.

Problems of succession, management, and ideology showed up pointedly in the NIE's budget hearings. The NIE was to receive most of the research work being carried on at the time by the USOE, a total of $110 million in contracts and grants. Mr. Nixon had envisioned $250 million and with USOE programs of $110 million already transferred, NIE director Glennan requested a fiscal year 1973 budget of $140 million with an extra $30 million for new initiatives. The Office of Management and Budget reduced the requested amount to $110 million. In March 1973, the director, anxious to undertake new projects, requested a fiscal year 1974 budget of $162 million.

Sproull et al. (1978) summarize the series of steps in the federal appropriations process that began in 1972 with the envisioned $250 million and ended eleven months later with a $65 million allocation and the resignation of the NIE director, and the chair of the National Council on Educational Research. The following is a chronology.

1972
October: $110 million recommended for fiscal year 1973 by Conference Committee (of the House and Senate)

1973
March: $162 million (fiscal year 1974) requested from House Appropriations Subcommittee.
June: $142 million recommended by House Appropriations Committee for fiscal year 1974
September: $50 million recommended by Senate Appropriations Subcommittee for fiscal year 1974
October: $75 million recommended by Senate Appropriations Committee for fiscal year 1974
November: $75 million recommended by the Conference Committee for fiscal year 1974

1974
February: $25 million (supplemental) requested from House Appropriations Subcommittee
Feb–March: $25 million requested from Senate Appropriations Subcommittee
April: $130 million requested from House Appropriations Subcommittee for fiscal year 1975
May: $0 supplemental recommended by Senate Appropriations Committee; and $0 supplemental recommended by Conference Committee
June: $134.5 million requested from Senate Appropriations Subcommittee for fiscal year 1975; and $100 million recommended by House Appropriations Subcommittee for fiscal year 1975

Glennan announces tentative fiscal year 1975 and 1976 allocations. $80 million voted by full House for Fiscal year 1975; and $65 million by Senate Appropriations Subcommittee for fiscal year 1975
(Glennan resigns)
September: $0 recommended by Senate Appropriations Committee for fiscal year 1975
(Haggerty resigns)
November: $70 million recommended by Conference Committee for fiscal year 1975 (pp. 164–165)

When considering the 1974 allocation, the House Subcommittee decided that the NIE was probably not ready for the new money. They reasoned that the NIE could not undertake new programs, because it had not received its 1973 allocation until October 1972 and seven months later, had obligated only half the allocation. The committee took this as evidence that the NIE was not ready to undertake new ventures and recommended only $50 million for fiscal 1974.

In March 1973, Glennan took his $162 million request to the Senate Appropriations Committee, which raised the $50 million House recommendation to only $75 million and commented:

To date…NIE has done little to assert its role of leadership. The committee is discouraged by what appears to be a total lack of understanding of purpose on the part of the agency. Persistent questioning by the Committee as to NIE's long and short range goals prompted little more than vague, often obscure, references to educational exploration. (Sproull et al., 1978, p. 78)

Glennan was unable to convince Congressional appropriations committees that "an emphasis on comprehensive thinking through of problems and vigorous attention to research design will provide…foundations for a truly productive system" (Sproull et al., 1978, p. 105). The inability of the NIE to come up with a convincing argument for its existence in the face of persistent questioning was embarrassing, as this exchange between Senator Magnuson of the Senate Appropriations Committee and the NIE Director shows:

Senator Magnuson: Do they (the school people) come and ask you for advice?

Mr. Glennan: Nobody comes and asks us for advice. That is, as far as I know.

M: Nobody asked you for advice on it.

G: No sir.

M: They don't ask you for advice and if they don't ask you, I don't know why you should be involved with it.

G: We would be producing knowledge that would be available to people who ask.

M: You said nobody asked for it.

G: To my knowledge, no one specifically.

M: What do you do with the knowledge?

G: The knowledge is made available.

M: But nobody asked you for it. (pp. 92–93)

According to the authors, "the visions of budget growth created by Moynihan, Levien, then HEW Secretary Elliot Richardson, and the other believers in NIE less than four years earlier had vanished in the cold light of the appropriations process" (p. 84). The inability to come up with a paradigm was reflected in priority changes. In February 1971, the NIE had three priorities, in December 1972, NIE had eight priorities. Later the eight were changed to five. The authors describe the "analysis paralysis" inside the organization occasioned by the continuous search for a lucid agenda. In fact, the planners never found one that would generate support from local districts.

This is not a balanced story of the NIE. It is only one account and it can be argued that the NIE did not fail, that even under assault, it persisted into President Reagan's years and supported several interesting and successful projects. But it is a story of an effort that was not deemed useful to people in schools and classrooms and so never accrued the credibility that would have freed it from the onus of earlier and similar efforts. It also tells a story of how education's system works and how filled it is with groups and coalitions, and ideals and aspirations, all overlapping with one another.

What the NIE stories teach us is that groups who seek to extend their influence must cast their efforts in ways that assist those whom they are trying to influence. With the ESEA, giving money and resources directly to schools made sense to teachers and administrators. The "excellence movement," to be described next, also gave administrators and teachers increased reason to do what they wanted to do and in fact were already doing. The NIE on the other hand might have been a good idea, but its logic was not sufficiently compelling, it offered little to those further down the system, and its backers were never able to gather enough support to make it successful.

THE THIRTEENTH MAN

Bell's (1988) book is a personal account of his tenure as President Reagan's Secretary of Education from 1981 to 1985. Under President Carter (1976—1980), education had been removed from the Department of Health, Education, and Welfare and elevated to a Department with a cabinet-level secretary. President Reagan wanted to reduce the federal bureaucracy in general, and the Department of Education, which in his opinion should never have been created, was a major target. When he was hired, Mr. Bell was told by the president's recruiter of

> the great distinction that would be mine if I could...walk into the Oval Office and hand the President the keys to the Department of Education and say, "Well, we've shut the abominable thing down. Here's one useless government agency out of the way." (p. 2)

In recounting his initial conversations with the president, Bell tells of Mr. Reagan's openness to turning the department, which at that time had a budget of $14,700,000,000 and a staff of 7000, into a foundation that would provide assistance to schools without the accompanying direction. Mr. Bell promised the president only that he would try to eliminate the department. The President did not insist on its demise.

Bell was loyal to the President, but he was also committed to several ongoing programs, and he used his bureaucratic skills to resist efforts to reduce aid to college students, cut appropriations for disadvantaged and poor children, and appoint conservatives to positions in education. He tried to fulfill his promise to the president. But he found little enthusiasm among key legislators, who were sympathetic to his political position and supportive of him personally, but who could not support the effort. The Department of Education had strong support by groups interested in the survival of particular programs, and legislators were not interested in either taking those groups on or reopening the education issue. As the senate majority leader told Bell, "We can't abolish the Department of Education. We just went through a big fight a couple of years ago to establish it" (p. 94).

Ever the conservative, Bell disdained the "ineffectual federal education programs and the absurd number of separate aid programs to schools and colleges — 120 of them — with a huge array of rules and regulations ... " (p. 68) by reducing the more objectional federal regulations and softening the enforcement of others. He also combined several separate programs, including the $3.5 billion Title I grant to schools attended by the poor and educationally disadvantaged, into block grants — based on the principle of "assistance without surveillance." The result was Chapter 2 of the Education Consolidation and Improvement Act of 1981, which placed thirty-two of the department's categorical programs, mostly from the ESEA

> into a single authorization of grants to States for the same purpose set forth in the provisions of law ... but to be used in accordance with the educational needs and priorities of state and local educational agencies as determined by such agencies. It is the further intent ... to financially assist state and local educational agencies to improve elementary and secondary education ... for children attending both public and private schools, and to do so in a manner designed to greatly reduce the enormous administrative and paperwork burden imposed on schools at the expense of their ability to educate children. (Knapp, 1986, Appendix C)

As Bell recounts, he encouraged support for the idea by presenting it as a temporary measure in the transformation of the department to the status of a foundation.

The second action, which turned out to be an important program for him, for education, and for President Reagan, was his "excellence" effort. When he was appointed, Bell shared the prominent feeling that schools were infected with declining academic standards, low teacher pay, low esprit de corps, a lack of basic skills among students that showed up later in high unemployment, and a general "loss of zest and drive and spirit" (Bell, 1988, p. 115). His goal was to create "a tough, powerful, persuasive report on the condition of American education [that would include] recommendations for change" (p. 115), that would reflect his concerns, and that would capitalize on the role of the Department of Education. Bell recounts the effort to convince a skeptical White House staff of the need for a national commission and his subsequent and successful efforts to select the members.

The resulting report, *A Nation at Risk* (1983), offers a broad, simple, and direct paradigm based on a few important and already widely shared ideas. Its first premise is based on the popular perception that America had lost its competitive edge.

> Japanese make automobiles more efficiently...South Koreans...built the world's most efficient steel mill...American machine tools...are being displaced by German products....(pp. 6–7)

Whether America was financially and economically declining was and still is debatable, but the perception that foreigners were making better products and thus taking American jobs and markets was sufficiently widespread that one could say it aloud without being challenged.

The second premise is that our students are neither working as hard nor learning as much as foreign students. This assertion was buttressed by data on international tests, by declining SAT's, and by an increased need for remedial instruction, as in the statement "some 23 million American adults are functionally illiterate by the simplest tests of everyday reading, writing and comprehension" (*A Nation at Risk*, 1983, p. 8). Evidence of scientific and technological illiteracy was juxtaposed to the assertion that it takes educated people to deal with modern technology (p. 10).

The conclusion to this syllogism was the causal connection between premise one, declining productivity relative to competing nations, with premise two, low educational effort. The conclusion was that our economy is failing "because" our educational system is failing and further that for America to succeed economically it has to succeed educationally. The commission went on to recommend increased homework, higher graduation requirements, a basic high school curriculum including science, language arts, foreign language, and math, increased teacher training and salaries, and a longer school year. *A Nation at Risk* (1983) has all the ingredients. It evokes the religious, democratic, and economic underpinnings of education, and it refers to the "intellectual, moral and spiritual strengths of our people" (p. 7) and to the "value of individual freedom" (p. 7). It calls up religious and democratic values and combines the fear of closed factories with the value of hard work. It even evokes the perennial disdain for "frills": "The public has no patience with undemanding and superfluous high school offerings" (p. 17).

The report advocated both quality and equality; i.e., "The twin goals of equity and high quality schooling have profound and practical meanings and...we cannot permit one to yield to the other" (p. 22). But an underlying agenda of the commission was to increase academic requirements and correspondingly to decrease the emphasis on equity that had dominated educational discourse since the mid-1960s. When the author of this volume presented to the commission a report on some side effects of the school's efforts at equality, one of the commission members said in the ensuing discussion, "We've had enough equality; now we want some quality" (May 25, 1982, Washington, D.C.). No one dissented. Most important, the report capitalized on a quiet wave of reform that was already going on further down the system. State departments, anxious to motivate low-achievers, had already started testing programs, and local schools, reacting to community accusations that they lacked control and standards, had already started tightening student conduct codes and bolstering the curriculum.

The way that federal events move into schools is explained in subsequent chapters. For now, the lesson is that the educational system at the federal level includes presidential aspirations, Congress and congressional appropriations processes, other federal agendas such as espoused by the Office of Civil Rights, associations of federal employees, multiple interests and lobbies, fate, chance, and everything else that can be shoveled into a bag of political realities. At the center are the national interests expressed as desires for increased quality and equality. From all the shifting, compromising, translating, and retranslating comes something called federal policy, which moves down the system and into the schools.

THE STATE LEVEL

Education is more directly a state rather than a federal responsibility, and is frequently a state's largest undertaking. Each state has an educational bureaucracy that administers school funding, curriculum, certification, number of school days, testing, transportation, insurance, etc. Many federal programs are administered through state agencies, and the number of people at the state level who are involved in federal programs and on the federal payroll can exceed, as it does in Michigan (in 1991), by 3 to 1 the number of people on the state payroll. Each state department is managed by a chief state school officer responsible to an elected or appointed board or to the governor. The paradigms so important at the federal level translate easily into the states where equality and quality and relations between education and productivity are as important as they are at the federal level. State educational scenes are full of interest groups, lobbies, and legislators who work on various programs and policies intended to improve education and, as the argument goes, the social order.

The purpose of this section is to elucidate system characteristics as they operate at the state level, to describe how the states define problems and how their problem-solving efforts overlap with adjacent levels. "State" is a confusing term. It implies centralized decision-making and an enforcing bureaucracy. Although each state has those elements, it seems that the state is less a monolith than a center of activity where multiple interests work out their agendas. The presence of the governor and legislature, state and federal funds, the bureaucracy, and sometimes the courts make the state a natural arena for such activity.

States differ—Marshall, Mitchell, and Wirt (1986) argue that each state has its own educational culture and each its own special context of power and influence wherein policy is made. Each state has its assumptive world for explaining how events happen and how influence is exercised. Those authors attribute the uniqueness of states to history, culture, and "slightly differing ways" (p. 366) in which principal players interact. In order to "get things done, one has to understand a state's particular culture." In their studies, the authors found numerous "stories of mistakes, violations of rules, and failures to act and think within the assumed...policy culture..." (p. 374).

Murphy (1974) explored differences among states relative to their expenditures of ESEA funds in his *State Education Agencies and Discretionary Funds*. His book describes the continuation of ESEA's Title V, which Bailey and Mosher describe as

> grants to stimulate and assist States in strengthening the leadership resources of their State educational agencies, and to assist those agencies in the establishment and improvement of programs to identify and meet the educational needs of states. (Bailey and Mosher, 1968, p. 57)

The public reasoning behind that was explained by USOE Chief Francis Keppel in his 1964 congressional testimony:

> In the long run, nothing we in education can do...can be more important than strengthening the capacity of our states to respond to the educational needs of our time.... In this nation of fifty states with vast and independent enterprises for education, the federal government must participate—not in domination, but as a partner in a vital enterprise. (Bailey and Mosher, 1968, p. 3)

According to Murphy (1974), there was more to Title V than Keppel made public. During ESEA planning, state interests felt bypassed with Titles I and III, which directly funded both districts and supplemental centers that were beyond the purview of state departments. They were also upset about Title II's direct aid to private schools. Initially, ESEA backers needed state support and, according to Murphy, Title V was the price ESEA backers paid to the Council of Chief State School Officers for that support. Independent of this quid pro quo, ESEA backers had strong reasons for wanting to change state departments. The ESEA represented a deliberate policy of underwriting the growth and reorientation of state departments of education, which had historically been independent of, and opposed to federal influence.

ESEA backers believed that state departments should treat local schools as part of an overall state system. They believed further that state departments were being held back by staff who were recruited from the ranks of local administrators and who were more interested in assisting and advising than managing and evaluating the local schools. They believed that these people with their modest views and small-town backgrounds would not lead state departments into the kind of reforms envisioned. In effect, this was an extension of the "better people—better outcomes" argument that accompanied ESEA into the USOE.

Francis Keppel explained it this way:

> Some state education departments are poorly staffed, too highly bureaucratized and politically dominated. Some are characterized by intellectual incest: the personnel, in training and experience, seem to have come from the states' own educational system, and often from small school systems. (Murphy, 1974, p. 4)

Among other goals, Title V in part was designed to press state departments into a more cosmopolitan perspective. The ESEA funded sabbaticals and further training for staff as well as personnel exchanges between the state and the USOE.

Murphy (1974) explored what states did with the Title V money and what impact the money had on states. Of the three states studied, Murphy argued that Title V had the most impact on South Carolina, a state that in 1965 was characterized by all the elements that ESEA staffers wanted to change: a segregated school system with black schools demonstrably inferior, and a powerful legislature with a "clubbish mentality" serving the state's powerful elite. As seen by the USOE, South Carolina's state department was a low-key operation, with a staff that was either transient or composed of "wornout schoolmen, often political supporters of the superintendent, who viewed (the state department) as a resting place before their final retirement" (p. 82). The primary agenda was to see that state laws on attendance and financing were followed. The superintendent was not inclined to disturb the status quo.

The opportunities provided by the ESEA money coincided with the governor's efforts to "change South Carolina from a rural, agriculturally based state to an industrialized, urban one" (p. 93), to attract industry, to improve conditions for the poor, and to provide a progressive image to businesses seeking relocation. The combination of these elements and the $20 million that ESEA funds brought, according to Murphy (1974), a new attitude to South Carolina's State Department of Education and a new relation between the state department and the schools. From 1965 to 1971, the state department tripled its size, from 166 to 450 staffers, undertook planning, and "shifted away from providing services at the request of the schools toward exercising leadership through persuasion" (p. 83). Among the projects undertaken with Title V funds and the funds that were given to states to administer the ESEA were teacher training, a testing service, and an instructional materials center. The money was also used to increase staff and raise salaries.

Murphy (1974) argues that the money made a difference, but did not foment the rational and centralized planning that ESEA originators had envisioned. Instead, traditional political realities and normal bureaucratic processes divided up the money before it could be used for centralized, rational planning. A successful staffer explained how he was able to capture a large share of Title V resources: "I was never bashful about asking the superintendent for more money. Some were content to let things just rock along and they didn't get much" (p. 89). Personal preferences and individual values also contributed to priorities. Early hopes for "problem analysis...delineating values, exploring alternatives, and developing solutions" (p. 104) never materialized. Instead, "Title V was used mainly for the expansion and marginal adaptation of [state education agencies] to meet short-run demands on the agency" (p. 87).

Murphy (1974) compared what happened in South Carolina with what happened in New York, the largest department in the country, where the money was used for "expansion and marginal adaptation of on-going activities to meet pressing problems" (p. 68) and where

> a striking number of Title V projects were designed either to put out small fires, to avoid them in the immediate future, or to fund previously conceived ideas. There is little evidence that the advent of Title V resulted in a rethinking of agency priorities or generated much original thought about the long-term needs of the [state education agency]. Stated differently, U.S. Commissioner Keppel's hoped-for thorough overhaul did not take place. (Murphy, 1974, p. 68)

As the story goes for New York, Title V was a bureaucracy-to-bureaucracy program with the USOE sending the money but exercising little control. People in the N.Y. State Department were encouraged to write proposals for how the money might be spent, and Title V priorities were established only after the money had been allocated in the ensuing competition. Staffers figured out how they were going to spend the money and then decided how such expenditures fit with the state's larger purposes.

The planning process of course included more people, further decentralizing the system. When ideas and resources enter the system, they encourage the proliferation of parties. The rhetoric of reform implies increased control, or perhaps coordination; or it implies at least the kind of rational planning envisioned by ESEA backers who disparaged their USOE predecessors for limited vision and abilities. But as the resources make their way into and down the system, control gives way to diversity and coordination gives way to political realities. Initial purposes are not ignored, but educational goals are sufficiently broad to allow for varied interpretations and approaches. Groups further down are thus able to take incoming programs and turn them to their own purposes without modifying the goals or even the language.

Another matter is the federal government's ambivalence about control. As noted earlier, Mr. Nixon retreated from Mr. Johnson's educational goals, and Secretary Bell's notion of federal involvement differed from that of his predecessors. Turnbull and Marks (1986) studied the effect of Secretary Bell's 1981 efforts to combine categorical programs into block grants and to give the responsibility for the design and implementation to local agencies, whose personnel have the most direct contact with students and parents.

According to those authors, the Block Grant Act left states with responsibility for several elements, such as designing allocation formulas, filing applications with the U.S. Department of Education, designing and reviewing local applications, keeping records for fiscal audits, and evaluating program effectiveness. Among school districts affected by that legislation, state-required paperwork and state surveillance were reduced, although states continued to offer technical as-sistance and some modest evaluation. What districts wanted most from the states was assistance in filing applications, and although state visits continued, they were described as low-pressure meetings with no single format attached. Infor-mation was exchanged and requirements clarified but no one reported changes being implemented as a result of the meetings. The authors indicated that the interactions tended to "revolve around forms" (p. 31) and "virtually no local respondents could think of activities that they would like to support with their Chapter 2 grant but that they were not allowed to fund" (p. 38).

The interaction across agencies was presented as friendly and helpful, but there was some skepticism as to how long such cordial relations could last. As one state's Chapter 2 coordinator explained:

> Under Chapter 2 we changed our approach to administering funds and now we're doing an about-face again. Under the antecedents, we were regulatory. Under Chap-ter 2, we took the philosophy: we will assist, be helpful. Now we're monitoring, getting more regulatory.... Initially, we didn't evaluate or review applications; we just checked that the dollars added up. We didn't have approval authority, so why bother? Now the law says "certify" [local applications], so we need more informa-tion. It's typical fed! The longer it exists, the tighter it gets. (Turnbull and Marks, 1986, p. 30)

The tightness, however, does not refer to overall department coordination, but to the control exercised by vertically integrated channels extending from the federal to the local level. Nelson (1975) gave an example of this vertical integration in his study of decision-making in the Michigan Department of Education. He found the State Superintendent continually exhorting staff to "get to know your counter-part" at the federal level. That counterpart, the person in charge of the particular effort at the federal level through whom funds passed to the state was, in the Super-intendent's view, a staff member's primary referent. On the other end of the funding channel were the people in the schools to whom the state was sending money. The department was full of vertical channels reaching up to the federal level, down to the local level, having little to do with other parallel channels that also ran through the department. As such, the states did not become centralized bureaucracies as much as they became container agencies filled with various parties interested in different, sometimes competing, efforts.

CHOICE IN MINNESOTA

For increased detail about how educational groups operate in states, we have Mazzoni's (1987) study of events in Minnesota in the early 1980s, a story that even at this writing in 1991 is not complete, but which illustrates the way educational policies originate. It also illustrates the place of basic values rel-ative to policies, and the place of educational politics in state government. As

Mazzoni tells the story, Minnesota had since 1955 provided a modest tax credit for private school tuition, a credit that had been passed quietly by key lawmakers with obligations to Catholic constituents. In the 1970s the Minnesota Catholic Conference (MCC), in the interest of increasing the tax credit and gaining some transportation assistance, allied itself with a second group, also interested in private schools, the Citizens for Educational Freedom (CEF). Downplaying the strictly Catholic aspect of the effort and emphasizing the values of "Freedom, rights and equity" (p. 218), the two groups had been successful in raising the tax credit for private schools in 1976 and 1984.

State support for private education expanded with a 1982 report by the Citizens League, whom Mazzoni (1987) calls, a "good-government group" interested in school reform. The League's report suggested three structural changes for schools, "deregulation, decentralization and choice" (p. 220). Choice meant that students could select any public school and that parents could purchase educational services from private schools. The Citizens League downplayed the potential benefits to private schools and stressed the benefits of choice to low-income families, arguing that they deserved the same opportunities open to the more affluent families. The effort was joined by Public School Incentives (PSI), a group formed to create alternatives to public schools.

The effort, even with support from the Minnesota Catholic Conference and the Citizens for Educational Freedom was not successful. It was strongly opposed by traditional educational groups who combined into an opposing coalition known as the Minnesota Friends of Public Education. But as Mazzoni pointed out, the MCC-CEF effort "had succeeded in shaping the parameters of debate so that educational choice could be found attractive by other reformers as a response to the demand for improved school quality" (p. 221).

Others interested in choice soon joined the effort. In 1986 the Minnesota Business Partnership, a group of the state's important business executives, commissioned an educational study by a private consulting group. Among the report's recommendations was one advocating greater choice, e.g. "Stipends for 11th and 12th graders to attend any state-approved public or private program" (p. 222). Placed within the governor's "Access to Excellence" plan allowing 11th and 12th graders open access to secondary schools and institutions of higher education, open enrollment became the focus for several groups desiring public school reform. Supporters stressed the democratizing and equity aspects of providing poor people choices and stressed the advantages from deregulating what they regarded as inadequate schools. The backers of "choice" also stressed the fact that choice was to be primarily among public schools.

Opponents, who included the teachers, administrators, and school board groups, disparaged the proposal as untried, unnecessary and nonsensical in rural areas which had only one school. These opponents were also angry about not being included in the governor's deliberations and began to attack the plan on the kind of details that insiders understand best, such as athletic transfers, transportation costs, district planning, and desegregation. They perceived the choice option as a direct threat to the established educational system. The debate was characterized with what Mazzoni calls "intensity, divisiveness, and passion" (p. 227).

Open enrollment meant more students; it meant revenue gains for some schools and districts and less for others. Nor were students, dollars, and power the only stakes. Schools, communities, and life-styles seemed at issue in small-town, rural Minnesota. Ideals were contested along with interests, with debate over whether market competition would contribute to or subtract from the quality of life or education. Excellence and equity were invoked by both sides in arguments over whether client choice meant expanded access by the poor or enhanced elitism by the rich (p. 227). As Mazzoni tells the story, the proposal became a public but not a popular issue that its chief beneficiaries rallied behind. It eventually lost by one vote in the Minnesota House Education Subcommittee where traditional educational lobbies exercised their power and where open enrollment was amended out of the annual education bill. Several related issues, most notably an economic downturn, which left little discretionary money to initiate the program, contributed to its defeat.

Mazzoni's story (but not the complete story of choice in Minnesota) ended in 1987 with a governor abandoning "choice," more cautious about educational reform in general, and establishing a centrist coalition to set future agendas. Left intact, however, was an older bill that since 1982 had allowed students to take courses in local colleges and universities. The house majority leader had long favored this initiative and felt that schools had not done enough to encourage students to use it. She took advantage of the opening offered by choice to expand the postsecondary option (p. 226).

Mazzoni includes all the elements: a reform-minded governor, interest groups and coalitions of interest groups, trial bills, legislators, and professionals watching to see what will, in the end, work. The educational professionals themselves are among the most active and vociferous of those concerned about particular measures. For system purposes, there is little distinction between those with and those without formal status.

As an example of the way special interests are represented by those groups with and without formal status, consider Nelson's (1975) story of Michigan's Mandatory Special Education Act of 1974 (P.L. 198), which stipulated that local and intermediate school districts should provide special services to all handicapped persons ages 0 to 25. Searching for the impetus of that Act, Nelson found that Michigan's legislature had passed it very grudgingly in response to a coalition composed of special education professionals, the Michigan Association of Retarded Citizens, and a particularly active subgroup, the Parents of Mentally Retarded Children. A key legislator reported that the coalition spokesman told him, "'If you're not going to pass it, we're going to' and they had the petitions drawn up and circulated and that's what got the thing moving" (p. 217). The legislator went on to say that:

> "You don't find anyone more militant than a parent who has a special ed kid and feels that the kid is being shortchanged. These people have a number of organizations.

The special ed professionals themselves are kind of an unbelievable group. They're militant as hell and they wrap themselves in these handicapped kids and march everywhere. That's where the push comes from. [They] are so successful that their own superintendents will wash their hands of them, really, there's no control...."
(p. 220)

Special education directors in opposition to their own superintendents and boards and the special education director of the state department (against the wishes of the state superintendent) were part of the coalition. In this discussion of the system, "the state" does not refer to a centralized agency taking directives from the legislature and money from the feds to distribute. Instead, it refers to an arena in which self-interested lobbyists, legislators, professionals, and nonprofessionals, press their favored programs into the formal organization.

Multiple and competing interests around selected issues characterize education at federal and state levels. They also characterize every important element in the system. In *America Revised,* Fitzgerald (1979) described social studies textbooks as emerging from a coalition of publishers, authors, and textbook "commissions" in such states as Indiana, Texas, and Florida. Along the way the content of books gets pushed this way and that by B'nai B'rith's Anti-Defamation League, the John Birch Society, the NAACP, school boards in racially sensitive cities like Detroit and New York, the National Council for the Social Studies, and various intellectuals, some in government, some in universities, who propose their differing notions of America's history. Writers and publishers have to wend their way through a minefield of conflicting interests to develop a defensible and salable account of our country and culture. Fitzgerald added several examples of how textbooks change to satisfy various groups.

Poor Columbus. He is a minor character now, a walk-on in the middle of American History. Even those books that have not replaced his picture with a Mayan temple or an Iroquois mask do not credit him with discovering America, even for the Europeans. The Vikings, they say, preceded him to the New World and after that, the Europeans, having lost or forgotten their maps, simply neglected to cross the ocean again for five hundred years. (p. 8)

Educational reform is another rainbow idea that attracts public and private groups. In the early 1980s Theodore Sizer, Dean of the Graduate School of Education at Harvard, was part of a three-year study of secondary schools. That study, backed by the National Association of Secondary School Principals and the National Association of Private Schools resulted in the book *Horace's Compromise* (1984).

At the center of Sizer's book was the composite teacher, Horace, having the energy that he should have put into teaching drawn off by organizational and maintenance matters. Horace's students were similarly burdened. Instead of attending to their own intellectual development, they were trying to keep up with the inane routine that the school called the curriculum. Sizer concluded his book with a plea for "essential schools," where students and teachers work around a coherent notion of intellectual development and within a school structured to support the notion. Sizer's ideas are neither complicated nor revolutionary; instead they are based on the age-old argument for a liberal education. He argues too that all students will respond to a limited and higher-quality curriculum.

The positive response to his ideas encouraged Sizer to form a group of secondary schools that would implement the ideas. Housed at Brown University and backed by Exxon Corporation, by the National Association of Secondary Principals, and by some donors affiliated with a private university, the Coalition of Essential Schools grew in a few years from fourteen to fifty-eight member schools (some private, most public) before it joined with the Education Commission of the States, a Denver-based coalition funded by state departments of education. The Education Commission had been searching for a secondary school reform program and adopted Sizer's ideas and his Coalition. By the summer of 1990, five states had adopted a model based on Sizer's ideas. That Sizer's initiative should be made up of so varied a set of supporters and participants is characteristic of the system.

NO PASS, NO PLAY IN TEXAS

One final story is of reform in Texas. McNeil's (1987) story has all the elements: a reform-minded governor, a blue ribbon panel, a logic connecting school reform to increased productivity, established interests, reformers, and conflicting parties pledging allegiance to basic values. In the early 1980s, Texas, with an economy suffering from a decline in oil price and real estate values, was open to the idea that "public education should somehow be responsible for economic recovery" (p. 199). In 1984, the democratic candidate for governor made educational improvement an election issue and among other things promised to raise teacher pay by 20 percent. But as McNeil explains, after being elected, the governor was unable to obtain the money to fund the increase and instead of raising salaries by the promised amount, he sponsored a broad education reform package that included among its provisions a "no pass–no play" rule

> to counter teachers' frustrations that their students were missing class for pep rallies and athletic games, especially in rural areas on Thursdays and Fridays, athletes would be held to strict grade requirements before being allowed to play in sports during each six week grading period. The provision not only gave teachers more leverage over class attendance and student activities, especially in varsity athletics; it sent the message to parents and students that the educative purposes of schooling are to be taken seriously. (p. 204)

In other words, athletics would henceforth be subservient to academics. The coaches reacted by mobilizing their local supporters to obtain

> extensive media coverage of star players, band members, drill team members, and cheerleaders whose tears were flowing over exclusion...based on failing grades.

Some high schools had to cancel games because of insufficient players. In small towns coaches became political leaders on state school reform. (McNeil, 1987, p. 206)

Arguing that it was those students most at risk who needed sports to encourage scholastic effort, they "descended on the state capitol in grief and anger to protest linking performance in competitive sports to students' passing grades" (p. 202). The no pass–no play provision stood, but according to McNeil, the furor contributed to the governor's election loss to a challenger who campaigned against the rule.

SUMMARY

Our educational system includes all sorts of people: the President, the Congress, the associations of federal employees, federal and state bureaucrats, reformers, courts, governors, teachers, interest groups, and coaches, all projecting their views into the system and, they hope, into the schools. Each of these has its own problem, and each phrases that problem in terms of quality and equality. But those terms are tossed around so indiscriminately that except as expressions of emotion, they are mostly neutralized. What remains are the interests: the president is interested in a reform initiative; the Congress is interested in dividing up money; the governor wants to improve schools so the state can attract industry and jobs; the business people want trained workers; the Catholics want choice; the teachers want money; the football boosters want an exciting Friday night. For any single group, the trick is to turn its interests into a program that is adopted by the formal organization. It helps if the program helps students, but all groups argue that. The point is neutral. In our system of overlapping groups, the initiatives that work are those that can be retranslated into terms that serve the purposes of groups down the line. Some are more successful. The ESEA forced its agenda onto schools by giving them money, plain and simple. "Excellence" worked because the schools wanted to do and were already doing what it advocated. The NIE did not work. Even its originators were suspect of its logic and motives.

What comes out of this system with its numerous and crisscrossing efforts is the formal organization, which is the sum of the programs hammered out by competing interests. As a compromise package, the formal organization rests uneasily. There are always more interests in the system than the formal organization can accommodate: more people who want special programs and who can point to others' getting them, people who want some time in an already full school day for particular groups of children. The people who run the formal organization are naturally conservative and cautious—they have to be. The schools they run are at the center of several noisy and contentious factions who want resources, attention, and time that are presently being given to someone else. If that someone else is deprived, she or he too may become contentious and noisy. One has to be careful to seek consensus, to winnow out gracefully the radical and threatening elements, and to test the wind for appropriate responses. The next two chapters describe schools as they respond to initiatives from federal and state levels.

7

Back to the Schools

INTRODUCTION

Each of the system's groups has to accomplish two things: it has to achieve goals and it has to overlap its efforts with contiguous groups. The two activities are always interwoven and often coterminous, but this book tries to treat them separately in order to draw out elements that are common to the system. In previous chapters, separate parts of the system are described. This chapter concentrates more on the way separate parts overlap. The descriptions show federal and state programs as they enter schools and affect the behavior of administrators, teachers, and students.

Change is a favored topic among educational researchers, and several have studied federal and state efforts as they enter schools and classrooms. Such studies are useful for elucidating the system because they focus on a single issue from the perspectives of several groups. Wolcott's (1977) *Teachers versus Technocrats* tells of a school district, aligned with a university-based and federally funded research and development center, creating a comprehensive management plan and taking the plan into classrooms. The resistance to the plan by teachers is at the center of Wolcott's story.

A similar effort was described by Popkewitz, Tabachink, and Wehlage, (1982) in their *The Myth of Educational Reform*, a story about Individually Guided Education, a classroom management and instructional plan created by another federally funded, university-based, research and development center. The authors describe the plan and the way teachers adapted it to their own schools. The authors argue that IGE's success was a function of how easily it lent itself to retranslation into terms that served the purposes of administrators and teachers, and parents and students.

A larger federal effort, generally deemed unsuccessful, was the Experimental Schools project, an effort designed to improve several schools through comprehensive community planning. The 1970s project awarded several million dollars to ten school districts over five years. Among the elements provided by the grants was a field researcher to trace the effort at each site. Five field reports are cited in this chapter.

Also to be used is Auletta's (1982) study of a single class in the Manpower Demonstration Research Corporation. He described how this federally funded and nonprofit corporation taught job attainment and job skills to long-term welfare recipients, ex-convicts, ex-addicts, and delinquents. Auletta tells a story of an effort that succeeded under the most difficult circumstances.

These studies were not selected because they depict conflict, but in fact most do. The conflicts occur when the operation of one group is changed, often shaken, by the intrusion of energy, money, and influence. Because each group is bound into the overall system, it does not have the option of departing and has to adjust. In the ensuing change, one can see how groups overlap, how initiatives are generated, and how much of the system is open to influence. One can also see the emergence of groups and coalitions that no one expected.

TEACHERS VERSUS TECHNOCRATS

Of the more popular innovations of the 1960s and 1970s were attempts to connect teaching and learning to planning and assessment. At the time, it was much bandied about by federal and state planners that "the public is demanding accountability." What "accountability" might mean and whether "accountability" is what the public demands of schools were open to question. But the USOE was trying to implement change and state people were trying to extend both federally funded programs and their own influence into schools. To assert that their efforts were being undertaken on behalf of the public seemed reasonable.

One of the more popular management models, called program planning and budgeting systems (PPBS), was brought to the federal government in the early 1960s by Secretary of Defense Robert McNamara. PPBS was an attempt to connect distant planners with on-site events, budgets with production, coordination with evaluation, and costs with benefits. Bailey and Mosher (1968) explain the background of PPBS inside ESEA:

> The extraordinary concern of the drafters and amenders of ESEA with reporting and evaluating procedures cannot be understood apart from a general movement within the Federal government ... for a new and concerted emphasis upon program evaluation. President Johnson had been greatly impressed with the cost-benefit studies conducted under the leadership of Defense Secretary Robert McNamara in the early 1960s. A program planning and budgeting system (hereafter PPBS) had been developed ... (and) ... had enabled the Defense Department to create (some would add "the illusion of") a rational structure for making planning decisions. (pp. 179–180)

The story told by Wolcott (1977) in *Teachers versus Technocrats* is of a district superintendent assisted by a university-based and USOE-funded research and development agency trying to implement a PPBS plan in Oregon's South Lane School District.

The matter began in the University of Oregon's Center for the Advanced Study of Educational Administration, a USOE- (later NIE) funded research and development effort. In the Foreword to Wolcott's book, the director of that center explained his dual concerns, first for the "lack of correspondence between

curriculum planning and the delivery of instruction and teacher evaluation practices" (p. ix), and second that his

> Center was being criticized severely by [the USOE] for failing to engage in work
> that could be legitimately called "development"...continued funding for the Center
> would depend upon our willingness and ability to initiate such work. (p. x)

The center staff developed a variation of PPBS appropriate to classrooms
and called it SPECS (School Planning, Evaluation, and Communication System)
and convinced the superintendent of the nearby South Lane School District of
its worth. The superintendent did not need much convincing. He believed that
a more tightly controlled organization was essential to improving instruction:
"I just couldn't have gone on for 20 more years in education without trying to
change and improve it....It needed to be better organized" (p. 81). In general,
the people whom Wolcott calls "technocrats," those in the USOE, the Center,
and the district's central office, shared the belief that too much of what goes on
in classrooms is under too little control, and agreed on SPECS as a solution.

Following the PPBS logic, the university plan was a five-step process designed to disaggregate and evaluate each element in the educational program.
First, the district's operating programs would be disaggregated "to the level at
which intensive...planning and evaluation could take place" (p. 21). Second,
each component would be analyzed and monitored for costs. Along with asking
about costs, planners would ask about each component's importance. Third, evaluation processes would be added, and the three processes, planning, monitoring,
and evaluation, would be applied to each component. Fourth, the community's
goals would be broadly defined and fifth, the community goals would be fitted
with the operating programs.

One can understand the support that such a plan would generate among
those outside the classroom concerned with: (1) what is going on, (2) how well
are goals being achieved, and (3) whether individuals are doing what is desired.
One can understand equally the opposition generated among teachers wanting
to preserve their flexibility. The plan required them to maintain an accounting
system in which they would (1) list students, (2) match each with instructional
objectives, (3) match objectives with learning activities, (4) assess student performance relative to activities on appropriate tests, and (5) develop summarizing
data for the class by objectives.

Program directions were written thus:

> 3. At the end of each program included in the "Record of Student Performance"
> use the right side of document 6.20 to summarize group performance on each
> objective. Enter the total number of students who worked on it in the column
> headed "Total." In the remaining columns, enter the number who achieved various
> degrees of mastery of the objective, the number who demonstrated various degrees
> of effort to achieve it, and the number of students for whom complete data are un-
> determined (U). If, in addition, a summary for each student's overall performance

on the objectives, and tasks in the program or unit is desired, use document 6.10 to summarize the data recorded on documents 6.20 and 6.21. (p. 19)

The lines were drawn. The "technocrats," not directly in contact with students but feeling responsible for their learning, saw themselves as requesting only that teachers disaggregate classroom events and subject each event to scrutiny. SPECS would enable planners and administrators to demonstrate that they were in charge of events and more particularly that they could connect events to outcomes. But many teachers saw themselves burdened with an impossible and useless task.

> I've heard teachers say, "I'd quit if I could find another job. Look at all this damn stuff."
> I can't possibly do all this pretesting. Having these goals, and knowing what I want to accomplish, this is all good but if you've been teaching very long you do those things anyway.
> It's the Mickey Mouse in triplicate that gets to me.
> Frankly the whole thing turns me off. I don't mind the objectives and the performance objectives. But this business of testing and writing! Junk, junk and junk. I just throw lots of it in the wastebasket.
> This whole program looks marvelous on paper, but things just don't work out according to the plan. (pp. 39–40)

There were several points of conflict. The teachers suspected that the program was intended primarily to assist the superintendent's career. They also considered university consultants both overly ambitious and ignorant about teaching. The combination of complaints encouraged several teachers to openly resist.

The resisting teachers, finding their concerns attributed to a mere communication problem by administrators and university planners, turned to their professional association, which formed an investigating committee. The committee was headed by a principal, himself dubious of the program. The committee documented widespread, but not universal, opposition among teachers. The teachers took the results of the investigation, emphasizing the oppositional parts, to the board of education, which backed the superintendent and the program. The local paper picked up and publicized the dispute, to the embarrassment of district administrators.

Equally embarrassed by the publicized dispute was the university group seeking to "sell" SPECS to other districts. During the investigation, the teachers had obtained a list of other districts interested in the project and wrote to each, giving an account of South Lane's problems. The opposing teachers also "bird-dogged" the superintendent, who was on the lecture circuit extolling the benefits of the program. A leader of the opposing teachers explained the tactic.

> Now the superintendent is spreading nationwide the glories of his work with SPECS. ... That's the same thing he did here that got us so mad—telling things to the board and the press that were not true. So we want to be a thorn in their side. It's our

professional obligation to warn unsuspecting school districts throughout the United States.

We'll bird-dog the superintendent's every move and contact any district that he goes to. We don't just want to send out negative information, but we do want to let people know what happened. (pp. 99–100)

Since no superintendent and board wants to invite teacher problems, interest in SPECS by other districts dropped dramatically.

Teachers' communicating with teacher organizations in districts that were considering a similar plan was a setback to the university group that had contracted with an independent agency to disseminate project materials. The agency's "educational services" division was then eliminated. The negative publicity also encouraged the South Lane school board to declare a partial moratorium on the project in preparation for the state department team that, at the request of the teachers, was coming to investigate. The board and superintendent then agreed to ease off on the reporting of individual students and subsequently on the paperwork required of teachers, but they kept elements of the program that they wanted.

Problems existed not only outside the classroom, but within the project itself. The idea of aligning community goals with classroom activity was simply not done.

During the Matching Workshop held in the summer following Year Four, a teacher asked: "Where are the district-defined program goals for the courses I teach?" The SPECS coordinator answered, "There aren't any. You'll have to generate them, like we did last year for courses that didn't have district-defined goals. Then teachers next year will have a starting place for working up goal statements." Another teacher at the workshop observed with dismay, "If you think about it long enough, you can justify drawing any line to any point relating what we do in school to what the community wants." (pp. 78–79)

Reactions to the program were not all negative. In fairness, some teachers endorsed the program.

All the kids in my class this year can do their "facts" [multiplication tables] and I think it's because last year their teachers knew what they were trying to accomplish and did so. This year I could get started right away. I have been able to reach an objective in math that I've never reached before. (p. 197)

Other teachers found the plan helpful, but not the associated paperwork. Five years into the program, the results of a teacher survey to assess whether the program should be phased out were more positive than might be expected. Strongly in favor were 31 percent; strongly opposed, 19 percent (p. 75). Most teachers said they would continue to use the pretesting and posttesting components of the program, although not the attendant record-keeping. The superintendent got high marks from central office staff for getting the district more organized.

In addition to events in the district, Wolcott (1977) described several problems inside the university Center and between the university group and the school administrators. A problem for the university people was internal continuity. By year three of the program, national interest in accountability was diminishing and NIE problems, as Chapter 6 describes, were having their effect. The Center's funding was being reduced and staff were leaving without being replaced. The changing nature of the project and the shifting staff made it difficult to continue long-term research or determine how results would be used.

At the same time, university developers and university researchers were unable to reach consensus on what constituted a positive outcome.

> It became gradually evident that the researchers intended to provide no feedback at all to the developers. The developers had anticipated gaining new allies to help move SPECS forward but they realized now that they had only added another burden to their task. They viewed the research team as sort of a parasitic sub-unit that intended to contribute nothing to SPECS except an independent assessment of its impact. (p. 90)

Distinctions between researchers and developers, important inside the university, meant nothing to South Lane administrators, who wanted to know, "Are [the university people] helping us or studying us?" When a questionnaire sent to teachers from the researchers included items about the administrators' motives, the superintendent decided the university people were studying them and he told both developers and researchers, "Get the hell out of my hair" (p. 74). As he made the final payment, the superintendent said, "That's our last payment... I'm tired of our being examined. People have used us as guinea pigs and it's hurt us. THAT ENDS OUR COMMITMENT" (p. 193).

In 1976, the project ended with the university group withdrawn or dispersed, the NIE reorganized and interested in other projects, and general interest in accountability diminished. The project, the university group that backed it, and the acrimony faded away, as Wolcott said, "without dramatic collapse" (p. 239). At the end, South Lane's administrators and teachers were calling for more open dialogue about common problems.

ANALYZING SOUTH LANE

Wolcott's (1977) story illuminates several points about the educational system. One is that not only do groups emerge unexpectedly, but they are free to seek allies with whom to pursue interests. As expected, each proclaims its interest in quality, equality, or both, but those are sufficiently broad as to encompass a plethora of disparate endeavors. Groups receiving unwanted interference from outsiders are free to enlist other groups in their cause—and they do. South Lane's opposing teachers called on and skillfully used their local and state professional organizations, the newspapers, the state department of education, and kept the superintendent's attention turned toward the conflict rather than toward managing teachers. Wolcott gives his readers a lesson on why school administrators are so cautious.

A second point is about formal authority. Consider the superintendent, ostensibly in charge of the district, "the educational leader" as superintendents are wont to style themselves. He surveys the situation and decides quite reasonably that education in general and in the local district in particular lacks organization and, further, that increased organization would result in increased learning. From the position of formal authority, and with the backing of his board, the superintendent implements a program to tighten the organization, a program thought to not only improve student learning but appeal to his cost-conscious community. The program is developed by experts endorsed by the United States Office of Education and a respected university. All the trappings of legitimacy are present.

But in the face of internal divisions, teacher opposition, bad publicity, defection by district administrators, and changed federal priorities, the project falls apart. So does the support for the project. One can say that SPECS was a bad idea. Some teachers did not think so, but perhaps it was. Or if it had been implemented differently, if the technocrats had been a little less technocratic, then teachers might have accepted it or a modified version of it.

Wolcott saw the problem in terms of the split between those inside (teachers) and those outside the classroom: the Center people, the administrators, the NIE, the technocrats. Wolcott believes that this teacher/technocrat division "permeates the entire educator subculture" (p. 118) and that "technocrats are normally in the majority and sometimes occupy all the professional positions" (p. 118). Given their mission to plan and administer classroom events and given their assumption that tighter, more predictable, and controlled classrooms are superior, they need an abstract plan through which to exert control. SPECS was such a plan. Wolcott's sympathy clearly lies with the teachers. He believed that rational plans are invariably imposed on, rather than created by, teachers (p. 195) and that they take neither the classroom control problem nor the personalized nature of teaching into consideration.

But in fairness to the technocrats, South Lane's teachers were not universally opposed to SPECS. Some found the program a useless burden; others, even those who opposed SPECS in principle, found it helpful in organizing their teaching (p. 194). Wolcott noted this split saying that a disadvantage for teachers, in their disputes with technocrats, is that the teachers are not of one mind (p. 194). Yet the descriptions show that neither are the administrators nor the university group of one mind. South Lane's high school principal was head of the association committee that investigated the teachers' complaints. Sympathetic to the teachers, he tried to mediate between the superintendent and the teachers and in doing so incurred the animosity of the superintendent, who considered him disloyal. The elementary principals too, when the matter came before the association, voted with the teachers (p. 173).

In South Lane one can see elements that undercut attempts to reform education through restructuring the organization, such as the tendency of groups inside the formal organization to seek allies outside to assist in countering the formal organization's authority. The overall system is much larger than the formal organization; in the event of a dispute, elements that are part of the system but outside the formal organization are invited in, or invite themselves in. Thus entered into South Lane teachers' unions, both local and state, the newspapers, and an ad hoc investigating team within the district and another from the state department. The arena filled up; the unit of analysis shifted from the formal organization with its designated roles and authority lines to the system filled with a fractious lot of equal and contending groups. The superintendent, when backed by the board, has authority over events within the formal organization. But when events are no longer contained within the formal organization, when matters slip out of the formal organization and into the system, the superintendent is only one, and sometimes not a very important one, of several contending parties. Elements from the larger system, when activated, can neutralize authority inside the formal organization.

The question that this raises is of the usefulness of the formal organization as a unit of reform. Attempts to reform education by changing its formal organization are too numerous to list, but they all assume that problems of education are in fact problems with the formal organization and that reform of the formal organization can cure the problems. Educational reform becomes ipso facto organizational reform.

From Wolcott (1977) we see other elements that undermine reform attempts, such as the tendency of individuals to choose how they will behave relative to the reform. In South Lane a teacher could side with or oppose the superintendent; a principal could side with teachers; a university developer could oppose university researchers; Wolcott, himself a professor at the University, wrote a book criticizing the university's efforts. Free conscience and free choice undermined formal authority. In effect they allow the individual to hold dual or triple roles and to play them off against one another. Thus a teacher could use her union membership to oppose her superintendent. A second element, emanating from the first, is the tendency of reforms to escape from the formal organization and go into the larger system. When the union, the newspapers, and the investigating team from the state department entered, it was no longer a matter internal to the South Lane schools, no longer subject to formal restraints. When an event that is internal to the formal organization escapes into the larger system, it is literally out of control. At that point authorities inside the formal organization do well to back away from advocacy.

That is what happened in South Lane. The technocrats backed off and allowed individual teachers to decide on their degree of compliance with SPECS.

> Each teacher could develop a personal strategy for coping with the issue and could decide just how involved to become with it. There could be no single, unified response from so many teachers who had so many different interpretations of what was happening. (Wolcott, pp. 194–195)

The effects of these two characteristics, free entry and exit by parties and freedom of choice and conscience by everybody, mean that issues are seldom solved until they turn into something that the federated interests can abide. Wolcott's (1977) final assessment was that

> PPBS as such never came to South Lane. SPECS evolved in the course of its implementation from an ambitious and comprehensive design for managing an entire school system to a set of districtwide procedures for curriculum planning and recording pupil progress. Since those processes were already part of the school program, the changes were only in degree and emphasis. (p. 80)

A study of an effort similar to SPECS pursues these ideas, freedom of choice and association, as creating a dynamic and shifting set of alliances influencing the system and the formal organization. *Education and the Myth of Educational Reform* by Popkewitz, Tabachink, and Wehlage (1982) is another story about connecting classroom teaching with rational planning. The authors argue that the results were quite different because, from the beginning, teachers were allowed to turn the program to their own ends.

INDIVIDUALLY GUIDED EDUCATION

Like PPBS, Individually Guided Education (IGE) was an effort at increasing rationality. IGE was "a systems analysis approach to coordinate organizational, instructional, and curricular aspects of the school in a potentially efficient and rational system for making school programs more responsive to individual variations in learning" (p. 4).

In the 1970s IGE programs were being developed in several sites, one at the University of Wisconsin's USOE/NIE-funded Research and Development Center. Wisconsin's people undertook their efforts in response to several concerns, among them that (1) elementary curriculum is not sufficiently sensitive to students' individual differences, (2) there is insufficient use of tests, (3) teachers and administrators spend too little time on cooperative and creative planning, and (4) the school day is too inflexible to allow for individual instruction. IGE was designed to combine efficient management with the psychology of individual differences.

> IGE ... links the appeal of individualism with the harmony and efficiency of scientific management. Systems management, behavioral objectives and criterion referenced measures seem to be backed up by research on individual cognitive differences and needs. The unitized school and the Instructional Programming Model combine systematically to provide for students who learn at different rates and at different times; by offering varied groups and materials as different routes to specified objectives, this system appears to be responsive to different learning styles. (pp. 33–34)

IGE was also designed to respond to two of the perennial concerns about schools: that they lose track of individual students and that they are not sufficiently accountable for their efforts. Wisconsin's version of IGE included systemwide planning and instructional improvement committees within buildings, and instructional groups of three to five teachers, each assisted by instructional and clerical aides and responsible for 100–150 students. It also included estimation of objectives, both for the class and for the child, criteria for satisfactory achievement, testing of objectives, grouping and regrouping according to test results, measurement, and record-keeping.

Teachers were required to

> plan and implement an instructional program suitable for each student or place the student in a preplanned program. Vary (a) the amount of attention and guidance by the teacher, (b) the amount of time spent in interaction among students, (c) the use of printed materials, audiovisual materials and direct experiencing of phenomena, (d) the use of space and equipment (media), and (e) the amount of time spent by each student in one to one interactions with the teacher or (other types of) activities. (Popkewitz et al., 1982, p. 32)

The authors studied reputedly successful IGE programs in several elementary schools and, in their book, treat each school or district in turn. In the first district, the director of elementary education heard of the plan and passed it to a well-liked principal of a school with high-achieving students and satisfied teachers. The plan in that school combined two major concepts, IGE and "open schools." The authors dwell on the tendency among school people to shovel two or more sometimes opposing approaches into a single improvement effort. Central to IGE was the assumption that learning is a continuous and upward series of concrete steps. Under that assumption were two different approaches. One is the belief that children should be allowed to make learning decisions and that if they are given sufficient opportunity, children will make the right decisions. The second is that teachers should use tests to steer student efforts. Students found deficient in measurable skills should be taught skills and tested to see if they have learned them. The authors note that the contradictions between these two assumptions were not examined by program implementers or by teachers. Instead, they were thrown together as if they were not contradictory.

At a second school, the program was adopted by a staff that had been "individualizing with continuous progress" for some time. There, IGE included packaged materials that students worked on individually. The worksheets and learning packages were organized by levels of difficulty. Student attention and progress was monitored by the teachers. At a third school, the plan was to divide the teachers into groups of four to six and students into groups of 125–150. The students were assessed and given skill packages similar to those in the first school.

The authors argue that teachers accepted IGE at these schools because IGE served their own ends. In fact, IGE served everyone's ends. Administrators liked the appearance of rationality in instructional decisions, teachers liked the increased contact with each other, and they liked the IGE logic, which helped them explain their efforts to parents. Parents accepted and understood concepts of individualization, continuous progress, meeting children's needs, positive self-image, and accountability (pp. 58–68). And for students,

> repetition and routine in worksheet instruction provided students with a feeling of satisfaction and security. They could immediately get a 'grade' and find out whether they could move on to another objective or level; the criteria of success seemed clear and unambiguous. (p. 69)

The students enjoyed the appearance of progress that did not require too much effort, and they further enjoyed a system that allowed them to talk quietly while doing worksheets. IGE's inconsistencies were ignored in favor of solving problems of school and classroom management, teacher morale, parent relations, student order, and organizational communication.

At a fourth IGE school, 150 students were assigned to groups of four to six teachers. IGE consisted of ability grouping, skill development, and worksheets that progressed in difficulty. Teachers there saw no inconsistency in placing students in worksheet activities while stating that "children have both the competence and the right to make significant decisions concerning their own learning" (p. 53). According to the authors, the "views of schooling that emphasize the 'natural' tendencies of children and views that stress the systematization of learning are not seen as inconsistent when teachers have developed practices and an institutional language to guide their work" (p. 53).

Unlike South Lane's administrators, the administrators of the IGE schools did not push the teachers into compliance, but let them decide on their degree of involvement. And unlike SPECS, IGE fomented no revolt that gained the attention of outsiders. The authors argue that IGE was successful only because separate groups could turn it to their own ends. Every group up and down the system liked the answers IGE provided to ever-present questions, "What are we doing?" and "How can we tell people what we do?" (p. 155). Whether the students learned more or less, or more of what was desirable and less of what was undesirable, was not known or, according to the authors, not even asked. Hence the reference to mythology in the book's title.

IGE translated easily into the different perspectives and purposes depending on the school. The schools varied as to clientele and students' social class, and these variations elicited different perceptions from teachers as to what the students "needed," their prospects for success, their social pathology, a portrait of the world for which they were being prepared, and appropriate academic treatments. Teachers' perceptions of students and what they needed affected their teaching and their way of talking about their efforts. IGE adapted easily to cultural differences. Thus the teachers in schools serving poorer students could assert that IGE was providing students with order, discipline, basic skills and so on. Teachers in schools that served more affluent students could argue that IGE was serving their individual needs to achieve and excel.

The authors argue that one of the erroneous assumptions of IGE is that students' individual differences exist apart from the school and the students' cultures.

> Individual variation is a psychological abstraction which isolates human traits, ap-
> titudes and attitudes from the school setting, cultural environment and social cir-
> cumstances in which children function. It assumes that "individual differences" exist
> apart from the social setting of schooling and that they can be treated in a logical
> and administrative fashion. (p. 173)

But teachers, although they appeared to go along with IGE, did not accept the belief that students' individual differences exist apart from the school
environment or the students' culture. So in each EGE school studied, the staff
adjusted IGE to fit preconceptions about that school and its students. Apart from
the forms and appearances, then, little changed. "In none of the six schools were
the existing conditions of schooling changed; instead the old conditions were
given a new source of credibility and reasonableness through the symbolic form
and practices of the reform itself" (p. 173). The authors sympathize with the
teachers and argue that IGE's originators were wrong in assuming that schooling is neutral. As the authors argue, "schooling gives form to certain social and
community interests and is not at all a neutral endeavor" (p. 168).

Finally, regarding students, what came through most strongly to the authors
was not learning and effort, but the appearance of learning and effort. According to the authors, IGE's progressive language masked burned-out teachers who
could not keep up with record-keeping, meetings, and planning, and who did
not monitor student progress as much as maintain the machinery. IGE masked
also the fact that students learned to appear busy while doing little. The authors
describe the students in one school exerting "periodic bursts of effort to keep
up with the requirements" (p. 51) and in another:

> A child came to show the teacher her work. She had done the mastery test and
> said "Look, I got 96." The teacher commented to the observer. "There's no way she
> could get 96 because she doesn't add or multiply." The pupil sits down with a level
> three book. She quickly thumbs through as though she's trying to look industrious,
> but she doesn't know how to read it. She looks up at the observer and says, "I
> finished the book. I made 100 and nobody helped me." (Popkewitz et al., p. 75)

Two efforts to change schools from without have been examined. Both
were promoted by federal funds channeled into university-based R & D centers, both focused on disaggregation. SPECS disaggregated the curriculum; IGE
disaggregated presumed student differences. Both were technological and both
developed outside schools and handed to teachers, albeit in different ways. Both
were designed to solve organizational problems of coordination, control, and
evaluation. Both books cited here describe improvement efforts that wended
their way down the system and became co-opted by targeted groups. The failure
of SPECS was that one group pushed its authority beyond what other groups
would tolerate. The success of IGE was that no group was pushed; instead, each
was allowed to continue standard practices while turning the reform into what
it wanted.

In South Lane and in IGE schools, local groups sifted through initiatives,
selected the elements that served their interests, and discarded or resisted the

others. Although the results were other than envisioned, both cases illustrate the system as a set of overlapping collectives, each seeking to solve particular problems, each quick to seize and turn an initiative into an opportunity, each appropriating terms such as accountability and efficiency, individualization and choice. One would expect that in the ensuing negotiations acceptable definitions of these terms would have been worked out. But as *The Myth of Educational Reform* (1982) indicates, it is more convenient to ignore the varied meanings of these terms, leave specifics to teachers and students, and concentrate instead on operational fluidity. Only if organizational fluidity is achieved is the reform counted as a success. If organizational fluidity is not achieved, the reform is counted a failure. In effect, organizational considerations co-opt educational considerations.

EXPERIMENTAL SCHOOLS

The Experimental Schools (ES) program, funded in 1971 by Congress and run by the USOE, was designed to assist small, rural school districts to implement comprehensive change. The projects were to be locally designed and were to involve:

> a fresh approach to the nature and substance of the total curriculum in light of local needs and goals...reorganization and training of staff to meet particular projects goals...innovative use of time, space, and facilities...active community involvement in developing, operating and evaluating the proposed project...(and)...an administrative and organizational structure that supports the projects and takes into account local strengths and needs. (Herriott, 1980, p. 3)

As it was reasoned, comprehensive change emanating from a community was more likely to succeed than were categorical efforts planned by the USOE and implemented by states. Under the ES arrangement, the small districts designated "experimental" would create and embark on comprehensive improvement plans of their own design. The USOE would provide up to 15 percent of the annual budget to support the efforts. Three hundred small districts applied and ten received grants.

The projects included the presence of a full-time field researcher to document the effort in the hope that expected success could be emulated in other districts. When combined, researchers' reports offer interesting perspectives on how changes are initiated, how agencies from different levels operate together, how districts implement change and, in this case, what finally occurred. Five of those research accounts are referred to in this chapter.

In the five districts, the initial idea for applying for ES funds belonged to the administrators, primarily superintendents, who saw the funds as a way to help with expansion and upgrading that in most cases were going on anyway. Shiloh, Virginia, was initiating a building and consolidation program and needed money for retraining teachers, purchasing equipment, and adding personnel. The superintendent seized on ES as a source of needed funds. He obtained the permission of the board, approval of teachers, and help from university consultants to develop his plan.

River District, Wyoming, had just been created from five smaller districts and the administrative team saw the program as a way to unify program, personnel, and evaluation. In South Umpqua, Oregon, and Constantine, Michigan, administrative teams initiated the response. In Quilcene, Washington, the superintendent was concerned about teachers "isolated into stagnation" (Colfer and Colfer, 1979, p. 200) and saw the program as a way to create a more unified, resourceful, and dynamic system.

The five reports concentrate on organizational problems that occur when outside money and influence are interjected into schools. Overall, the reports are quite disparaging of the effort. Colfer and Colfer (1979) reported from Quilcene on "the specific steps by which a small school district, caught in the conflicting web of federal wishes, state regulations, and citizen demands, absorbed and diffused a large federally funded effort at planned change" (p. iii). Donnelly (1979) reported Constantine's effort as "undermined by dissension between administrators and teachers, a strike by teachers, lack of commitment to the planned goals, inadequate leadership and a lack of community participation and support" (p. 1).

Hennigh (1979) termed South Umpqua's effort a "success," but qualified the term by documenting the "gross underestimation of impending difficulties on the part of everyone concerned" (p. iii). Messerschmidt (1979) concluded his study of River District, by describing declining interest and support for the project, a lack of local commitment, discontent with USOE/NIE policies and personnel, and "reduced financial incentives for participation" (p. 192). Clinton's (1977) study of Shiloh, Virginia, concluded that residents used "informal methods of social control such as gossip and social shunning to curb the activities of change agents and to reject their innovations" (p. 4).

Those were the final assessments. At the outset, people in each district expressed enthusiasm and pride at having their schools selected from so many applicants. The studies illustrate what educators do when they have additional resources. They target particular groups of students and direct resources at those students, thus further differentiating the organization. They also add programs that are currently "hot," which in the early 1970s included individualized instruction, outdoor education, a new social studies curriculum called "Man: A Course of Study" (MACOS), and career education; most of these included humanizing, equality, and self-actualization among their goals.

In Shiloh the money would be used to fund a "diagnostic center housing specialized services" (Clinton, 1977, p. 105). The staff would include a reading specialist, nurse, guidance counselor, and contract personnel in speech, hearing, social work, and counseling. Each school was to have a diagnostic center for reading and math. In Constantine, the central idea was humanizing the curriculum, and the plan included individualized, personalized instruction in reading and math. Local and regional resources and cultures were to be emphasized. River District planned programs in career and cultural education. South Umpqua revised its curriculum to include "local history, Northwest Indians, public services, colonial crafts, nature trails and field trips to other small towns" (Hennigh, 1977, p. 111). Several then popular curricular programs, such as MACOS and "People and Technology" were purchased from publishing houses. Instructional leaders and classroom aides were hired.

In Quilcene, the program consisted of reading improvement, career and cultural education, improved and individualized reading packages, expanded facilities for vocational arts and crafts, athletics, refurbished facilities, and elementary and secondary libraries (Colfer and Colfer, 1977, p. 245). New classes were added in reading, vocational and manual arts, science, and careers.

Reform was prima facie equated with disaggregation of students, differentiation of curriculum, and implementation of the latest programs. Accompanying the three thrusts was the need for increased coordination by administrators. Coordination is necessary in efforts spanning several overlapping groups because the members have to know how their work is being received and interpreted by others.

SOUTH UMPQUA, OREGON

South Umpqua is a good district to discuss in detail because it was not troubled by the financial problems or the erratic administrative behavior reported in some other ES districts. South Umpqua's staff had worked hard to improve the district and had been rewarded by voters who consistently approved the budget and rewarded by the state, which had given their newly consolidated district full accreditation (Hennigh, 1979).

South Umpqua's final plan, negotiated with the teachers' association, focused on grades K–3 and on the high school. The funds gave the staff a chance to do what they always wanted: add programs for students. Teachers submitted 120 projects, 100 of which were approved. "The thrust [of these] was usually toward helping students adapt to the problems of small town living." The added components included staff development, evaluation, cultural and field experiences, assessment tutoring, peer counseling, and block scheduling. Content additions were made in social studies, reading, art, drama, outdoor education, and civics. Twenty-four additional staff members were hired in addition to half-time aides for each primary grade. According to Hennigh (1979), over the program's five years, during which 25 percent of the school district's funds were covered by federal funds, the district improved in several areas. Reading, math, language, and spelling scores all increased. College applications and acceptances also increased. Music, art, drama, reading, tutoring, and cultural programs were judged by school personnel and parents to be successful.

As the story goes, either those accomplishments occurred too gradually to be attributed to ES or they resulted from an influx of new residents who cared more about their children's school achievement than did established residents. Rather than working on programs and receiving credit for success, ES was engulfed in problems involving staff, the community, and local USOE/NIE problems. The ideas of a rural area as a community and of a rural school district as serving the needs of the rural community are appealing. They have a nice ring and can be sold by federal planners to Congressional appropriations committees. But in fact, each community is a loose amalgam of always wary and sometimes competing interests. There are common notions, of course, that each child should receive an education and that schools as presently organized are reasonable. Beyond these assumptions are myriad possible disagreements and the ES program triggered them. Whether more or fewer problems existed than at other times is impossible to discern. But in the minds of many, ES fomented or was associated with the problems.

One problem was resistance by teachers to a program that was initiated by administrators. South Umpqua's staff had been looking forward to a routine year and were not pleased with the prospect of the additional work that the planning grant required, particularly since they had not been consulted. During the planning time, the administration had to meet deadlines, and it had to do so with consensus. The hundreds of required meetings with representatives from the community, students and staff were emotionally charged with "some...teachers nearly bursting into tears" (p. 91) from frustration.

The recently consolidated district was trying to present itself as a single administrative unit which, in fact, it was not. Jealousies among the separate communities were always an issue.

> If the Myrtle Creek junior high principal requested and received new wrestling mats, for example, it was predictable that the Canyonville principal would argue forcefully for new mats also...a teacher's proposal in one school might turn out to be an administrator's [problem] in another school. (p. 92)

Furthermore, in the original ES idea, planners envisioned that the resources would draw participants together into a forum where they would make decisions and take actions by consensus. Participation and consensus are appealing in theory, but in practice are difficult to achieve. In addition to cross-district jealousies and teacher suspicion of administrators, teachers were unable to decide among themselves how to allocate resources. Hennigh's account describes faculty meetings (similar to Lightfoot's (1983) account of Milton Academy) where definitions diverged, action was not agreed upon, and discussions drifted off. In one meeting,

> teachers seemed reluctant to offer suggestions in spite of repeated requests from the superintendent....After several such requests, he noted that some of the school had expressed concern about integration of the mentally handicapped into the classroom. This brought out first a few, then quite a number of responses. "When I taught in California, we integrated the classrooms and the progress the students made was just remarkable." "Where I student taught, we had the handicapped students separately half a day and with all the other students half a day. It worked out fairly well." "Teaching the handicapped requires special skills most of us haven't had the training for." The meeting ended inconclusively, and I did not hear discussion of it afterward. (Hennigh 1979, p. 93)

Equally nonconclusive were the meetings of the community coordinating council set up so citizen groups could "oversee" the effort. The administrators had tried hard to recruit interested people and were eager to hear their comments, but questions about the council's authority relative to the district's other efforts and about the role of the project relative to the rest of the district's efforts went unresolved, while the discussions drifted around. At the meeting where the central office administrators were to present the final program, only two of the committee's citizen members showed up.

The open discussion of the schools relative to ES gave community people an opportunity to express whatever they thought was wrong with the school. In small towns, school administrators' salaries are frequently a source of envy and in South Umpqua the superintendent, who was receiving a $10,000 bonus from the USOE, was accused of "selling out the students for cash" (p. 93). And predictably enough, some parents were suspicious of the term "experimental." "I don't want my children experimented on" and "What experiments are they conducting?" (p. 93). Those who feared higher taxes feared that the community would be left with ES to support after federal money was withdrawn. Others criticized the program as another federal "bureaucratic boondoggle" (p. 99). A retired teacher was quoted as saying, "When are they going to give the teachers a chance to teach?" (p. 99). Incorrect change from a young waitress in a cafe might incur the comment that "the schools are going downhill" (p. 99).

> By January of 1973, local residents also were beginning to express their political power by organizing around the issue of student discipline. One afternoon a teacher phoned a logger's wife and said "the schools were endangering the health of the students and if parents were concerned about the health of their children they had better do something about it, fast." Friends called acquaintances and a meeting of about 20 parents was held in the logger's home. At a later meeting 120 were present. (p. 100)

Thus was initiated a "Concerned Citizens for Education" group led by a young minister, which set out to investigate everything from administrative salaries to discipline in the bathrooms. Local people spoke of "things being out of control" at the school. The investigating committee posted parent patrols in the halls and lavatories. A school board member ran a newspaper ad inviting people who had complaints about the schools to call him at his home to discuss them. Predictably enough, the school was accused of not stressing the basics.

Experimental Schools was only one of several topics discussed by the investigating committee, but people agreed that "it was the new federal project that had gotten people stirred up" (Hennigh, p. 101). The administrators attended to each concern, and responded to each new issue. Gradually the controversies waned, but lingering suspicions contributed to the district's budget defeat the following spring. A reduced budget was later approved, but the following year other employee groups saw the money from ES going to hire additional administrators whose jobs they thought were superfluous. These employees believed that because the district was receiving ES money, they wanted some, and so pressed the board for salary increases.

Finally, several teachers had resented ES from the beginning. It was administrator-initiated and called for extra effort by teachers; it generated another layer of supervision over teachers and furthered their growing militancy. As of the 1973-1974 school year, the district's teachers asked for an 18 percent increase in pay; shortened school year; an increase in travel pay; written statement of the reasons for transfers, demotions, or changes in scheduling; binding arbitration; and greater power to discipline. Added was a provision that "the administration could not introduce any new or experimental programs into the curriculum without first informing the faculty and obtaining its permission" (p. 122). Most inflammatory was the attempted firing, later reduced to transfer to an elementary school, of a popular and winning high school coach. The ensuing public hearings had parents taking sides, some defending him for being a "wholesome individual who inspired good manners and morality"; others said he "shouts and throws things on the floor in the classroom" (p. 125). According to Hennigh, the combination of issues contributed to the budget defeat.

Another controversy rose in one of the ES-funded electives, "myth and legend." A teacher showed a controversial film, *Horror House* and was subsequently accused of being a witch. Additional objections were made to the showing of the film version of Shirley Jackson's *Lottery*, a story of human sacrifice in a small town. And the new fifth grade social studies program, "Man: A Course of Study," which portrayed other cultures, instigated rumors that schools were teaching bestiality, wife swapping, infanticide, parenticide, communism, and secular humanism (p. 158). A prominent citizen put the distaste for studying other cultures this way.

> I want you to have my opinion. They say that ignorance is bliss. Well, sometimes it's true. Maybe it's true that there are people in Africa who chop off their mother's heads, or cut off their big toes and throw them in the stewpot. But I don't think we need to know that. I don't feel the least bit smarter when I learn such things. (p. 159)

Each conflict generated opposition and each generated a committee trying to respond. The controversial films were shown publically, and private textbook analysts from out of state checked the controversial passages to see if they were antithetical to community values. There were more hearings at which petitions were presented, countered, etc.

Hennigh's (1979) assessment of all this is optimistic, even philosophical. He reasons that problems of cohesion bedevil all organizations, and the task of South Umpqua's administrators was to handle them. The administrators did handle them, the district did not fall apart, the superintendent did not get fired, and for his defense of the programs even received an ovation from teachers. A residue of resentments lies around all school districts: resentments about administrator salaries, particular teachers, textbooks, property taxes, student behavior, athletics, and so on. These resentments can break out any time around a soft spot. ES was a soft spot and a lightening rod for floating resentments. Reading Hennigh's account, one can understand the wariness of the small-town principal, quoted in Chapter Four who, when asked what his community wanted of their schools replied, "They want it clean, quiet, no trouble."

Hennigh's account is useful for its portrayal of how local issues overpower a federal initiative. But like others who studied ES, he limited himself to organizational conflicts and did not describe successful classrooms where ES programs might have worked despite problems with organization and administration. It may be that school classrooms are too private and school organizations too public. The former are as likely to obscure success as are the latter to exaggerate failure. Hennigh, like the rest, ignored what was happening in classrooms and made project coordination the subject of his study. When conflict wrecked consensus, and the contending groups and issues derailed the plans, ES was judged a failure. Robert E. Herriott (1980), who evaluated the total program, attributed the failure to ES's inability to function successfully within the culture of the federal bureaucracy in a manner sympathetic with the cultural morals of [those it was attempting to help] (p. 14).

There are good reasons for making organizational change the criterion of success. Federal agencies that provide money to local schools want assurance that the money will be spent as intended and that funded efforts have good effects. That is not unreasonable considering what federal staffers have to go through to obtain funds from congressional appropriations committees. They have to appear as if they know what they are doing, that parties further down the system will accept the planners' directions, and that the outcomes will be favorable. Accompanying educational improvements there has to be increased organizational intelligibility. But to several of the system's major groups, planning, coordination, and organizational intelligibility are not important. They mean little to teachers, less to parents, and nothing to students. They are useful primarily to those administrators at central office levels and above who have to communicate with state and federal agencies.

Furthermore and as discussed relative to South Lane, rational plans cover only the formal organization, not the elements from the overall system. The planners in South Lane did not know the teachers were going to head for their union and then the newspapers. The planners in South Umpqua did not know that the teacher was going to call the logger's wife and the logger's wife would call the minister and the three would start a time-consuming investigation. Nor did the ES planners at the federal level foresee all the events that derailed the NIE. No one foresaw the groups that would emerge or the issues they would bring in. If the formal organization were the system, or if it were at least coterminous with the system, then those controlling the organization would also control the system. But the system is much larger than the formal organization; it contains all sorts of people who think and do as they please rather than what the superintendent says. Rational planning, coordination, and orderly communication are perennially problematic.

CONSTANTINE, MICHIGAN

Educational reforms usually begin with a somewhat exaggerated description of both present and envisioned states of affairs and a logic that connects the pre- and postreform eras. In 1971 Constantine's description and its logic proceeded thus: schools and teachers are at present too subject matter–oriented. Teachers lecture their way through the subject matter in an impersonal and authoritarian manner to students who, inundated with impersonally presented facts, are lost, confused, and unhappy. In Constantine, Michigan, ES was projected to correct the students' unhappy state by developing "an educational process based on interpersonal relationships rather than a 'subject centered' orientation" (Donnelly, 1979, p. 19). "Authoritarian patterns of instruction…(would be replaced)…with egalitarian, interpersonal relationships" (p 15).

> Basic to this approach is that learning will be conducted in a compassionate and supportive manner where teachers guide, motivate, and encourage learning rather than dictate or lecture. The teacher will help each student develop to his potential as he uses acquired skills in interaction with persons and things in his daily life. To promote such interaction, the teacher must serve as a resource person with a focus on the learning environment rather than on the teaching act and the subject content. (Donnelly, 1979, p. 15)

Following the practice of enlisting slogans to stimulate innovations, associated with the present state of affairs were such harsh terms as "dictate," "lecture," and "authoritarian." Associated with the envisioned state were such euphemisms as "compassionate," "supportive," and "interpersonal." Underlying the associated logic was the assumption that students' performance is a function of their attitude, and improving their attitude will improve their performance. If they feel they are being dictated and lectured to, they will respond negatively. If they feel personally supported, they will respond positively.

Such slogans provide terms around which specific components can be organized and a language with which educators can explain their efforts. They also obscure the more unpleasant aspects of the endeavor, such as that schools are coercive and competitive, that students' social-class differences show up in their achievement, that learning foreign languages, math, and science is hard work, and that those unwilling to do the work will, unless favored by luck or family resources, find themselves denied access to society's preferred positions.

Constantine's program included personalized instruction in reading and math, expanded guidance programs for middle and high school, a wilderness program to present challenge and thus improve students' self-image, supplemental instruction in elementary school, staff development, adult education, and travel outside the community. The latter was deemed important to students growing up, but unlikely to spend their lives, in that rural community.

The project was to be organized, run, and evaluated through the district's extant structure with the addition of a few supervisors. A project coordinator was hired to work across the district, and some teachers in each building were given time away from students to coordinate project activities. Outside consultants were hired to assist with the new ideas, and several then popular programs were purchased for classroom use. Naturally, the improvements were to be carried out via extant authority lines. Indeed it is characteristic of developed systems in general and education in particular that suggested improvements, even those that propose to alter authority lines, are channeled along those same authority lines.

Donnelly (1979), the outside researcher assigned to describe ES in Constantine, tells two separate stories. The main one is how ES efforts got bogged down in ongoing disputes among the district's parties.

> The project was undermined by dissension between administrators and teachers, a strike by teachers, lack of commitment to the planned goals, inadequate leadership and lack of community participation and support. Many components of the plan were abandoned and the final defeat came at the end of the final year in a decisive rejection by the voters of a tax increase which would have provided local funds following cessation of the federal funding. (Donnelly, 1979, pp. 1–2)

ES began with a teachers' strike, the first ever in the district. Among the teachers' complaints was that ES obligated them to additional work without additional compensation. Animosity built up between the superintendent, acting for the board, and the teachers, who enlisted parents, mediators, state employee associations and even USOE people for their side. The strike lasted only the first week of school, but a residue of hostility dogged the program: teachers were reluctant to do extra projects and the superintendent, according to Donnelly, was bitter and isolated himself from teachers. The district embarked on a search for the correct mix of humanizing and individualizing, but the parties were unable to come to any agreement about these central concepts.

Animosity between teachers and the superintendent was one of several ongoing problems. Others were the conflict between the project director and the principals; the opposition to humanizing on the part of the high school principal, who resigned halfway through the project; and the departure of the middle school principal, who was a project supporter. The high school guidance counselor, who had been the mainstay of the school's effort to "humanize," also left. Rumors circulated that the superintendent and both elementary principals were out hunting jobs. Several elementary teachers resigned or went to the board claiming they could not work with the elementary principal.

An elementary principal, himself responsible for many of the programs, blamed the goals. "The more individualizing and humanizing attempted in a school, the lower will be the achievement scores" (p. 137). Furthermore, he explained that "we all got tired. I got tired, the teacher-coordinators got tired, tired of the in-service, tired of the Experimental Schools program" (p. 137). Newer teachers claimed that they were not using techniques from ES but using those they had learned before they came to the district. They felt little pressure from administrators to adopt techniques that the project outlined or recommended (p. 131).

> I'm not currently relying on Experimental Schools concepts nor much on my training while in college.... I find I've gone back mostly to common sense. We're being fed a lot of psychology.... We're afraid to make a move without considering whether we are doing something wrong to the kids. As for the projects here, I think we are much more confused about how to improve education than when we started. We don't know which way to go. We have so many in-service workshops. No one can make up his mind. (Donnelly, 1979, p. 140)

A high school science teacher, an early proponent of humanizing, saw humanizing as a complete failure.

> It failed because of the continuous battle between teachers and the board.... It failed because of the workshops which forced teachers to be unwilling receivers of useless concepts. Some teachers did not understand, and probably never will understand what humanizing is all about. Those teachers thought humanizing meant eliminating discipline and control in the classroom. Thus when they let students run amuck, they blamed it on humanizing.... Humanizing doesn't mean lack of structure and discipline. But those teachers couldn't figure that out. Then, when it didn't work for them they could say it was a failure and return to their old ways of doing things, satisfied that they had tried. (p. 141)

Exacerbating the confusion about terms was the fact that although one of the major goals was to raise reading and math scores, they declined during the life of the program, and the decline was blamed on humanizing.

During the fourth and last year of ES, the reading program had been changed several times; the districtwide and coordinated math program had been abandoned; penmanship was abandoned except in one elementary building; the travel component was under criticism; the careers component was discarded in elementary schools and never started in the high school; outdoor education was not functioning; and horticulture never started despite purchases of equipment.

On the other hand there were several successes. A guidance counselor was assigned to the middle school. Early childhood, pre-K, and adult ed programs were all working by the fourth year; wilderness and adult programs, penmanship, travel, and art in the high school and music in the elementary schools were all deemed successful. Donnelly attributes these successes to the "interests of teachers in implementing them and the relative freedom teachers had from the administrators" (p. 139). Teachers either did not allow themselves to be impeded by the coordinating efforts or by disagreeing colleagues, and they were able to implement their programs as they wished. Again, the wisdom of using the formal organization as a unit of reform is opened to question. Reformers might consider looking less at the organization and more at the separate parts, wherein education takes place. The system allows pockets of excellence to continue despite organizational problems. What happened in Constantine is reminiscent of what happened in Lightfoot's (1983) story of Carver High in Atlanta, a difficult school that nonetheless contained some long-running and excellent programs.

As evidenced in South Umpqua and Constantine, a part of the educational system is open to intrusion by one or more of the system's less predictable elements, and new programs, generated from without, are likely to excite the recipients. South Umpqua's and Constantine's citizen groups, aroused by costs and rumors of undisciplined behavior, investigated curriculum, discipline, and salaries. In Shiloh, the separate communities that had been consolidated into the district were jealous of one another's facilities and used ES to air their grievances. In Quilcene, Washington, which had three superintendents over the course of the project, "the experimental schools project...thrust the school into central focus. Old hands on the faculty pointed to the superintendent's fate with knowing nods, indicating the expected fate of all school persons when the community was aroused" (Colfer and Colfer, p. 214). In River District, Wyoming, the citizen committees set up to help plan and oversee the project became frustrated over their unclear roles, and later administrators and teachers tried to ease them away from active participation.

The ES districts had additional problems, most attributed to federal interference. From the combined studies, a picture of hesitancy and inconsistency emerged around the relations. Federal administrators were regarded by these Westerners and Midwesterners as foreigners from the East. The latter never created workable relations with the former. In Quilcene, the NIE staff, according to Colfer and Colfer, were primarily interested in comprehensive change and assurance that the money would not be used for routine upgrading. Accordingly, the care taken by the USOE/NIE to assure this comprehensiveness was interpreted by the district people as the federal bureaucrats meddling in their affairs and a violation of their understanding that the money came with "no strings attached." "Viewed from Quilcene, both Abt associates and the National Institute of Education were large eastern bureaucracies staffed by Ivy League hotshots who spent their time composing incomprehensible memoranda" (Colfer and Colfer, 1979, p. 120).

> The presence of external evaluation was felt at every turn. A looming, impersonal and inscrutable machine from the East which asked for endless data and offered in return an incomprehensible technical assistance plan did nothing to ease the growing anxiety over the idea of being evaluated. (p. 211)

In River District, Messerschmidt (1979) says that the relationship with the Washington people was generally bad and attributed it to the Washington bureaucrats' having

> little prior experience with school or rural communities...(and coming)...with a definite mission in mind, prodded by their own personal needs and the agency's need to demonstrate accountability to higher authority in Washington, to the ES and NIE directors and ultimately to the Congress itself. (p. 114)

Frequent changes in the Washington staff did not help. Nor did the third project officer, who made herself popular by blaming the problems on her predecessors. Staff changes within the district were paralleled by staff changes in the NIE. The director of the NIE resigned in 1974, and there was a general declining interest in ES on the part of NIE staff to whom the project was given. Donnelly (1979) says that in Constantine, initially the feds were more interested "in the mechanics of the process...than...the conceptual framework upon which the ...process was built" (p. 25). After the project's second year, when the NIE's internal problems became its chief concern, the organization kept up its financial obligations but stopped its visits and its advice.

ES was generally regarded as one of the USOE's ill-conceived efforts and no one in the newly formed NIE wanted to be burdened with its expected failure. In South Umpqua, Hennigh (1979) had relatively little to say about federal relations except that they were fairly good, although the federal project officers tended to come and go. Clinton (1977), whose study is almost entirely of how local people reinterpreted the federal initiative to pursue their own agendas, concluded that "external initiatives are not particularly effective in achieving developmental change" (p. xi).

The issue of different agendas was what Herriott (1980) concentrated on in his summary assessment of ES in the ten districts. He used the term "goal displacement" (p. 15) to refer to the way purposes change at various levels of the system and the frustration of planners unable to see their plans carried out or positive results that they can attribute to their efforts:

> The intent of most federal education legislation is the eventual improvement of pupil knowledge and skills. However, as programs are being designed to reflect Congressional intent—particularly as they are being negotiated with the local educational agencies responsible for their implementation—one can easily lose sight of pupil change as the major program objective. Over time, such goal displacement occurred within the rural ES program as implementation problems at both the federal and local levels led to a shift from an emphasis on pupil change to one on school system change, and finally to one simply on limited change in particular curricular components. Thus it was not surprising to find no consistent evidence of pupil change that could be attributed to a district's participation in the program. (Herriott, 1980, p. 15)

It seems unfair to judge ES efforts solely on the basis of their inability to coordinate broad changes. Communities are composed of several, often competing, groups. ES did not create teacher militancy, student unrest, taxpayer resentment, or community unhappiness over consolidation. Any large-scale change coming into the community was bound to catch the fallout of these issues. The problems of ES were not of its making. The system is constructed so that different parties can add their own realities and subtract or ignore realities they dislike.

As in any system, the key to success is the continued influx of energy and resources. Experimental schools brought extra resources and programs into those districts, and teachers were able to take and make use of those resources. ES also brought the expectation that the varied parties with varied interests would work in harmony. However much such harmony appeals to orderly impulses, it is of use primarily to administrators, who have to explain events inside the system to those outside the system, and for preventing simultaneous and contiguous events from backing into one another. To make coordination the criterion of success obscured the good that ES might have generated between teachers and students in classrooms.

For an additional example of federal programs extended into classrooms, we may consider Auletta's (1982) study of a federally funded program in New York City. In *The Underclass*, Auletta (1982) described a single classroom, within a broader antipoverty effort. He concentrated on the interaction of teacher and students, and on the effect of the program on the students' lives: this enables the discussion here to examine federal initiatives as they move down into classrooms. And because it was an adult program, with the students going directly into the job market, the results could be seen quickly.

THE UNDERCLASS

The Manpower Demonstration Research Corporation, funded through the U.S. Department of Labor, was designed to provide training and subsidized work to those whom it was hoped would be able to escape poverty, welfare, and crime. Among the twenty-six students, who for their participation were given $105 (1979 dollars) per week and assistance with placement, were

> people who have been murderers, muggers, stickup men, chain snatchers, pimps, burglars, heroin addicts, drug pushers, alcoholics, welfare mothers and swindlers. Their teacher...is a former heroin addict, drug peddler, welfare cheat and near alcoholic, and has spent several of his thirty-nine years behind bars (p. 3)
>
> Not untypical of the students is Joe.
>
> "I had a personal problem," Joe says. "I was unhappy in my family." He dropped out of school. At sixteen, he was arrested for stealing a car. He started smoking marijuana, graduated to heroin and eventually entered a rehabilitation program for addicts. He straightened out, and went to cooking school by day and worked as a porter at night, finally latching onto a job as a cook at a fast-food restaurant in Manhattan. He was happy but after a month he forged a company check and was fired. He bounced around....Joe also returned to crime, and not long afterward he was convicted and sentenced to five years on Rikers Island for sticking up a store. Or consider Pearl, an able lady, who dropped out of high school when she gave birth to a son, who married, divorced, remarried and began to drink heavily and "in a drunken rage knifed a woman fatally, and she served eighteen months in prison." At the time of the study was both in poor health and on welfare. (Auletta, 1982, pp. 3–8)

The seven-month training program that Auletta (1982) studied consisted of typing, office practices, English, math, clerical, and life skills. The latter was designed to teach students to "use an alarm clock and telephone, follow dress codes, cash checks, say 'please' and 'thank you,' tell the truth about their pasts, write letters, conduct job interviews" (p. xv). Auletta describes the histories of the students, who in general were brought up by the kind of people they became. He details their drinking, drug abuse, violence, and belief that white people in particular and the system in general were against them.

Despite the unpromising participants and dreary surroundings, the program had some success. Seven months after it ended, Auletta (1982) described the sixteen students who had either left or been asked to leave prior to graduation and the ten who did graduate. Of the sixteen, one was back in prison; two were working as messengers; one was a shipping clerk; one making dolls for a company; one a street peddler; one a security guard; one a copy clerk; and one back on drugs. The salaries of those working was between $125 and $150 (1982 dollars) per week. Auletta was unable to find seven of the dropouts, but he found their acquaintances, who implied that the dropouts had drifted back into drugs, crime, and welfare. The graduates were noticeably more successful. Among the ten, only one had disappeared and only two were unemployed. Of the remaining seven, one was a clerk and word processor making $185 per week; two were clerks; one a financial aide; one a secretary; and one a draftsman. The most successful was a financial aide at New York's City University making $250.00 per week (pp. 210–219).

The heroes of the story are Howard Smith, the instructor, and the students, who found the forbearance to put up with the $105.00 a week, the plodding courses in English, math, and typing, and "five afternoons and three mornings each week, in dreary, unheated classrooms with windows caked with dirt and naked pipes crisscrossing the ceiling" (p. 3). Nothing magic happens in Howard Smith's classroom. Except for flashes of humor and warmth and hints that the students are a more able lot than their histories indicate. The activities and dialogue are frustratingly pedestrian, particularly for students accustomed to the street's action and movement. While federal funds kept the organization alive and administrators attended to the details, Howard Smith was free to help these "hardest to reach" students begin a responsible and regular life.

The program was closed down in the federal cutbacks of 1981; reinforcing the point that even if successful, there is no assurance of continuation. But continuation of the program is not necessary for success. What is important is that a good teacher and students accomplished some things despite organizational problems. Making organizational survival or change the unit of analysis and the criterion of success can obscure the good that goes on inside classrooms between teachers and students. Had the ES researchers concentrated on students and teachers rather than on interorganizational coordination, they might have judged ES a success.

SUMMARY

Schools are never sufficiently individualized, equal, excellent, or efficient. So education's reform mill never lacks grist. Reform and change are initiated by energetic individuals who in Trotsky's terms "sift themselves through the sieve of events," (1959, p. 121) and seize offered opportunities. Some of these individuals are in education's formal organization; others are not in the formal organization, but are in the system. A problem for reformers is that they tend to see education's system as coterminous with the formal organization. Therefore they try to channel their reform efforts along organizational lines, passing them down from the state to the superintendents to the principals and so on. But they mistake the nature of the system.

The descriptions show that there are many more groups in the system than there are in the formal organization. Reform efforts give birth to additional groups and they give the groups outside the formal organization a chance to participate on an equal footing with those inside. Changes have to be filtered through groups that the planners forgot or ignored: groups who may or may not agree with either the intended change or with the change as intended. They also exacerbate problems or activate resentments that have simmered for years. The activity and controversy generated by these parties outside the formal organization who suddenly find opportunities to enter the formal organization can derail a change or reform, particularly one that makes coordination a criterion of success. Making the formal organization the target of change may also mislead one to think the effort failed, when in fact it succeeded.

Furthermore, certain elements within the system are impervious to change. Change does not make it easier to impose the schools' version of reality onto students, or to convince teachers to give up personal autonomy or administrators to be less wary of their communities, or communities to accept the expertise of school staff. Nor can envisioned changes eradicate conflict between the bureaucracy and notions of individual fulfillment. Nor can reform and change alter two of the system's basic characteristics: the tendency of individuals to follow their own conscience and make their own choices, and the freedom of individuals to join with others to press their views. Change does not alter these two constants—it provides opportunities to exercise them.

There are good reasons why the system derails change and reform. But the derailing should not obscure the fact that it is only through reform and change that energy, ideas, and resources come down into the schools. Those energetic individuals, to whom Trotsky (1932/1957) referred, are often on the margins of the formal organization; they see opportunities for improvement, mobilize support, garner resources, and form alliances with those inside to try out new ideas. Change and reform bring the system alive. We might consider the formal organization apart from the system and ask whether left to its own it would continually try to improve. The answer is probably not, except in bureaucratic ways. It would be more coordinated, controlled, predictable, and probably more meritocratic—a textbook bureaucracy perhaps—but it is questionable whether the bureaucracy by itself, without the assistance of groups from the larger system, can improve teaching and learning.

8

Quality, Equality, and Reform

INTRODUCTION

In the educational system the same ideas tend to float among all levels at the same time. Teachers, administrators, planners, researchers, and lobbyists go to the same meetings, read the same journals, and carry on a broad discourse through which ideas emerge. The popular ideas are likely to generate simultaneous initiatives at several levels. As federal and state versions move into the schools, they join with already developed versions of the same ideas. For example, in the early 1960s local teachers and administrators were talking about poverty, race, and minority achievement just as was President Johnson—more likely before President Johnson. The president and his staff articulated the issue in a way that suited the operation of the federal government, but the rapid success of the ESEA can be attributed to the fact that it helped local schools do what they cared about and in many cases were already doing. This point is extended in this chapter, where it is argued that the 1980s federal initiative on excellence succeeded, to a great degree, because it matched what the states and schools were already doing. The chapter also describes how broad initiatives are distilled before they finally arrive in classrooms in the interaction of teachers and students.

Two studies are included in this chapter. Both were undertaken as part of a broader effort to trace the 1980s reform movement. In *The Thirteenth Man,* Bell (1988) recounted that when he was Secretary of Education, he had felt that schools were infected with declining academic standards, low teacher pay, a lack of basic skills, and a general lack of "zest and drive and spirit" (p. 115). He had formed a national commission that studied and reported his concerns. The report, *A Nation at Risk,* called for increased academic requirements and increased rigor across the nation's schools, especially secondary schools.

The publicity generated by that report put pressure on state departments and school districts to examine their secondary curricula. Among the side effects was some NIE research money to study reform efforts. The author of this volume and Christopher Wheeler obtained a grant for that purpose and were given permission to pursue the reforms in two school systems. Part of the original agreement was that the districts would not be identified in any national publications and so Cusick termed his system Salem County, and Wheeler termed his system, Delaware. The material in this chapter is drawn from Cusick and Wheeler (1987).

Both districts are fairly large, ethnically diverse, enjoy good reputations, and both were at that time reputed to have upgraded their curriculum in the ways suggested by *A Nation at Risk.* Delaware and Salem County had been through several changes in their secondary schools. Both districts had spent considerable energy accommodating their increasing minority populations and both had bused for integration. Both had grown rapidly from the 1950s to the mid-1970s and declined since the mid-1970s to the 1980s. In 1986 Delaware had 24,000 students, down from a mid-1970s high of 40,000. Salem County had 100,000, down from a mid-1970s high of 120,000. Both were well-regarded in their respective states and both were well-organized, well-run, and well-staffed. Cusick pursued the reforms in one of Salem County's twenty-two high schools, Suburb High. Wheeler pursued reform through Delaware's secondary system, which included four comprehensive and three alternative high schools.

In general, Cusick and Wheeler found that although the reform movement was generally thought to have begun with *A Nation at Risk* (1983), Salem County's and Delaware's efforts preceded that document by several years, and the publicity associated with it had little impact on either district. The long-term efforts of both districts to handle integration, accommodate minorities, raise standards, and maintain order and attendance continued right through and beyond the period during which *A Nation at Risk* was being publicized. That document did not initiate new efforts; it was turned into ways that supported ongoing efforts. Therefore, rather than follow specific activities emanating from that report, Cusick and Wheeler focused on long-term changes in the schools. The account of events in Delaware is taken from the half of the report that Wheeler wrote and is largely in Wheeler's own words.

REFORM IN DELAWARE

Delaware is a heavily industrialized midwestern town full of auto and auto-parts factories. In the auto industry's booming years, 1945 to 1975, Delaware enjoyed unprecedented prosperity and its per capita income was among the nation's highest. In 1986, when the study took place, auto sales had declined, there was 30 percent unemployment, and the high-paying factory jobs, formerly available even to marginal students, were few. The city was not only increasingly poor, it was increasingly African-American. Along with a ten-year decline in student numbers, the schools' white population had gone from 66 percent to 52 percent. Minority families, whose workers had the least seniority in the auto factories, were particularly hard hit by layoffs.

Delaware in the 1960s and 1970s had gone through the same racial conflicts that Grant (1988) described in Hamilton High. In addition to trying to keep the school under control, teachers in the 1970s developed a more open, diverse, and student-centered curriculum. As it was then reasoned, such a curriculum could awaken the students' latent motivation and natural propensity to learn. A long-time teacher explained:

> We felt that the curriculum was not responsive to students.... We developed a student selected series [and] tried to find the strength of the teachers and develop courses that responded to those strengths. As a consequence, we had quite a proliferation of courses that I don't think had too many threads. (p. 5)

The whole idea was to get away from the tracking that left African-American students together in lower-achieving classes, inviting charges of racism. Placement was predicated on students' abilities, not race, but the district wanted to get away from the blatant segregation that accompanied school placement.

New exigencies demand a new way of thinking, a new logic. The new line therefore was: The problem with tracking is that choices are made for, not by, students and the organization's underlying racism is reflected in the choice. If students, who are not naturally racist, were allowed to make their own choices based on their abilities and interests, they would do so in such a way that integration would follow naturally. To implement the new line the schools opened their departments to many more teacher-created electives and allowed students to choose among them. Social studies departments were adding courses in "Minorities in the USA," "The Colonial Experience," "Radicals, Reactionaries, and Revolutionaries," and "Vacationland." Science departments added house plants, small animals, consumer chemistry, and over twenty different electives in each high school. As the social studies chair in one high school explained, "They were terribly interesting courses,... I think we really began to open things up and we were doing things that were really interesting and exciting for ourselves, also for the students" (p. 7).

Several problems were associated with what teachers called the "salad curriculum." First, the new courses had not generated additional interest and effort among students with low skills. Second, a course was theoretically open to any student. But students tended to gather according to ability and race, just as they previously gathered according to assignment. Distinctions, as one teacher explained, "still existed but they went under the table." The intended integration of whites and blacks did not occur. Third, teachers were trying to be more sympathetic with students and so eased academic requirements, but they found that even more able students were gravitating to easier electives.

> Every single course was to address listening, speaking, reading and writing...I taught a course that was for kids having problems with print and with meager language skills called "girltalk." The material was a total package. But the next people who taught "girltalk" thought it meant "girls talk," so it became sort of a rap session. Skill development fell by the wayside, listening skills, speaking skills, the whole range fell by the wayside. (p. 8)

With formal differences among courses abolished, teachers pegged course level and content to whatever students could handle. The result was an increase in courses that previously had been remedial but now were accorded full status. As the social studies chair explained, "Easier courses began to get taught. For example, courses like 'USA Vacationland' were taught with no text" (p. 7).

Fourth, the salad curriculum exacerbated the perennial dispute among teachers over whether students need to know a little about a lot (survey approach) or a lot about a little (posthole approach). The freedom of teachers to turn their electives into anything they wanted encouraged the posthole approach. Hence there was the criticism:

> Students get a narrow view of the subject...a course like "Wars of the United States" was entirely dependent on the instructor. [He] could talk about what led to the wars or just talk about the battles. There was no control of content. We would see students walking across the stage to get their diplomas and we would shake their hands knowing they didn't really have a basic knowledge of history. (p. 8)

Finally, the salad curriculum did not satisfy students of parents who wanted academic rigor. By the mid-1970s, the most advanced courses at Delaware high schools were taught as independent studies for between three to eight students. The middle class continued its exodus to the suburbs. Teachers felt that parent disgust with the salad curriculum contributed to the exodus.

THE OFFICE OF CIVIL RIGHTS ENDS THE SALAD DAYS

With the baby boom ending, Delaware, like most school districts, was losing students and in the mid-1970s had to close some schools and draw new boundaries for others. Along with the closing and redefining Delaware had attempted, even before the integration order, to correct some of problems with the salad curriculum. The district ended social promotion and added a year-end test to determine promotion from grades 1–11. The district began to require a competency test for graduation from high school. The test could be taken in the spring of ninth grade and if failed, again in January of the tenth grade, and again until the test was passed. The curriculum of the competency classes was whatever a student needed to know to pass the test. Because failing students also tended to be those that did the most switching among the schools, their skill levels on the tests eased the receiving school's task of placing them.

The salad curriculum, choice, and proliferating electives ended on August 25, 1975. On that day the Delaware School District was found to be in violation of the Civil Rights Act of 1964. The finding was in response to a discrimination suit filed by Health, Education, and Welfare's Office of Civil Rights. The verdict gave the district ninety days to end de facto segregation or face the loss of federal funds. No one seriously contemplated losing federal funds. The superintendent and staff responded to the verdict with an open letter explaining the situation to the community; there were long public hearings, visits to districts in similar situations, and a public opinion survey, which revealed that 79 percent of the respondents preferred voluntary to forced integration. Finally, after negotiation and litigation, Delaware's integration plan was accepted by the Office of Civil Rights.

The center of Delaware's plan was a curriculum differentiated according to the needs and abilities of students. As it was reasoned, forced busing was unacceptable, but parents and their children would freely choose integrated programs in distant neighborhoods if the programs were made sufficiently attractive. The central idea was to create a series of programs that would draw black and white students together. With the programs placed around the city, white students would volunteer to go into formerly black schools. Black students would volunteer to go into formerly white schools. Selectivity to the point of tracking would be avoided, because the students would not go to magnets for an entire day, only for selected subjects. In effect, the plan treated the entire district as if it were one school with several parts, students crossing among the parts of the district just as in former times they had crossed among the parts of a building.

At the elementary level, students were offered magnets in creative arts, environmental studies, Montessori, music, and reading. The elementary magnets were built around team teaching, small groups, individualized instruction, and nontraditional classes. At the secondary level, the plan included magnet programs within each of the four comprehensive secondary schools. Three special schools, two for marginal and disaffected students, and one for students wanting acceptance into better colleges were also created. Each comprehensive secondary school offered its own magnet, one in math and science, one humanities and social studies, and two in specialized vocational programs. Two of the special schools were designed to give nonattending and troublesome students minimal skills and keep them away from the comprehensive schools where they caused so much trouble. The Academy was designed for parents who might have followed their friends to the suburbs had the school not given them the program they wanted for their children.

In order for the magnets to draw students from their home schools, incentives were included. Exclusivity was a major incentive. Admission to magnet schools and magnet programs was based on scores. Selected students were offered free transportation. More qualified teachers were recruited or assigned to magnet programs. The districtwide curriculum was used to distinguish the magnet curriculum from the general curriculum. Magnet programs had to be protected, and teachers in schools where their particular expertise was not part of the magnet were not allowed to teach advanced courses. The same reduction and consolidation took place at the middle schools. Central office staff were added to serve magnet programs.

Magnet teachers were evaluated more closely. If they were unable to attract and retain students, who presumedly were looking for solid instruction, they were replaced. Magnet classes were smaller, and had a stable set of students. In the secondary schools, magnet students were free to leave the buildings as their schedules demanded and were thus distinguished from those remaining.

Their classes were held in distinct parts of the building, and they could eat when their coming and going allowed. The counselors processed their schedules first, giving them options denied non-magnet students who were scheduled later. Furthermore, their programs required parental signatures, thus bringing parental participation into decisions affecting students. Administrators stated that places in the honors and magnets were open, but those not in the gifted and talented sections from elementary schools were rarely included. One joined Delaware's selective track early.

Some magnet programs failed. The medical careers program at a heavily African-American school in a poor area, placed there purposely to attract white students, failed to attract a sufficient number of high-achieving students. As the science teacher who taught the magnet courses in another school explained:

> You're unable to get enough academically successful students to go there to make it a viable program. The teachers there are highly qualified and they're good. But they're suffering because it's a black school...white students are reluctant to go there. (p. 18)

Magnets in marketing and careers, designed to appeal to students who were not college-bound, also failed for want of students. Ambitious and energetic students, both African-American and white, wanted college preparatory, not vocational, classes.

Shifts in society, sooner or later, overlap their way down the educational system to changes in schools. On the way through the hierarchy, several groups join in, each promoting its own interests. In Delaware, a coalition of these groups took advantage of a shift created by declining population, middle-class flight, and court-ordered integration. The coalition centered around students with enough ability and ambition to be termed "talented." Their parents sent them to school open to effort and compliance. Teachers liked to teach them and gave them attention.

Administrators provided them the programs they wanted. Counselors drew those students into their schools to attend the magnets, and then tried to keep them there for other classes. As one explained, "I'll find some students who are going to take a magnet course and I'll schedule their magnet second and third hour and arrange another suitable course for their fourth hour." Finally, competitive colleges recruited them. Up and down the system, from parents that raised the students to colleges that recruited them, was a vertically integrated channel of groups interested in promoting the education of more able students.

TWO MAGNET SCHOOLS

Wheeler described two of Delaware's magnet schools, one the 7–12 Academy, a second, the School for Potential Dropouts. The academy was a competitive-entrance, college-preparatory, privatelike school that offered its 800 students a structured program replete with dress codes, behavior and attendance requirements, mandatory parental involvement, and classes for the gifted. The academy's racial balance reflected Delaware's black-to-white ratio of students. The academy offered no remedial courses and accepted no special students. Students applied in the sixth grade and had to be doing at least sixth grade work on standardized tests. The school maintained more stringent graduation requirements than those at the comprehensive schools. And unlike the comprehensive schools, the academy had a six- instead of five-period day.

Teachers praised the academy: they had students who wanted to learn, an administration that backed them, and the freedom to teach what they thought was important. Teachers spoke well of the school and predicted success for their students. In their nonteaching time, they coached school sports, ran activities, plays, trips, and events, and unlike the teachers in the comprehensive schools, many of whom worked out-of-school jobs, only one of the academy's thirty-eight teachers worked a second job.

Wheeler noted several behavioral differences between the academy and the comprehensive schools. Unlike the latter, the academy's halls cleared before, not after, the bell rang. In class, teachers lectured and students took notes. Average daily attendance for these mostly college-bound students was 96 percent and tardiness was rare. Teachers in their free periods shared ideas among themselves and talked about "never leaving this place" to return to their comprehensive schools. Teachers also endorsed the system of administrative and peer review for students. If a student was thought to not be working hard, she or he was sent back to the comprehensive school. Another student, equally qualified, was waiting for an opened place.

Special schools were available not only to the higher-achieving students. Delaware's School for Potential Dropouts served 509 students who had a history of poor attendance, low or nonexistent GPAs, and other demonstrated deficiencies. Approximately 450 began the year, another 300 entered to replace dropouts, and in 1986, 100 graduated. Inside the school for potential dropouts, students had no lectures, no bells. The methods were individually packaged instruction, self-guided study, short-answer questions, and continuous testing. When students completed the work and passed the test, credit was granted. Students asked for help when they needed it. A typical classroom had seven or eight students working by themselves while the teacher conferred with one or two more.

Instruction that has been individualized is immune from the chronic absenteeism that causes students' ejection from their comprehensive schools. If students do not show up, the materials are left waiting for their return. If a student fails, the class is retaken with the same methods. Students at the school for potential dropouts had to show progress to stay enrolled, and the school insisted on progress, not on steady attendance, although the chronically absent were dropped. Periodic absenteeism was tolerated. Some students enrolled only until they caught up and then returned to their home school. Others continued until they graduated or dropped out.

The school attempted to latch onto and make use of what little the students would do. The school's short-term perspective and limited goals matched the students' limited attention. As the principal explained, "We're trying to graduate them...we hope to improve their self image and give them some skills to use in everyday life." He was personally sympathetic with these students and their situation.

> Jobs are the biggest problem and we can't do much in that area. I grew up in West Virginia in a working class family who adopted me and my two brothers. I can see the other side of it, how the economy creates a situation where a kid doesn't have a thing to do once he comes out of high school. I know what it feels like to be in that setting. (p. 53)

Even with a high school diploma, the staff considered those students' prospects bleak and repeated the sentiment frequently. But they had volunteered for the assignment—they appreciated the orderly atmosphere, the lack of busyness, the decreased noise level, the chance to work with one student at a time, and the absence of discipline problems. If a student caused trouble, he was gone the next day. A coalition of administrators, teachers, parents, and students enabled the district to attain a specific end, in this case, to retain errant students and demonstrate that it was doing something for them. Delaware offers an illustration of how a school organization reacts to changes in society. It differentiates students, specializes staff, and creates coalitions of groups to pursue separate interests. Problems are addressed; uncertainty is reduced; stability is preserved.

PROBLEMS WITH SPECIALIZING

Differentiating the curriculum to accommodate students at either end solved some problems. It added evidence to the district's argument that it accommodated everyone, and it retained the middle-class parents who were inclined to take their children to other schools. It relieved the comprehensive school from the chronically absent and troublesome students while it offered those students an alternative to rules they could not abide. But solving problems for the educationally minded on one end and the more troublesome on the other created problems for "general" track students and staff who were not favored with special assignments. Wheeler argued that the matter of how to educate the two-thirds of the student body who made up Delaware's general track went unattended and unresolved.

Delaware had more good teachers than magnet programs could accommodate, and reasonably enough, general track teachers felt excluded. In the competition for the good classes, not all could win and those that did quickly consolidated their advantage. Magnet teachers dominated the districtwide English Committee. Administrators protected teachers' assigned magnet classes, even during layoffs forced by declining enrollments. As one of those left out of magnets explained:

> They started the humanities program in 1976 and the same teachers are in it today. There is some politics going on. For example, when they pink-slipped teachers, two

of them were in the humanities magnet. It was interesting to learn that when they recalled teachers, they went down the list just far enough to include those two. (p. 60)

That teacher went on to explain that it was not only teachers but students too who were left out.

> Those who really get left out are the ones who used to be called the general track students...that's the largest group of students. They're the ones who need as much or more as the special and gifted kids...special education, it gets lots of support. Bilingual has five computers while the English department just wants one but can't get it. For the gifted kids they organize programs. And the teachers...who teach in it happen to be the better teachers. So weaker teachers are placed in the general program. It's a self-defeating system.... (p. 34)

General track teachers were the most upset.

> We lose good students. Our own counselors send them [to the magnet]. Last year I had an excellent geometry student and this year he's taking courses over there. My ninth grade geometry class is not comparable to last year's because they sent 38 or 39 students to take the magnet program.... We lose good kids and as teachers we're not challenged. (p. 59)

Perhaps most hard hit were the vocational and arts classes into which the administrators, to comply with federal law P.L. 94-142, were mainstreaming special education students. This fulfilled the mainstreaming requirements and provided students for courses that, because of Delaware's increased requirements in English and math, were losing students. But it left those teachers angry.

> I have 15 learning disabled and emotionally impaired students and they have so many hangups; you speak crossly to one of them and he starts to cry. They create a lot of problems. They just can't function in the classroom. All I'm doing is disciplining. I have more special students than some special ed teachers and I ought to get paid for it. It takes too much time. It ends up being nothing more than babysitting. (p. 42)

And a building science chair explained

> [the magnet] is not doing a whole lot different than we are, at least in their basic courses. But when the upper kids leave, you're left with those that have less facility and are less stimulating. You've lowered everything; you're now concentrating on the average and below average in science classes. (p. 59)

The magnet programs, combined, served approximately 30 percent of the students: 5 percent in academic magnet programs, 12–15 percent in special education, 5 percent in vocational magnets, and 5 percent in programs such as NROTC, drama, art, and music. For the remaining students not in magnets, not selected out on some competitive basis, or not protected by advocate groups, the situation was difficult. Teachers believed that parents did not support education and that these students were likely to be lost when they entered the world. They were anxious to help these students but seemed unsure of what to do. The regular track classes were taught with what Wheeler called scripted lessons, oriented toward competency/coping skills with little interaction around the subject. When explaining their efforts, they resorted to vague goals of coping and awareness, e.g., "I'm not preparing them for any kind of particular lifestyle but rather I help them be aware of what is going on around them" (p. 35). Class content was equally vague.

> I take as much liberty as I can with content. I try to relate the things I am talking about to situations that they could possibly encounter. For example, I talk about prejudice in terms of applications for jobs and interview situations. I have an article written by [William] Raspberry that talks about the use of proper English in interview situations. I'm going to pass that out and talk about it...I try to make a conscious connection between what I'm teaching and the real world. (p. 65)

Delaware had made several changes in school organization. It developed a series of magnets, stopped social promotion with competency and graduation tests, implemented a curriculum that distinguished more and less difficult courses, and put an end to the salad curriculum. But none of those changes nor their sum altered the fact that interaction between teachers and students is still open to negotiation and is heavily weighed by students' class, culture, interests, and abilities, and by teachers' obligation to impose some intelligible order on a diverse group. District policies altered the conditions, but did not alter the freedom of teachers to bring themselves into their classes, the freedom of students to elect their level of compliance, and the obligation of teachers and students to work out a compromise. Wheeler selected classes from different levels of the curriculum to demonstrate several types of accommodations.

MR. O'DAY'S MAGNET HUMANITIES CLASS

Mr. O'Day, white and in his mid-40s, taught a two-hour block class in the academic magnet. During the first hour, O'Day lectured, asked questions, and engaged students in spirited discussion of the influence of the Babylonian Exile on Jewish theology. He lectured on how Zoroastrianism influenced the prophets of Israel to reformulate the monotheism of ancient Hebraism into a dualistic theory in which Satan became the adversary of God. O'Day extended the discussion to Zoroaster, his life, religious teachings, his political influence, and the influence of his followers. O'Day also introduced current information, noting that long ago Zoroastrians left Babylonia (Persia) for India, where most of them now reside. Zubin Mehta, the conductor of the New York Philharmonic, he pointed out, is a member of that religion, and the well-known theme music of the movie *2001: A Space Odyssey* is a tribute to that religion. Throughout the lecture, O'Day asked questions and encouraged students to interrupt with their own, which led to several lively discussions. After a short break the class resumed at 11:30. The second hour, in which O'Day and the students examined a selection from Aristotle, was as stimulating as the first.

MR. JACKSON'S SOCIAL STUDIES CLASS

The bell rang at 10:35, signaling the start of this fourth-hour social studies class, "You and the Law." Half the desks were empty, but the classroom filled to three-quarters as students wandered in. Mr. Jackson talked to a small group of students. At 10:39 he closed the door and started to speak. The students quieted down. On that Friday, the class reviewed the material for Monday's test on amendments to the Constitution. Jackson had a list of terms on the board under each amendment. He pointed to each term and asked if anyone had questions. He explained that they would be required to define key terms and describe circumstances that led each amendment to become a part of the Constitution.

Fewer than half the students were listening. Three females and one male were otherwise occupied. One female was going over her checkbook; another stared into space; a third was fixing her hair. A male had his head on the desk, his eyes open. Occasionally the students asked questions. No one took notes. The discussion ran out.

At 10:59 Jackson told the class to take out a ditto sheet describing different Supreme Court cases. The students were to review these so they could say what the courts decided and why. Only two or three students at each table bothered to look for their sheet. Others looked on with someone, talked quietly, or stayed withdrawn. For the next ten minutes, Jackson read the single page handout, pausing often to ask if the students understood. One asked a question.

At 11:09 the review session was over. Jackson said, "Okay, now you can catch up on the gossip...." The noise level rose. The class ends at 11:20 (pp. 26-27).

MR. RESTON'S ALGEBRA I CLASS

John Reston's Algebra I class was getting underway. Several homework problems were on the board, to which Reston turned to complete number 3. "How many got this right?" he asked. Six raised their hands. "Terrible," he said as he went over the problem carefully. When he got to the last question, he paused, "This is the most difficult, let me show you where most of the hangup comes." He proceeded to explain the problem and judging from the head nodding, several students remained confused.

Within a few minutes, Reston moves on to a short review of how to add and subtract fractions without a common denominator. Stern and serious, he calls on Kevin, an African-American male, who mumbles an answer. "Take your hand away from your mouth. I can't understand what you're saying." Kevin repeats the answer. "Good. That's right."

After a brief review, Mr. Reston introduces the lesson for the day. After explaining the major principles, he assigns number 29. He circulates while students work, checking their progress. One female has no pencil—he gets a neighbor to lend her one. Another female has her head on her desk. He stops and tells her it's "OK," but she should try to listen because she may want to get into the lesson later on. He stops and asks the class how many got to the last step. Five raise their hands. "We've got to do better than that," he says and heads to the board. He and the students then work out the answer together, and he assigns number 27. He circulates again, commenting: "Good." "That's right." "Almost." "I've got three right answers." "I've got four." Now everyone finishes the problem and gets the right answer. Reston then assigns a set of problems that the students work on while he circulates, giving individual attention to different students. The girl with her head down has opened her book and is working. Three minutes before the bell, he calls for attention. He goes over a new problem and asks them to look at one like it tonight while they finish what they didn't get done today. It will be the subject for tomorrow's lesson. The class ends.

MR. ADAMS'S MODERN LITERATURE CLASS

The bell rang at 9:55 but nothing happened. Twelve students sat, stood, or moved around from one group to another chatting, while Mr. Adams shuffled papers. Then he got up, went to the front, and started to call roll. As he did, six more students, one at a time, entered the room. It was then 10:00.

The next five minutes were taken up with a series of exchanges between Adams and individual students over why they were not in class yesterday or the day before. "I couldn't get out of my job." "I had to work on the play." "I couldn't get a ride to school." One refuses to answer. At 10:05 Adams announced that the main activity of the day would be a review of the short-answer test, given three days before, that covered Harper Lee's *To Kill a Mockingbird.*

Within a few minutes, Mr. Adams launched the real lesson of the day—his views of U.S. society. A question within the lesson required the answers, "courts." He used the occasion to ask, "Do you believe you can get a fair trial in this country?" Silence. "If you have money you'll get off." He followed it up with, "Do people in this country believe that all men are created equal? No, they don't." A few more answers were spent on the general topic and a few more arguing over whether partial credit should be given for partially correct answers. Adams then launched into a critique of the state legislature, the use of metal detectors in schools, and Delaware's policy of having a police officer in each high school.

Returning to the test, he asks for answers to a few questions. To his direct question, a white female replies. "I don't know." "Why don't you know?" he yells. Another white female starts to answer. Mr. Adams says, "People, please ignore anything she says." She stops in midsentence. Adams turns to an African-American male student, puts his hand on the boy's shoulder and says, "Brother, can you give me the answer?" He could not and so Adams gave it and moved on. After a few minutes, Adams says, "Who was W. E. B. Du Bois?" An African-American student gave a partially correct answer. Adams replies, "That's why they kicked me out of history. I taught real history. You're not learning real history, you're learning lies. History is supposed to belong to all of us but it's taught from a white perspective." He then spends fifteen minutes talking about Du Bois, racial oppression in the United States, the need for African-American students to confront their white history teachers, and tries making revolutionaries of them. He closes the lesson announcing that Wednesday and Thursday will be "reading days," and that "anyone who talks will get a zero, and those who read will get an 'A' for the day." The bell rings.

Relative to its prior, unprecedented prosperity, Delaware was undergoing difficult economic times, and the schools had to accommodate a declining, poorer, and blacker population, retain its middle-class students, and respond to the Office of Civil Rights's desegregation demands. It also had to prepare students for life without the automobile factory, which would have hired them no matter what they had done in school. Faced with conflicting demands and pressured by outside forces, the district resorted to classic management techniques. It upscaled the curriculum, specialized the staff, and recruited new markets. They also lavished a disproportionate share of their resources on a small percentage of students at the top and at the bottom. Wheeler argued that those techniques worked at the extremes, but made conditions more difficult for students left in the middle, where chronic problems of low ability, little motivation, and disinterest were accentuated.

Delaware illustrates why the system is always unequal. Larger social and economic events open opportunities. The better or luckier teachers, more talented students, their ambitious parents, and advocates of particular groups take advantage of the situation to move the formal system in ways that suit their purposes. Other teachers, students, and parents, less lucky or less advantaged, are no better and perhaps worse off than before. The open and competitive educational system moves the formal organization around, leaving it always unequal and thus always open to more shifting in order to correct the inequalities. This line of thinking is continued with Wheeler's account of Delaware's reaction to *A Nation at Risk* (1983).

DELAWARE REACTS TO *A NATION AT RISK*

As Wheeler tells the story, *A Nation at Risk* did not alter Delaware's efforts or direction, but provided a convenient aegis under which to continue what it was already doing. Delaware's deputy superintendent explained:

> When I first heard the news [of *A Nation at Risk*] on television, I knew it was an issue we would have to address. I expected the press would be calling the next day to find out what our response was. I also knew school board members would be asking about the report. They'd want to know how we measured up to what [the report] was saying. Around 6:00 P.M. . . . I was resting on my couch in my office and it came to me. I went to the superintendent the next day. (p. 5)

The deputy superintendent recommended the creation of a district committee on secondary schools. The committee, composed of staff and community people, attempted to show how the district was ahead of and already responding to suggestions made by *A Nation at Risk*. The committee's recommendations described changes and subsequent improvements in each major academic area and added recommendations that the district was already planning. The curricular recommendations read thus:

> The citywide high school English Committee studied the English curriculum in detail for more than two years and recommended the English module program which the board adopted in April, 1982...a competency test in reading has been required since 1970. This requirement was significantly strengthened in 1978 with the adoption of the Promotion and Graduate Requirements. Steady increases in language arts test results have been reported to the board. (pp. 10–11)

Furthermore, the committee took the opportunity to raise several sensitive issues outside the framework of contract negotiations, which are serious business in Delaware, a bastion of the United Auto Workers and the site of the state's first teachers' strike. The computer elective for the middle and high schools and the six-hour day funded by the state were sensitive issues. Both were taken out of contract negotiations and placed under the district Committee on Secondary Schools. At the same time, staff people took the opportunity offered by the report to lobby their superiors about particular projects. For example, the district science coordinator had been encouraging biology teachers to develop a common set of exams and a more standardized high school curriculum. He had already obtained funds to develop test items and establish a districtwide bank. He used the standards committee to sell the idea to the directors of elementary and secondary education.

The committee also provided the central staff the opportunity to raise several important issues. One was the equity fund, which at that time approached $20 million in a district with a budget of $125 million. To administrators, the fund reflected prudent management, but the union had the opinion that the fund had been extracted from teachers' wages, and further, that $3–4 million was sufficient equity. With negotiations coming up in the fall, the union was, according to an administrator, "smacking its lips" about the fund. The Excellence Committee was an opportunity to clarify the fund as to size and as to conditions under which it could be used.

The committee also raised the sensitive issue of teacher assignment to magnet programs. As part of the magnet plan, a free hand was given by the union to principals and department heads to recruit teachers without regard to seniority. That negotiated agreement had lapsed, and selection based on seniority had been bargained back into the contract. Principals used the committee to advocate for reinstatement of the lapsed policy. Teachers too used the committee. Their union wanted an updated evaluation policy and wanted it developed and piloted outside the annual negotiations process. The reform committee's subgroup of teachers advocated a new evaluation instrument and pushed to have it agreed upon in advance of negotiations and later incorporated into the master contract.

The superintendent took the sum of the committee's recommendations to the board and had them approved en bloc, without an accompanying timetable. This board approval, which he received just as he wanted, enabled him to push the recommendations he favored, to study those that needed further work, and to ignore those he did not like. Had the board adopted the recommendations one by one, with an accompanying timetable, the superintendent would have had to implement them amid open discussion and even with a reduced budget. As it happened, he retained maximum control over the implementation.

As Wheeler tells the story, the authors of *A Nation at Risk* were not the only educators concerned about standards and quality. Delaware had for some years been working with testing, academic requirements, curricular coordination, reduced electives, and more stringent promotion, attendance, and discipline policies. *A Nation at Risk* did not spawn new reforms or even the reexamination of old ones. Instead, it provided an opportunity for the district to publicize and continue what it had been doing all along.

Wheeler's story describes how the system's groups, some within, some without the formal organization, turn events to their own ends. He also tells about the school organization, which has to continue amid the machinations of competing groups. Some organizational elements are open to change. The mix of specialities, the assignments of people, and the resources given to particular groups are negotiable. Some things are not negotiable. The formal organization is a bureaucracy. It can group students several ways, but it has to group students. It can assign teachers several ways, but subject specialty has to be respected. Discipline and order have to be maintained among students. The community has to be treated warily. Even as they open a dialogue, the administrators have to take steps to ensure that they remain in charge. The natural inclinations of students have to be treated warily. Events that include up to several thousand students, as they did in Delaware, have to be coordinated with rules and regulations. So even while the several groups seek to further their agendas, they must do so in ways that will not too much disturb the bureaucratic order that makes sense of the myriad events.

Any change therefore has to be incorporated into bureaucratic processes which, however pedestrian, are consistent, equitable, and reliable. The bureaucracy serves as the guardian of equality for students not favored by ambition, talent, or assertive parents. Advantage-seeking individuals and groups would run off with the whole endeavor were it not for the bureaucracy insisting that all children, even those who do not want to come and whose parents do not care if they do come, show up and take the required curriculum. The bureaucracy insists that class sizes and expenditures per pupil be relatively uniform and that all students be treated in a consistent manner. The bureaucracy insists that females be given the same opportunities for athletics as the males. It coerces people into thinking about benefits education offers to society at large when they would prefer to think about benefits that accrue to them personally. The bureaucracy advocates for society at large. It also advocates for the students who have no advocates.

Of course, there is inequality in the formal organization because some teachers are better, some students are smarter and more willing, some parents take a more active interest in their children's education, and because special interests garner a larger share of resources and rewards. But the bureaucracy tries to keep the inequalities within bounds. It forces some uniformity onto the separate and competing interests and so decreases inequalities that would result from unbridled competition. There are thus two forces for change within the system. One is the separate groups agitating to further their ends and increase their advantages. The second is the bureaucracy trying to force a measure of uniformity on the competing groups without too much alienating the more influential.

Reform in Salem County and Suburb High

Salem County's school district was adjacent to a major eastern city and reflected, as did Delaware's, the social and economic surroundings. In 1986 among its 100,000 students, the district had many from wealthy and well-educated parents; many more from the middle class, also well educated; and some from rural as well as urban and poor areas. It was a progressive and highly regarded school district with a long history of supporting education.

The study took place inside one of the district's more diverse secondary schools. In 1986 Suburb High served 1735 students, 65 percent white, 30 percent African-American and 5 percent other. Serving some of Salem County's most and least affluent students, Suburb High was in 1986 at the center of several important events. Cusick's original intent was to trace the effects of *A Nation at Risk*. But in Salem County, long-term efforts to improve the district's secondary schools had begun several years earlier and continued right through and beyond the period *A Nation at Risk* was receiving its greatest publicity. Those long-term efforts to satisfy important groups, improve discipline and attendance, implement the state testing program, and differentiate and coordinate the curriculum became the focus of the study.

In the mid-1970s, there were several reasons for working on secondary schools. With *High School and Beyond* (1986) suggesting that private schools were superior to public schools, public school people, including state departments' staff, feared that the middle class would desert its schools. There was also the general perception that there was too little administrative scrutiny of classes and too much teacher and student autonomy. It was reported in several studies, Cusick's (1983) among them, that teachers could get away with not teaching, and students with not learning.

General awareness of secondary school problems led to changes, several of which were undertaken in Suburb High. That school had in the 1970s done many of the things described by Grant (1988) in *Hamilton High* and in Cusick and Wheeler (1987) in Delaware. In the interest of accommodating more and more diverse students, the schools had increased the number of electives, eliminated tracking and eased rules and regulations. According to long-time teachers, the changes resulted in diminished control and parents of better students taking their children to the district's less-integrated public schools or to private schools. Suburb High's principal at that time was popular, but according to a teacher,

> [He] had been part of the freeing up of the 1960s. He was a really good guy; the teachers loved him...a good counselor but not a good administrator. He'd make a policy and someone would come in and say "Hey, I know it's a policy but I have a bad back or a conflict and I just can't do it," and that would be the end of the policy. (p. 15)

Further, the school had suffered adverse publicity when a reporter from the adjacent city's major newspaper did a story on high school and reported that the school was infected with drugs. Staff regarded the story as unfair, but a new principal was brought in to change the school's image and the students' behavior. As the (then) principal explained:

> That newspaper story really hurt the school. Drugs were really not that bad but there was a real lack of discipline. Some lockers had been ripped off and some Black kids unfairly blamed. They had been expelled without due process and some of the expulsions had been reversed in the central office. When I came here there were no student policies. You know that student handbook? We started working it right away and when the teachers came back they got a stack of policies...on due process...on suspension...on expulsion. (pp. 16–17)

The vice principal put it more bluntly.

> The kids who could make the most noise were controlling the place. We threw 12 of them out real quick, and when the bad guys suddenly disappeared, word got around. People have to know that if their kids go here, no one is going to be patting them on the backside, stealing their stuff and holding them up in the bathroom. (p. 18)

Armed with a new attitude, a new district policy connecting attendance to credit and detailing every offense from skipping to gambling to harassment (bumping, tripping, threatening, etc.), and with sanctions imposed for each offense, the school calmed down. There were still, in 1986, problems one would expect from 1735 adolescents. But the administrators, armed with their intelligible procedures, kept the school clean and orderly. The problems did not overwhelm the procedures and personnel assigned to them.

THE STATE TESTING PROGRAM

A long-term change affecting the school was the state's secondary school improvement effort. Until the early 1980s, that state had offered a single state diploma to students taking standard requirements. But some of the state's larger districts were requiring more for high school graduation than did the state. State department staff members feared their agency was lagging behind the state's more progressive districts.

For starters, the state board hired a new state superintendent. According to a state staff person who worked on the reforms,

> the previous Superintendent had been a really nice guy. All the administrators loved him. He was one of them, an old coach but he didn't do anything. And at that time, 1976, the President of the State Board was hearing from the legislature that "the schools are graduating kids who can't read and write, and if the State Department didn't do something about it, the legislature would." The board wanted someone who would do something and D. came in and outlined some things. (p. 18)

Among the new superintendent's initiatives was a Commission on Secondary Education, composed of teachers, administrators, school board members, and members of urban groups. The commission then undertook a three-year study of the state's secondary schools. Their recommendations included increased graduation requirements and a state testing program for high school graduation. Like other reforms, the actual recommendations were phrased in terms that the system could accommodate. As the staffer explained,

> we held a three-year in-service for the commission and came up with some good things...but many just weren't feasible. For instance we considered a pupil teacher ratio of 80 or 90 to one but we had to throw it out. We had this one state assistant superintendent who sat in the corner and every time a recommendation was suggested, he would estimate the cost, tell the group and they would back away. (p. 47)

The commission made several recommendations, such as that students should take twelve core credits in advanced courses, that students stay in high school for four years, and that students with a 2.6 overall average be given a "certificate of merit." There were compromises. The 2.6 average was a compromise between the state superintendent who wanted 3.0 and the districts who wanted 2.5. The requirement for a credit in "fine or practical" arts was a compromise between those who wanted only fine arts and vocational educators who feared losing students.

At the center of the commission's recommendations was an itemizing of skills and competencies that each student should have by graduation. To generate the list, the state engaged a group of teachers, parents, and administrators, who compiled the items and put them under seven areas: English, math, writing, social studies, arts, survival, and career education. The state then proclaimed the list as an "index of competencies" and told districts to include it in their curriculum. The state also said that students would be tested on the items as a condition for receiving a state diploma. The commission had talked openly about the consequences of a state testing program and had accepted the fact that state tests would deny graduation to students unable to pass. To those students, the state would award a certificate of attendance.

Supporting the testing program was a belief by state people that the schools needed more control. As the staffer explained, "If you could get a group of state policy makers to be candid about the schools they would say that 'In the schools, it's all chaos. The schools need control, and testing is the best means of control. If we test it, they have to teach it." She went on:

> First you understand there was a lot of resistance to [the competency list and the testing], and second the state was afraid the locals wouldn't do it. So the state got approval from the legislature for 24 new positions, one for every district, and the job was to create a "curriculum competency match" which would identify just where every listed competency was taught in the district. The locals screamed and bitched and moaned about how the state was trying to control curriculum, but the legislature had empowered the state to act and the state acted. (pp. 12–13)

In the public hearings the state department held before recommending legislation, the state proceeded with tests in math, English, writing, science, and social studies but retreated from the tests for survival, career education, and arts. Beginning with English and math, they staggered implementation with some initial "no fault" years, when the tests would be given to students without consequences. The state board wanted to respond to their legislature, to their newer staff, to their more progressive districts, and to the middle class, whom they feared losing to private schools. The tactic was to specify and place the power of the state behind subject-matter tests for graduation.

THE TESTING PROGRAM IN THE SCHOOL

Salem County's graduation requirements already exceeded the state's, so the state's increases had little effect on the county. But the state tests had several effects inside the school. Most important, testing fits well with the idea of schools as rational organizations. Schools need a frame of discourse, an idiom, in which events can be discussed, problems phrased, and solutions proposed. Students' standardized test scores are an established frame of discourse in all schools. At Suburb High teachers talked glowingly about their students' performance on the SATs and on the Advanced Placement (AP) tests. They also taught students how to pass SATs or APs to assist their acceptance into good colleges. The state tests became the educational equivalent of SATs and APs for lower-achieving students. Even special education students had to pass the state tests, so preparing for and passing them became the educational agenda for those students. State tests also enabled administrators to measure progress across a district.

In addition to phrasing a dialogue around which the school could discuss its efforts, test scores became a topic for teacher in-service meetings. Even the social studies teachers who disparaged the tests for further segregating students along class and racial lines, accepted test scores as a unit of discourse. As the social studies chair said, "Our students scored only one point over the county average, and that's not very good so the district social studies coordinator came and gave us an item analysis. Now we know what to work on" (p. 54).

The discourse continued among the district's 22 high schools with the scores enabling each to measure its progress against itself and against the others. For Suburb High, located in the county's most affluent area, it was important to convince parents, who envisioned society's better places for their children, that it was among the district's best high schools. High scores were a means of assurance. Principals of schools with low scores were expected to raise them and were given a tangible goal.

Tests fit easily with the idea of students making cumulative progress, or as it was expressed, being "on track." It was not a fabricated notion. For aggressive students, the school record that they put together and present to selective colleges is extremely important. The principal gave an example of how important.

> We had one girl with 1300 on her SAT's, 3.7 average, two honors classes, high recommendations and she was rejected by Duke [University]. I don't think Duke is all that good a school, but the parents were upset, and we called Duke and asked why and they said she had taken sociology and psychology and not European history. Her electives were "light" as they put it; they also criticized her for taking Russian history and being in pom-poms...I mean you have to select every course if you want to go to those schools. (p. 49)

Whereas the more able and ambitious or fortunate have to watch their electives, grades, and SATs, those at the other end had to do reasonably well in basic classes, attend regularly, keep lessons and homework organized, and pass the state tests. If that could be done, then these students were also "on track." If a student were not "on track," the problem could be handled by one of the school's specialists, an attendance officer, vice principal, special education teacher, psychologist, or resource teacher. The state tests contributed to the school's idea of itself as a rational organization.

Finally, the tests enable the district to address differences between black and white achievement. African-American students overall scored one standard deviation below whites on the California Achievement Test. They also scored lower on the state tests. An accompanying problem in the district and in Suburb High, and an embarrassment to some socially conscious staff, was that the basic classes contained a majority of African-American students whereas honors classes were almost all white. Black-white discrepancies were a districtwide issue and the superintendent, hired two years previously, promised that by the end of his five-year term, this black-white discrepancy would be eliminated. Publicly recognizing the problem and promising something would be done about it contributed to the image of a rational and capable organization.

An additional advantage wrought by the tests was that students would have to prove literacy to graduate. School people are sensitive to the accusation that they give diplomas to illiterates, but it is possible to accumulate high school credits without reading, even in as good a school as Suburb High. A basic goal of the tests was to connect literacy to diplomas and eliminate the practices such as described by this social studies teacher in response to a question about his expectations:

> The kids have to participate, learn the material, internalize the material, think about it in relation to their own lives. If a kid can't do that but tries hard, then I'll pass him even if he can't read. (p. 39)

In sum, the state tests increased organizational coherence up and down the system. They enabled staff at all levels to give a common theme to diverse efforts. They added a learning agenda for students who came to school without one. They gave focus to the superintendent's efforts, goals to the district and particular schools, and provided a unit of dialogue among and between the schools and the central office. Within the dialogue, efforts could be discussed, comparisons made, and progress assessed. They also prevented illiterates from gaining high school diplomas.

Some teachers raised objections, not to testing so much as to elements that accompanied testing. At a department chair meeting when the principal brought up the topic, one chair responded with a comment about the irrationality of cumulative progress. "We get a bunch of kids, all with very low test scores, then we move them up and then we get a new bunch with scores just as low as the old bunch. Cumulative progress doesn't make any sense." Several teachers voiced the opinion that testing was a burden on an already crowded curriculum. Explaining lower than expected scores in her subject area, a math teacher said, "We have so many things to teach and we didn't cover the test. The scores came up low so now we just work on the tests." And too, some were skeptical of the superintendent's score-raising plans.

> Every few years they get a new superintendent and he has some new ideas and we get it for awhile. Now it's test scores and minority achievement. We'll get some in-service days and then we'll never hear about it again. (p. 45)

Central office staff members were sensitive to the problems associated with testing. The director of testing was concerned about the tests being used as a management rather than an assessment tool and about reducing education to test scores. He knew how easily "assessment goes over into accountability, accountability into management, and management into instructional design." He knew that at the lower ends of the curriculum, passing the test became an instructional objective rather than an assessment of progress, and worried about the effect of that action on the district's democratic goals.

> We'll have to segment off large numbers of kids, many of whom are black, who are having trouble passing. They will have to study for some terms or maybe years before they can pass and that separates them from the rest of the school.

Another of his concerns was the general misuse of tests.

> I get calls all the time asking me which is the best school in the county and I always tell them. "I don't know what the best school is but I can tell you the scores for a school'. But I don't know if that makes it the best school.

At the same time, he accepted the necessity of broad measures.

> Tests are used too much but they're a convenient way to describe a complex thing. We don't want to go into all the complexity so it's easier to say the scores averaged 87.3 than it is to try to understand what's going on in there. (p. 54)

Despite the cautions and objections, the state's high school testing program was easily and successfully integrated into the school. It served the purposes of several individuals and groups, and more important, it served several organizational purposes and supported notions of equality in a school and district where some students were very rich and some very poor. What is illustrated is that in the system, a successful change has to further the ends of important groups. In Salem County among the important groups were those administrators who had to ensure that the district treated students equally. Also illustrated is the way educational reform, which begins with social and economic ideals, turns into organizational change: in this case, a set of tests ensuring that those with high school diplomas are literate. The tests served the interests of important groups needing to communicate across the system and did not disturb activities of other groups, such as the students in the honors classes who did not have to prove they could read.

THE HONORS PROGRAM

Like the state testing program, Suburb High's "honors program" emerged from a complex set of issues. In 1986 the district's student population was declining from its mid-1970s high of 120,000. Some of the more affluent students were leaving for private schools, and more poorer and minority students were moving in from the adjacent city. Suburb High had to keep its reputation for excellence with its middle-class and affluent parents while it accommodated an increasing number of both lower-achieving and poorer students, many of them minorities.

Suburb High's former principal explained his own and the school's responses to combined demands for excellence and equity. First, he benefited from the board's decision to tighten secondary school boundaries to prevent whites from drifting to less-integrated schools. Second, he implemented a seven-period day, which was important to students who wanted to present a complete image to selective colleges. "The seven-period day would help me get more teachers, and then the kids could get everything in . . . even six academics and music and art." Third, he chaired the district's Honors Committee and used the position to push districtwide "honors classes" and implement them in his school.

"Honors" had originally come into the district from the state, which was funding "programs for the gifted." The district's director of gifted programs believed that gifted classes served too few students and was therefore advocating an honors program. Honors would not be a track, because one could be in an honors English without being in honors math or science, so the overt segregation that accompanies tracking was avoided. The requirements for admission to honors classes were (1) a "B" average in prerequisites, (2) eighth or ninth stanine scores on the most recent achievement tests, (3) teacher or counselor recommendation, (4) demonstrated interest, and (5) special consideration (for students who did not meet the preceding criteria). The last criterion was designed, according to several teachers, to satisfy what teachers called "the brag factor, e.g., "Parents want to go to cocktail parties and brag about their child being in honors." In 1986 60 percent of the school's students had one or more honors classes.

The former principal used honors classes to appeal to parents who feared erosion of quality. As he reasoned, keeping the children of ambitious and affluent parents was important to the school's success, and an honors program would keep those children. As he further reasoned, it worked. "The year I came there were 100 transfers out; the year I left, there were 100 transfers in. The year I came there were four national merit scholars, last year there were 19." An additional indicant of success were the parents of 100 students from the city paying the district per-pupil average of $4300 (1986 dollars) to send their children to Suburb High. The principal believed that the diversity occasioned by the arrival of immigrants and minorities had initially threatened the school, but intelligent policies had changed diversity from an unintended byproduct into a celebrated virtue. "We didn't write three lines that we didn't talk about the educational value of diversity and celebrate the diversity of the school."

Several parents active in the parents' association said they appreciated the racially mixed environment, and one senior on his way to Princeton commented on the virtues of diversity.

> You know what this school's about. It's the [intramural basketball league]. Everybody plays, Black and White. And after every game we go to someone's house and talk. I meet kids I'll never see in Princeton. Four years ago my parents wanted to send me to [an exclusive private school]. If they had I don't think I could forgive them now. (p. 68)

The honors program also created some problems. For one, it contributed to racial segregation. Honors classes were heavily white and classes for the lowest-achievers, heavily African-American. Several teachers, notably those in the social studies department had foreseen this. "Some of us didn't want honors; we thought it would segregate the kids by [race and] class and at the department meeting when (the former principal) asked, 'Do you want to adopt honors,' we said 'No.' And he said, 'You're going to get it anyway.' The principal offered his side of that story:

> I was hired to make some changes in the school and to do the things that had to be done, I had to take decision making away from the teachers...some left...some I got rid of...some retired. I had to hammer home that decision making is not by consensus. They thought they were going to vote on and approve (or disapprove) everything I did. And I had to tell them, 'We're not going to do it that way.' The leader has to be the leader. He has to articulate the program. That was my job. (p. 31)

There was also the matter of defining "honors." Honors did not reflect what the district's director of gifted programs had in mind when she helped initiate the program. In her opinion, honors had become a place where "they just select the best students and have them take classes with more material. They're just adding material and calling it honors." Teachers also questioned what they considered an inflated number of students admitted to honors classes, creating an "honors balloon." The accompanying complaint was that teachers had to reduce their expectations to a point where the class was no longer honors quality. As the science department chair said:

> Five honors math classes is ridiculous. We need two but no one is saying, "No." The trouble with honors is they tend to proliferate. There are too many kids showing up in the junior high who want and expect honors and the policy is to allow the students to enter if the parents want it. (p. 63)

As with Delaware's magnet schools, Salem County's honors program created distinctions among teachers. An honors class was a reward and better teachers, as defined by the principal and department resource teachers, were given honors classes. One teacher knew she was regarded as "good" because "they gave me another honors." Another considered himself punished because "they took my honors away." Another in response to the question, "Can a teacher slide here?" responded "Not and teach honors." Honors differentiated teachers just as it did students.

In addition to honors, the school contained other specialized curricula. In addition to special education, there was an alternative school for students unable or unwilling to accommodate school demands; an ESL (English as a second language) program for students who had recently come from foreign countries (many from Central America) and who spoke little English; and basic classes for students who needed the most remediation. Each program had its own constituency, curriculum, and teachers. The varied programs existed side by side, but without much contact with each other. Suburb High specialized; it did not coordinate across specialities. Because coordination of activities is generally assumed to be worthwhile and because the way schools organize is frequently selected as a target for reform, the next section discusses Salem County's efforts to coordinate its curriculum.

COORDINATING THE CURRICULUM

Curriculum is a school's attempt to take what society deems important and turn it into what students learn. Schools do not generate curriculum. Culture, colleges, parents, fads, conventional wisdom, combined with what teachers want to teach, all create curriculum. To impose some rationality, or an appearance of rationality, on all of this is not simple. In Salem County, there were several reasons for coordinating curriculum. First was the general feeling among administrators that there were too many courses, too much teacher autonomy, and too much inconsistency across classes, even in the same subject. Second, this 100,000 student district included a large and diverse population, and there was a potential perception that schools serving the more affluent were superior and were receiving more resources than schools serving the less affluent. The school board had to assure the public that the curriculum taught in the 76 elementary, 46 middle, and 22 secondary schools was reasonably consistent and that the schools serving the district's less affluent offered the same curriculum as schools serving the more affluent.

For several years, the district had been working to coordinate the curriculum. Each major area such as social studies, math, or science had a district coordinator who in the summer engaged teachers to write course guidelines, later approved by the board. The guidelines contained sample outlines for each course, lists of acceptable readings, suggestions for assignments concerning particular topics, and questions to accompany the readings and discussion guides. Ensuring that teachers followed the approved curriculum was what the administrators called "working on curriculum."

Overall, the efforts were deemed to have been successful. Suburb High's principal, herself a former English teacher, explained:

> This (curriculum) is a far cry from the early 1970's when English 9 could be all fiction or all drama depending on the teacher... writing was not emphasized, speech was generally ignored and teaching fiction dominated many classrooms... (now) there are still variations on how teachers organize and the subjects of speeches vary, but in speech class, students give speeches and in writing courses, students write specific types of compositions. (pp. 47–48)

Initially some teachers questioned whether the district would insist that teachers follow the approved curriculum. One of Suburb's teachers provided the test case when he used books that were not on the approved lists. The story, according to the teacher, was the following.

> The kids in this English class wanted to take one day a week for free reading... what could I say?... could I refuse? I gave them a list. No comics, no *National Enquirer.* The principal got wind of the fact that I was assigning books that were not on the county approved list. (p. 22)

The story according to the principal at the time was that "we needed to win that one if we were going to make (the curriculum) stick. If the district was going to organize, it was going to organize and stay organized. Otherwise the teachers would just ignore district regulations." The teacher insisted on using texts he and his students had selected. The principal brought the teacher up on charges of insubordination. The charge was supported by the superintendent and the teacher was reprimanded. He then appealed the reprimand, and amid long and widely publicized hearings, the school board suspended him without pay. He was placed in a vocational school, later reinstated in Suburb High's English department, but never given the honors classes. The events left that teacher embittered and critical of administrators, but the point that the district was serious about curriculum guidelines was not lost on anyone.

A department testing program accompanied the curriculum. In the late 1970s, the board of education had passed a policy requiring standardized two-hour exams in the major areas, social studies, English, math, and science. According to Suburb High's principal, the tests reinforced curriculum guidelines and provided an additional unit of dialogue among teachers. For instance, the four teachers who taught the required American history began with the county curriculum and adopted readings from the approved list. They also developed a common bank of test items from which each could choose.

Resource teachers enforced the guidelines. Those people were selected by the principal from teaching faculty, given two fewer classes, paid twenty days in the summer to work on curriculum, and given some secretarial help. They scheduled classes, chaired meetings, allocated supplies, monitored guidelines, and communicated with administrators. According to the principal these resource teachers were the key to an effective school.

> I've read all that stuff about the principal being the leader and I don't believe it at all. I think it's five years out of date. There's no way one person could run all of this. The principal can observe some classes, but can't really run the school from the top. That's why the resource teachers are so good; they're integrated all the way up, down and across. They're the key to the school. (p. 38)

Coordinating curriculum is a favored pastime of administrators, obligated as they are to demonstrate rationality and intelligibility to those outside the organization. Operationalized, coordination means getting the teachers to communicate about their efforts, placing some modest restraints on their propensity to teach what they feel like teaching, and giving administrators an intelligible way to talk about districtwide efforts. Coordination, communication, authority, and intelligibility are the substance of educational reform. They are what is left when the rhetoric of quality and equality and economic improvement is washed out. In that sense, educational reform becomes reform of the educational organization. Furthermore, the organizational reforms are conducted in ways that neither overly disturb influential groups nor interfere with the right of teachers to develop their own content and style.

ORGANIZATIONAL REFORM AND TEACHER BEHAVIOR

The argument is that changes in the organization that passed for educational reform were addressed to coordinating the school's busyness and density, satisfying external groups, and solving problems of coordination. They did not seriously affect the way teachers taught or students learned. They were organizational reforms that went up the system and across the schools, not down into the classrooms or into the personal interactions of teachers and students.

Suburb High offered 175 separate courses. The courses that every student in the district took, such as general science, English 9 and 10, government, and U.S. history, were district-regulated. As one social studies teacher explained about U.S. History, "It's all laid out, the objectives, the handouts, the movies, the tests. I don't have to do anything." On the other hand, many courses were electives with only a few sections. In these courses, the curriculum was less controlled and teachers exercised more discretion. For example, there were three sections of advanced placement English. On her reading list, one teacher chose *Agamemnon, Hamlet, Othello,* and *Rosenkranz and Guildenstern Are Dead.* A second chose *Hamlet, Cleopatra, Rosenkranz and Guildenstern Are Dead,* and *Waiting for Godot.* A third chose *Oedipus Rex, King Lear, Othello, Eurydice,* and *Waiting for Godot.* All the texts and many more were on district's approved list and each teacher was free to pick favorites.

Several more courses were "singletons," offered once a term or offered only by one teacher. Russian history, economics, advanced functions, airplane mechanics, clothing design, graphics, photo-journalism, and several language courses are examples. Guides for singletons were written by the particular teacher and reflected whatever she or he did in the class. The graphics teachers gave an example of how he created a curriculum. "When I came here the offset presses were up against the wall with a lot of junk piled around them. I hauled them out and created a program around them." And the auto mechanics teacher commented: "Not too many people understand what I do so they don't ask questions about how I do it." Freedom to select from a wide range of material and teach the way one wanted was not limited to teachers of advanced English or auto mechanics. The fact is that in that district, which had spent several years coordinating the curriculum, there was a great deal of freedom for teachers to select their materials and teach as they wished.

At Suburb High, the teachers behaved just as did teachers described in Chapters 3 and 4. They selected elements of the topic that interested them, students who were interested and responsive, and material that suited these. Their classes and students absorbed their attention and energy, and they gave the coordinating efforts only minimal attention. Even the English teacher who had been reprimanded and suspended, when one day Cusick complimented him on his planning and asked if other teachers were as thorough, replied, "I don't know what others do, I only know what I do."

Teachers also laced their classes with their values and views. In the space of twenty minutes, Cusick watched a teacher discussing Lady MacBeth's pre-suicide soliloquy give four asides: one on fate, one on responsibility, one on justice, and one on ambition. The poetry teacher taught the Irish poets she loved; the clothing teacher taught her favorite designs and her New York contacts; the family living teacher taught her experiences as a single mother; the honors geometry teacher taught his favorite theories; the economics teacher, his personal opinions on world affairs; the computer teacher created his problems; the art teacher taught about her favorite artists. The distributive education teacher had business contacts, a school store, and a national association of distributive education teachers and students. Each teacher had considerable latitude to create his or her curriculum.

Nor did district efforts hinder the teachers assessing their success in personal terms. One recounted how a former student, "not a good student and didn't have a lot of advantages, but she worked hard here and now she's working in

Bloomingdale's (department store) doing fine." Another recounted that she has just received a letter from a former student "to tell me he had just received tenure in Mt. Holyoke." Another recounting how he had, several years prior, taken in a homeless student: "Now he's a practicing attorney in the city." What unhappiness teachers expressed was not directed at the greater organization or administrators, but at there being an insufficient number of eager and aggressive students for the classes they wanted to teach.

The continued freedom of teachers was paralleled by the modest view that central office staff took of their efforts. The district social studies coordinator with his half-time secretary, said the idea of "controlling" the curriculum was ridiculous. "Schools are so different . . . teachers are so different. We can't do that." His chief responsibility consisted of selecting teachers to work on committees and synthesizing and reporting social studies efforts to the associate superintendent for curriculum. The latter agreed. In addition to stressing the teaching experience of each supervisor and resource teachers, she was careful to differentiate learning from instructional objectives. "Just because we have some ideas about what we want students to learn doesn't mean we control classroom teaching (and) just because we set learning objectives doesn't mean we set teaching objectives." And she saw the effort not as one to control curriculum, but to make some abstract sense of what was being taught in a district with 100,000 students, an abstract sense useful primarily to the superintendent and board in communicating with the district and state.

Furthermore, no teacher interviewed considered the guidelines or enforcing procedures a burden. A few voiced minor complaints, "Kids aren't automatons, you tell them something in September and two months later you ask them about it, and it's 'duhhhhhhhhh . . .' They just forget. The (guidelines) don't allow for that." A math teacher commented regarding the computer course guidelines: "It's too much. They give it to you but you have to make the problems and get it to the kids. They don't have to do that so their expectations are unrealistic . . . I have to add the problems to get the meaning across." Teachers accept reforms that come from above. They understand that the coordination is important and that the school and district have to make some overall sense. But coordination and overall sense are not their primary concerns. And when reform comes down to their classrooms, they make whatever adjustments are needed to fit the reform to their personal style.

For central office staff, the "district" was a political entity that had to present an intelligible and rational posture to diverse constituents. It also had to respond to events in the greater system such as increased minorities, state tests, and parents nervous about their children's future. The district did what it had to do with what it had at its disposal. It differentiated the curriculum, specialized the staff, and added necessary rules, regulations, and procedures so that the busyness created by differentiation could proceed. The district also worked to mesh its efforts with contiguous groups such as its clients and the state department. These changes enabled the organization to solve problems and not overly disturb either important groups or teacher discretion.

SUMMARY

President Johnson wants to reduce poverty; the U.S. Department of Health, Education, and Welfare wants to use schooling to transfer income to the poor; the Office of Civil Rights wants integration; state legislatures want to respond to criticisms from legislators; Secretary Bell wants to reduce the Department of Education's role. School districts want to respond to their diverse students. The middle class wants their children to succeed. Administrators want order; teachers want interested students; students want college acceptance. Every individual, every group, has an agenda—a problem that it is trying to solve. The school is where they come to find their solutions. The separate efforts as they are played out and as they overlap in the schools make up the system.

The formal organization emerges from the activity. Delaware gave the middle class its magnets and academies; the lower-achieving their special and basic classes; students unwilling to accommodate the comprehensive school were given one that did not demand that they show up every day. The superintendent increased his discretion, the teachers got some of the equity fund, the science director got his curriculum, and Delaware's deputy superintendent, so wise about public relations, became the superintendent. Salem County gave the ambitious parents honors, other groups their basic, special, and ESL classes. More difficult students were given their own school. Both districts segmented their groups and resources, particularized their offerings, and developed differential standards for varied groups. The formal organization of those districts was made up of a series of partly discrete, partly overlapping, responses to varied constituencies.

Specialization, that is, fragmenting the school into parts each designed to respond to a different group, is a conservative approach to change, usually less than called for by reformers. But it is reasonable for schools that reflect a fragmented social system and have limited ability to alter what students and teachers bring. Specialization serves another, seldom articulated, effect. It keeps reformers focused on the organization and away from classrooms where their presence could prove disruptive.

Lest the explanation here appear too sanguine, too functional, recall that changes described in this chapter were accompanied by disciplinary action against a recalcitrant teacher, administrative firings and reassignments, student expulsions, and a reward structure that left some teachers and students winners, some teachers and students losers. Not all administrators are retained; not all teachers assigned honors classes; not all students accepted by Duke. Schools present a benign image, but their rewards are limited and competition is harsh. The price of functional smoothness is borne by individuals who are not given the schools' best, whose views and services are no longer valued, whose opinions are discounted, and whose objections are overruled.

9

Conclusion

THE SYSTEM AND THE ORGANIZATION

The people are students, teachers, parents, administrators, lobbyists, policymakers, governors, presidents, and bureaucrats. The issues are curriculum, standards, autonomy, reform, quality, and equality. Running through the center, guiding and limiting the people and their activity is the system. What remains to be summarized are the characteristics of that system. With that task accomplished, the book will be finished, and the system will stand defined.

The concept "system" is simple enough. It is a set of overlapping collectivities—microstructures whose parts intersect to form a macrostructure. A human system has values and norms, a nature and logic, a way of processing information, and a way of defining and solving problems. The premise from the beginning has been that America's educational system is a discernible and predictable entity. It has a history and memory, a nature and logic; it socializes new members into old ways. Groups and their overlapping and problems and their solutions persist the same way across the schools and across the years.

The system's groups include those in the schools' formal organization: students, support staff, teachers, administrators, boards, and state and federal officials. It includes also those outside the formal organization who actively participate in day-to-day operations. Students' informal associations, parents, citizen groups, unions, newspapers, legislators, politicians, the President, and varied interest groups are all part of the system. The schools are not only lodged in and responsible to the larger society. The active participation by groups from society, the minimizing of distinctions between insiders and outsiders, and the crowdedness, busyness, and density created by the myriad groups, make up the system in which schools operate.

The system is much larger than its formal organization, but the schools are where the system happens, where groups come to develop identities, define problems, and seek solutions. What goes on in schools is the subject of the system's discourse. The curriculum, textbooks, electives, teaching qualifications, shape of buildings, length of day, and getting or allocating funds are the issues around which groups develop, coalesce, press, or oppose particular views. From the discourse comes the formal organization that then stands as the compromise, or aggregate of compromises, among the system's individuals and groups.

Even as a compromise the formal organization is an entity in its own right, with its own character, dynamism, and way of solving problems. Although ostensibly the United States has no national school system, there is a great deal of agreement about what a school is and how it should be run. At base, a school is a bureaucracy with a specialized staff, hierarchy, and formal authority. It differentiates students and teachers, relies on rules and regulations, and even for this most personal endeavor, it separates the role from the person. The bureaucracy keeps track of people and events. It accounts for and allocates resources. It provides the intelligibility, predictability, and the rational and progressive appearance that this large and busy endeavor needs.

The bureaucracy stabilizes the schools. It also provides a dynamic with which schools address change. New regulations and procedures are developed to guide and keep track of emerging issues. Specialization, the assignment of people and resources, is the way the schools handle honors or alternative programs, non-English speaking students, and chronic absenteeism. Along with specialization, the bureaucracy moderates among its interdependent parties. The teacher asks less than she would like to ask; the principal enforces only the rules that he can; federal and state staff adjust the regulations; the superintendent accommodates demanding parents; reformers ease away from too much disturbing of the accommodations that teachers make with students.

Along with specializing and moderating, the bureaucracy allows the schools to co-opt important groups. Schools open their doors to critics, who mollify their accusations in exchange for a chance to have access to students and carry out reforms more modest than originally envisioned. New proposals, suggestions, and reforms are taken into the organization, and outside critics become part of, instead of separate from, the organization. Specializing, moderating, and co-opting provide the dynamic by which schools keep themselves on an even keel within the system.

Although these processes seem reasonable and functional in a system that needs both stability and responsiveness, they combine to turn educational reform into organizational reform. When the rhetoric of reform is removed, what remains are more specialists and specialities, additional programs, changed procedures, and different evaluation schemes. The schools go on and the bureaucracy goes on, most likely expanded. The tenacity of the bureaucracy can be frustrating to those who see the bureaucracy itself as the barrier to educational reform. But education's bureaucracy works well relative to the overall system, a point that will be expanded upon as this chapter progresses.

There are some additional points about the school organization. One is the way that it treats its separate functions. At central office, state, and federal levels there are a great many rules and regulations about attendance, insurance, busing, building codes, and the categories into which students are to be divided. Matters of time, place, and designation are tightly controlled. The stability provided by these designations is a source of public confidence. One is satisfied that his or her child is "getting an education" if the child attends a standard school 180 days per year, is taught by certified teachers, and takes the required number of credits.

On the other hand, the soft and uncertain technology of teaching and the variety among students that obligate the formal organization to leave school staff and students sufficient autonomy to make needed personal adjustments. Judith and Clarence sit in the same room. It is left to Mrs. Zajac to adjust her efforts to their differences. Thus schooling goes on and public confidence is preserved while more difficult, obscure, and personal issues are left to be worked out privately among individuals.

Finally, the formal organization is not just another bureaucracy. It resembles most the large, successful corporations, described by Chandler (1990), that are vertically integrated, serve mass markets, practice economies of scope and scale, and expand by creating new services, acquiring more companies, and merging with competitors. Such corporations are run by mobile and professional managers and have interlocking directorates with broad-based boards of directors. These corporations create markets for their products; more to the point, they create demand for products that they then produce. They also remain internally flexible, allowing them to assign people and resources to emerging problems and to provide latitude to people at lower levels.

Even recalling Iannaccone's (1967) description of the educational system as fragmented by federal, state, and local governance, modern schools have adopted several corporate techniques. School districts practice economies of scale with their continuing consolidation, standard K–12 curriculum, and standardized purchasing practices. There are increasing numbers of specialists and a class of professional administrators that is quite mobile among large districts and, more regionally, among small districts. School taxes are mandatory for adults and school attendance mandatory for youths, thus ensuring the schools a steady flow of resources and customers. And like corporations that create demands even as they fulfill them, many of the services sold to students are created by the schools themselves.

Public schools have systematically discouraged competition, not only by expanding their services to match and underbid competitors (the expansion into preschool is a recent example), but by convincing regulatory agencies to back their services with law. Public schools have a near-monopoly on education as evidenced by school demographers who regularly predict the number of kindergarteners five years into the future from the number of births in the current year. At the other end, schools have successfully convinced colleges that only young people whom they have approved are worthy candidates for admission and likewise have convinced employers to make high school completion a criterion for employment, regardless of the job. On a broader scale, the educational system has succeeded in identifying what it is and does with the national good. School people may not have originated the notion of education as a solution to poverty, economic competition, or national defense, but they eagerly accepted those ideas and the resources that attend them. In fact, the only characteristic of a large corporate endeavor lacked by schools is an interlocking directorate. But with virtually no competition, such a directorate, essential to a large corporation seeking to minimize competition, is superfluous.

In sum, Americans have some broad ideas about education's formal organization. Schools are bureaucratic and use bureaucratic means for adapting and surviving. The organization co-opts outsiders and critics; it moderates both among competing parts of the overall system and among its internal groups. It maintains tight control of elements that lend themselves to control while leaving elements that do not to teachers and students. And even with its somewhat fragmented governance, it behaves as do large, successful corporations. With these few ideas about organizations in general and the school organization in particular, the elements of the system will be itemized.

FREE CONSCIENCE / FREE CHOICE

Two elements come through the descriptions, consistently at every level. The first is that individuals exercise free conscience and free choice. All the way up and down the system, individuals participate on their own terms and make their own adjustments and accommodations. They decide on their degree of compliance and their degree and mode of participation. Each member of the system is the best judge of his or her own interests, and each serves as his or her own referent. There is a distrust of expertise and a quickness to stake claims based on personal opinions. The educational system is not unique. Barnard (1938) long ago noted this tendency among individuals and groups to evaluate an event in terms of its contribution to their own purposes and notions of the organization. So our interest is not in arguing uniqueness of the characteristic but in showing how it works in education.

This characteristic is evident right from Chapter 2, which described the school opening its doors to the varied and conflicting classes and cultures of society. Across those classes and cultures are equally varied ideas about learning, authority, orderly behavior, the place of the individual in society, and about education and its place in life. Students bring these classes and cultures into school, reinforce them in peer groups, and then force a compromise between what the school in the form of the teacher asks and what the students in the form of society will do.

The school has its own definitions of appropriate behavior. Students may, however, using their class- and culture-based groups as referents and their friends as supporters, behave in ways different from that asked by the schools, and thus create different educational experiences for themselves in the same school, indeed, in the same classroom. The tension between what the students bring in and what the schools deem appropriate is what makes classroom control problematic and necessitates the teacher maintaining center position in the class. The tension that this characteristic generates between society in the form of students and the idealized society in the form of the school, is a fundamental and inescapable element. It affects everything up and down the system. It shows up more clearly with students, and most clearly, with students most at variance with the school.

Other elements support free choice and conscience as students exercise them. First are the schools' obligations to universalism and equality, which means that all students have to be accommodated and respected, even those who challenge one or another premise of the formal organization. Students have to adjust to schools but schools have to adjust to students. Second is the soft and uncertain technology of teaching and learning that undermines the school's efforts to counter the students' tendencies to engage in class- and culture-based arguments. Using personal freedom as a basic principle and only common sense as a criterion, it is almost impossible to prove that one person's opinion is superior to another's, even when the other speaks from a position of authority. Different approaches to the educational endeavor, a soft technology, and the doctrine of equality mean that the schools' primary content, reading, writing, math, foreign language, science, and so on, and its secondary content, order, respect for tradition, and authority are open to varying interpretations. Conflicting views abound, their number and intensity influenced by differing perceptions, opportunities, values, orientations, and personal preferences.

Students are not the only ones who exercise free choice and conscience. They show up more clearly among students because students are the most numerous and varied of the system's participants. Teachers too exercise freedom of conscience and make their own choices about how to behave in class. Mrs. Zajac and Mr. Richards, and Ms. Rosencranz and Mrs. Schiller are unmistakably individuals. No one would mistake one for the other. They share a role, a place in the system, but they behave very differently, even while doing the same job. Each has opinions on students, on appropriate behavior, on learning and content, and on how to talk and act toward students. Their behaviors cannot be traced back to the organization or to the actions of the administrators ostensibly in charge. Each is her or his own referent.

Teachers do not limit free conscience and choice to their dealings with students; they exercise them in dealing with administrators. As the descriptions from Chapters 5 and 6 indicate, teachers may or may not go along with the superintendent's reforms. When the Milton teachers found the headmaster-led discussion boring, they refused to participate, made off-the-point comments, and complained about his indecisiveness. The teachers in Constantine and River City found the Experimental Schools program more trouble than they wanted, or they judged it as something the superintendent was doing to enhance his career and, to the superintendent's consternation, refused to go along. The teachers in South Lane decided they knew more than the superintendent and the university people and opposed SPECS.

Individual freedom runs all the way through the system. Parents may or may not support the school board; superintendents may support or oppose the state department; state department staff may alter the intent of federal policymakers. People make and exercise personal decisions, enter and take part on their own terms, and regard these as their rights. Indeed, within the system, these are their rights. Students mix their classes, cultures, and friendships with school requirements; teachers adjust the curriculum to their predilections, create their student relations, and support or oppose the principal as they choose. Reformers decide schools need accountability, or principals decide that the teachers have too much or too little power. Teachers decide that the students need more freedom. Each member of the system is free to make his or her own decision and set out on a course of action.

Free conscience and choice are not limited to the system's professionals exercising professional judgments. From private citizens to presidents, all have their ideas about education. The South Umpqua teacher does not like what is going on and decides to call the logger's wife; the logger's wife calls the minister who then places himself in charge of the investigating committee. The state reading expert, acting as a parent, leads the group against the open school. Teachers make of IGE what they want and of SPECS what they want. They also make of the curriculum what they want, even in the reformed schools. Each is allowed to judge, speak, and to a great degree act for him or herself. Each participant in this system is also free to call on a supposed consensus to validate self-perceptions. Each acts as if "everyone knows" that students are out of control, teachers need accountability, schools need reform, and so on. At the base of every reform is the reformer's assertion that he or she knows better about what should go on in schools than the child's parent, the child's teacher, and the person administering the child's school. Empirical data may be absent, suspect, or ignored. That achievement scores rose did not deter Lincoln Elementary's parents from viewing open schools as a bad idea. That they did not like students' wandering around justified their opposition. They needed nothing else.

Each views the endeavor from the first person, singular, possessive. "It is my education"... "my class." "These are my students." "She is my child" and "I know best." The dropout, the parent, honors student, teacher and administrator, coach and bureaucrat, critic, and policymaker operate the same way. Each reserves proprietorship to some piece of the system. Each makes his or her own judgments and when the energy and resources are available, acts upon them. This tendency continually frustrates policymakers or reformers trying to divine a clear line between their abstract plans and classroom outcomes; they see their plans being altered as they are being implemented. Even as the university group was developing and promulgating SPECS, its members were dividing into developers and researchers.

In the views of many, the absence of control wrought by the exercise of free conscience is the characteristic most responsible for poor performance. Subsequently, they aim their improvements at restricting individual choice. Even for those not trying to instigate reform, but trying only to get on with the business of the day, free conscience is a barrier. The principal, the headmaster, and the superintendent want the parents to provide some common direction, the teachers to take collective action, and the students to legitimate and accept legitimate authority. But free conscience and free choice erode the consensus that legitimate authority needs.

Were free choice and conscience to operate unbridled and with maximum intensity all the time, the formal organization would deteriorate; intelligibility would be lost. But individualism does not tear the system apart, because it is not exercised at the same level, everywhere, or all the time. And when it is exercised, the organization has two safeguards. First, it is constructed to allow for personal choice. Willing students find enthusiastic teachers; unwilling students are pushed only as far as they allow themselves to be. Administrators do what they can and turn their backs to what they cannot. Parents unwilling to integrate move their children to private schools or other districts. Federal and state staffers work out disagreements; teachers accommodate students; administrators accommodate teachers and parents. Personal negotiating and personal accommodations disarm conflicts, mollify critics, and bring along dissidents. Personal interactions smooth out the hard edges of conflict.

Freedom of conscience is thus matched by an internal and personally executed flexibility that prevents individuals or groups from tearing the schools apart. The tolerance rests on the fact that everyone knows, tacitly at least, that learning is ultimately a personal and personalized endeavor, that the power of the organization is limited, and that the matter of learning comes down to what parents encourage, teachers teach, and students will do. The formal organization is not an educative entity but a container carrying the individual abilities and desires, and activities and expectations. Its central activity has to be worked out personally, so does everything else. In the personal working out, the overlapping occurs and the system goes on.

Second are the bureaucratic techniques of specializing and moderating that the organization uses to appease its more contentious groups. Reformers are given a chance to try out their ideas. Aggressive parents are given honors; the Parents of Mentally Retarded Children (PMRC) are given their own classes and teachers; chronically absent students are given a school that does not require regular attendance; reformers are given experimental or alternative programs. The most insistent of the groups are allowed to have what they want and still stay within the formal organization.

Freedom of conscience and choice are the source of endless problems. They are also the system's source of energy and renewal. Individuals, acting on their own and for their own reasons, add the passion, energy, and commitment that make education happen. It was a principal and an assistant superintendent who picked up IGE, a superintendent who picked up Experimental Schools. Mrs. Taylor and Mr. Ward ran their quality programs in one of Atlanta's more troubled high schools, year after year, through good times and bad. Theodore Sizer decided that schools needed reform and built his coalition. Al, Mrs. Zajac's principal, protected teachers from interference by the central office and Mrs. Zajac made her class come alive, even on the worse days. Elliott Shapiro wanted to do more for his students; Howard Smith made the Manpower program successful, even while the larger organization was folding for lack of funds and even for his least successful students. Federal policymakers convinced President Johnson to initiate the ESEA as an answer to poverty, and a governor in Texas made educational reform a political issue. Individuals exercising their free choice and conscience add vitality to the system. They also bring in the resources the organization needs to stay current.

Loyalty is not to one's designated role or to the formal organization that defines the role, but to one's personal inclinations and only secondly to the overall system, which protects one's rights to switch, create, and interpret roles. As such, roles are extremely elastic. Professionals are parents and parents are professionals; students are members of classes and cultures that hold views in opposition to the school; teachers and administrators may create groups that oppose superintendents and boards. The school board president in Washington decided to administer the schools, and for a time, she did. The board president had her constituency, to which she responded and in doing so opposed another school board member with a different constituency. The reading expert gave advice on structure. The logger's wife started an investigating committee; Clarence decided how he would behave in class. The Delaware teacher decided to teach revolution to his African-American students. Even within the university group pressing for SPECS, divisions occurred, with some more interested in studying the conflict than in pressing for reform. Individuals do not hesitate the exploit either the groups of which they are members or the formal organization to obtain some personally stated goal. They switch roles depending on their interests and views. Adherence to quality and equality underlies switching and expanding. Because no one knows more about quality or equality than anyone else, each can justify switching.

The system allows individuals to exercise more than one, and sometimes conflicting, roles simultaneously. Federal educational people are both members of the formal system and members of groups opposing the formal system. They may also be parents. The Texas coach is a district employee. He is also a member of the coaches association, his own community, and a voter. In the dispute over students' playing qualifications, he used his latter two roles to influence his former role. The teacher is an employee of the board and subject to the authority of the superintendent, unless the teacher does not like what the board and superintendent are doing. Then she is a member of the union, a concerned citizen, or perhaps a parent. The student is a member of the seventh grade class. He or she is also a member of a group with values opposed to those espoused by the teacher. A radical reformer may advocate a conservative education for her own child. The superintendent of South Lane, referring to the university group, asked the basic question, "Whose side are they on?" Indeed, whose side is anyone on? "Whose school is this anyway," in a system that includes everyone, where each can take multiple and even competing roles, a system that is crisscrossed with kinship and personal relations, and where each is free to switch and justify the switching with basic values? There are no insiders and outsiders. Everyone, by calling on basic values and asserting a right to free conscience and association proclaims to be an insider.

Personal responsibility and ownership follow freedom of conscience and choice. Rewards and costs are self-generated. Dropouts make their decisions about the worth of schooling and the price they will pay to get an education, just as do those who compete for honors and magnets. South Lane's principal knew when he sided with the teachers that he might not become the next assistant superintendent. Elliott Shapiro might have been fired for his actions, but he took his chance—as did the student who goofed off in Hamilton High, the

Sioux and the Cherokee, the African-American males, and Willis's (1977) lads. Each asserted that he knew what he was doing. One can argue that these people should behave differently, that they are wrong, ignorant, disloyal, young, brash, inconsiderate, that they don't understand, that they have too much freedom, or that they are being misled.

But those are individual judgments, based on the same freedom of conscience practiced by the dropout who insists that he may do as he wishes. The vice principal's admonition to stay and thus increase his economic chances is matched by the dropout's insistence that he can leave just as his uncle, brother, and sister left. It being the dropout's life, not the vice principal's, he leaves. For system purposes, the dropout's asserting control over his piece of the endeavor is no different from the teacher deciding to agree or not with the superintendent or Elliott Shapiro deciding to go to the parents and the newspaper. There are qualitative differences to be sure, but the purpose is not to evaluate decisions, only to point out that each of the system's participants makes his or her own and that the right to do so is one of the system's basic characteristics.

Administrators, headmasters, and superintendents publicly speak of the collective "we," but the "we" is weak in a system that provides each with a side door to slide out when the person determines that he or she knows better than the one ostensibly in charge. Even in the Baptist Academy, Peshkin (1986) found many of the students quietly sliding out the side door to free conscience. That is not to deny the formal organization's authority. Teachers show up on time, bus drivers follow their routes, students obey rules and regulations, graduation policies are enforced by guidance counselors, and teacher certification policies are enforced by the state. Administrators count students according to rules and fund programs according to guidelines. Matters of place, time, and designation are consistent and uniform. A remarkable degree of sameness lies across the structure and curriculum of the nation's schools.

A later section of this chapter attends to that sameness. For now, and based on the descriptive studies, the argument is that the sameness does not prevent a broad array of individual accommodations and interpretations. Students show up on time but control their degree of compliance. Teachers show up on time but the way they handle their curriculum and student relations is more their business than the principal's. Administrators add their opinions and biases to rule enforcement. Even after the English teacher lost his case, his administrative superiors did not know what he did in class, and he did not know what his colleagues did in class. When matters of time, place, and designation are settled, interpretations are left to individuals who follow their own judgments and elect their own modes of participation.

It is also true that matters of time, place, and designation are of concern primarily to those with formal status, such as students, teachers, and administrators. The system is full of people who are not bound by the building with its seven-hour day, transportation, and lunch schedule. Parents, lobbyists, legislators, interested citizens, critics, reformers, and special interests are also part of the system, playing out their roles according to their private interpretations. The interest groups are not bound by the constraints of the formal organization except that they are trying to bend it to their own purposes. It is true that schools appear narrow and restrictive, but their appearance is only the facade of a crowded and busy system where individuals, with and without formal status, do to a great degree as each sees fit. The freedom of conscience and choice is a basic characteristic of the system.

FREEDOM OF ASSOCIATION

The second characteristic is freedom of association, which allows individuals to form groups in which they pursue their personal judgments and inclinations. Free association is a basic American right, open to any and all, a safeguard of freedom, the vehicle through which citizens participate in public affairs, and the way minorities protect themselves against the majority. The tendency of people within the educational system to divide and subdivide themselves is a characteristic that shows up in every one of the studies at every level of the system.

One does not have to actively join associations. Learning is a private and individual endeavor. But education is also a public and cooperative endeavor and if the goal is to influence others, or even the preservation of one's right to behave as desired, then alliances must be entered into. One may determine his or her own compliance. If one wants to extend influence, he or she has to join with others.

The book's argument is taken from descriptive studies of schools and school situations but it can certainly be said that in fundamental ways our education system reflects our society:

> Americans of all ages, all stations in life, and all types of dispositions are forever forming associations. There are not only commercial and industrial associations in which all take part, but others of a thousand different types—religious, moral, serious, futile, very general and very limited, immensely large and very minute. Americans combine to give fetes, found seminaries, build churches, distribute books, and send missionaries to the antipodes. Hospitals, prisons and schools take shape this way. (de Tocqueville, 1839, p. 513)

Of the different types of associations in the system, the primary is the designation of the formal organization's participants according to role and status. Some are students, some teachers, some administrators, and some specialists of one sort or another. The organization stipulates relations among these people. State staffers send along their guidelines to district staffers, administrators direct teachers, and teachers direct students. Within hierarchial lines, those with the same or similar roles join around particular efforts. So teachers join to create a new curriculum, administrators and board members push an improvement, or teachers and students cooperate among themselves.

A second type of association is the personal but purposeful relations among those with formal designation and within the formal system. Judith and Mrs. Zajac constitute such an association; so do Mrs. Zajac and Clarence or Pedro. Elliott

Shapiro and his supporters in the central office constitute such a group. So do Cusick and Wheeler's magnet teachers, Mr. Smith and his class, the administrators in Constantine, Michigan, and the USOE staffers pushing the ESEA or the NIE. Ed Bell, the principal of Freedom Elementary, and his educator colleagues constitute such a group. So do all the interest groups that surround and monitor the federal operation in Washington. Each chapter in this book reveals participants deciding how they will behave and seeking out colleagues inside the organization with whom to act out their decisions. The formal organization is filled with these personal and purposeful associations, too numerous to be formally recognized, which operate inside and drive the organization.

The third type of association consists of those that join people inside with people outside the schools. The system is replete with freestanding, single-purpose associations that include parents, students, policymakers, critics, change agents, teachers, and administrators, combining their efforts to achieve some end. These are the most interesting, because they reveal the breadth of the system and thereby justify the assertion that the system extends far beyond the schools. Students maintain alliances with their out-of-school classes and cultures. Elliott Shapiro allies not only with some central office supporters but also with the newspaper and parents. The teacher calls the logger's wife and the logger's wife calls the minister and the three initiate an investigating committee, which the superintendent then joins. The U.S. president's staff joins educators and key legislators, business people join the governor's reform panel. The panel takes its proposals through the legislature. Coaches, first in their own association, then with like-minded citizens oppose the reforms and take the issue back to the governor. The USOE and the Office of Civil Rights work out a policy of busing for integration. Parents may, as they did in Pontiac, Michigan, in the early 1970s, form groups to oppose busing.

The Parents of Mentally Retarded Children (PMRC) join with special education teachers; Sizer and his private backers convince some school administrators and boards to go along with their proposals. The originators of the ESEA have no trouble finding school people equally concerned about the poor and who are willing to use education as a solution to poverty. A group opposing open classrooms is joined by a group wanting lower taxes. A group wanting funds for private schools is joined by a group wanting choice of public schools. Oregon's PPBS initiative was carried through by some federal staffers, a university, a school board, a school district, and its teachers and administrators. The opposition included some teachers and administrators, the newspapers, unions, and the Oregon Department of Education. Regarding this American tendency to blur distinctions between those inside and those outside government, de Tocqueville noted that those in government "are surrounded by the constant agitation of parties seeking to draw them in and enlist their support" (p. 173). People inside the schools regularly join people outside to pursue mutual ends.

Not only do those outside seek to influence those inside. Those inside and those outside are part of the same system. They adhere to the same principles of free conscience and free association, and they join efforts and act out their visions of education in the same arena. This constant shifting into multiple and overlapping groups and groups into coalitions is what makes school board politics, as described by Cuban (1975), so entertaining. It is also why school administrators tend to be cautious and to regard their communities warily. Their authority is always open to challenge by one or another group: either one of the system's recognized groups or a group organized for the purpose of opposing an administrative action.

Several of these associations spring from the schools' local base. Citizens and their boards feel they own the school. Indeed they do and therefore they have a right to join, and with or without being asked, to give advice and assistance to those who work in the school. Administrators have to behave warily. They are in charge only of the formal organization, not the varied sets of people and interests that operate freely within and around the formal organization. School administrators administer the schools, not the system.

Spontaneous associations that are formed around issues frequently blind-side those with formal authority. The reform-minded Texas governor and his blue-ribbon panel were thus blindsided by a combination of coaches and their supporters, as were the Lincoln teachers and administrators by the opposing parents, and the New York Chancellor by Elliott Shapiro and his parents. In the fall of 1990, the *New York Times* is reporting from Philadelphia that a "group of parents is suing a school system over its new program requiring students to perform 60 hours of volunteer work." (September 22, 1990, p. 22).

> "I don't want my son being told what to do," said Thomas Morales, one of the plain-tiffs, and a member of 21-family organization "Citizens Against Mandatory Service, Inc." "I went to school in a free America I want the same for my children."

Without difficulty, one can imagine the school staff, well-meaning and con-cerned about giving their students a sense of social responsibility, designing a reasonable program, one that according to the article has already proven suc-cessful in Atlanta. And without difficulty, one can imagine Mr. Morales and some other parents, also well-meaning and concerned, not wanting the school to add something else, opposing (according to the article) the choice of organizations in which the service was to be undertaken, and calling on personal freedom to justify their opposition. The administrators, the approving board and staff, several organizations willing to take the students, opposing Mr. Morales, his wife, their association, and their legal council: It is all so predictable.

That disputes get played out in court reflects the fact that the parties regard themselves as equals. Indeed within the system, they are equals. Expertise per se is not highly valued. And even when the court decision favors the plaintiff in a case against some action by administrators, the decision is not "against" the system, for the system includes courts, school people, and plaintiffs, the latter of whom are using the courts to effect a particular result. That both parties play out their disputes in the courts is proof of the system's inclusiveness and of its participants' equal status. Ed Bell, principal of Wolcott's (1978) Freedom Elementary, found this lack of respect for professionals irritating. He wished that the parents would recognize the expertise of the school staff and leave decisions concerning the children to them. But that is not the way the system works. Professionals' decisions and actions are always on the defensive against nonprofessionals, who regard themselves and indeed are, from the system's view, equals of the professionals. Not only do people have the right to express their personal opinions and work toward them, they do so with great frequency. Education being too personal and too important to be left to professionals, the movements and counter-movements of interest groups cut across the formal organization. For administrators in charge of the formal organization, but not in charge of the system or the associations that crisscross the system, caution becomes a way of life.

In sum, there is the formal organization with its bureaucracy, forms, functions, roles, and authority. Within and across the bureaucracy are the vertically integrated, single-issue, tightly coupled coalitions that protect select pieces of the curriculum. An administrator may exercise authority within the bureaucracy, but he or she is another among equals within the coalitions.

Just as the system is not limited to those with formal status, so ideas, energy renewal, and reform are not limited to those with formal status. Elliott Shapiro, a school principal, central to the formal system, may initiate renewal. So may Sizer, from his positions at Harvard and Brown, initiate renewal. So may Michigan's PMRC, who want special consideration for their children and the Suburb High parents who want honors. So may Mrs. Zajac, Judith, and Judith's father. More likely, those on the periphery are most free and most likely to become reformers, to form coalitions, co-opt those with resources, and bring in new ideas.

The ideas and energy come from individuals deciding by themselves and for their own reasons that schools need excellence, or integration, or honors, or special education, or that rural schools need to be brought up to urban standards. Ideas and energy come from individual assessments and are worked through on a line parallel to the formal organization. These associations that generate and nurture the ideas and energy are essential to the system. Within the associations, individuals outside schools transmit ideas, energy, and resources into schools. Within them, people inside garner resources and ideas from outsiders; individuals join with others to generate ideas and to press for reform. In these associations, the system's periphery joins with its center. Debates are conducted, people hone their visions, and education is renewed. Rational planning and formal authority are frustrated, but passion and initiative, reform and renewal are alive.

Individuals and their associations do the actual educating. The formal organization is not so much an educative entity but a container ship, a coordinating system inside which these individual associations define and take care of the teaching and learning, or fail to take care of the teaching and learning. One can think of a student, parents, and peer groups as a coalition that backs up the perspective the student takes toward the endeavor. A teacher does not face a single errant student but a coalition of people including the child's parents, grandparents, and friends, who do not much care about what the teacher has to teach or who would support the student's decision to drop out. Judith, her father, and Mrs. Zajac compose an association in which Judith's education goes on, an association qualitatively different from that created by

Mrs. Zajac, Clarence, and his family. Individual students, even in the same classroom, operate within different associations that shape their education. The lads play in school; Grant's drug-taking student goofs off with his friends. Suburb High's honors students seek out teachers and classes that will help them enter Princeton. The greater system and the formal organization allow participants to carry on associations that reflect their variety, abilities, beliefs, and inclinations.

Mr. Richards does not know what to do with students who refuse to participate or rather, participate on terms other than those he asks; who ridicule his efforts; and who take every opportunity to turn the class their way instead of his. Neither does Pamela's teacher, nor even the excellent Mrs. Zajac and the equally excellent Mr. Smith know what to do with the most difficult students. These teachers have many good days with such students; they even like them and are liked in return. But the chance of dragging those students away from their primary associations and into academic matters is sometimes and fleeting. The formal organization with its orderly classrooms, sunny optimism, and future orientation has a hard time penetrating or even influencing the associations in which many students live and in which their education takes place.

Freestanding associations operate and protect their interests up and down the system. At Suburb High, such a coalition was made up of (1) parents who want their children in honors, (2) students who want to attend competitive colleges, (3) teachers who want aggressive students, (4) administrators who want quality programs, and (5) colleges that recruit students who demonstrate achievement in honors classes. From production to distribution, the honors program was thus supported and protected by a vertically integrated coalition that operated freely within the school, the district, and the system.

With the actual teaching and learning carried on inside these freestanding and unequal associations, results are naturally unequal. The network that influences the education of Pedro, Clarence, Pamela, and the lads is no match for the network influencing the student on his way to Princeton. In an attempt to mitigate natural inequality, the formal organization offers all students the same curriculum, opportunities, and restraints; and equal measures of time, resources, and money. But an honest answer to the young lady who upon hearing of students who represented Suburb High on TV, "Do those kids go to this school?" would be, "No, they do not. Not the one you attend." The set of colluding interests that surrounds the students who won Sunday's quiz bowl is worlds away from that of the young lady.

Each of the formal organization's successful endeavors is likely to be ensconced within a network of supporting affiliates, some from inside, some from outside the formal organization. These endeavors extend back into supply from parents, and forward into distribution, with colleges and employers wanting their graduates. The educational system is replete with these vertically integrated channels, each composed of partisan groups interested in a particular endeavor. Individual teachers are often at the center of these coalitions. Suburb High's Distributive Education teacher had her students, her contacts in the local business community, her school store, a national association of distributive education teachers and students and, at that time, Big

Boy Restaurants, which was sponsoring a contest within the national association. So did the design teacher have her students, her professional supporters, and her contacts in New York's garment district. The coach had friendships in the community that insulated him from his superintendent's opprobrium.

The success of a coalition depends on its ability to protect itself by extending its influence. The Delaware teachers favored with magnet assignments gained control of important committees and extended their influence into the negotiated contract, so that in their case rules of seniority were abrogated. Free-standing associations protect Salem County honors programs, Michigan special education, Delaware magnet programs, and Texas football. Indeed if any single piece of the curriculum were examined, it would likely be found thus protected. The looseness of the formal organization is compensated by the tightness within these coalitions. The latter are seldom formally organized, but with limited ends, and close personal agreement among members, they do not need administrators, rules, and regular meetings. Hence they are less visible, and their existence and strength tend to be overlooked by those who desire change and who limit their efforts to the formal organization or to the formal organization's bureaucracy. But when these single interests are threatened by some proposed change, they can become visible, noisy, and contentious. They show up at board meetings, mobilize the PTA, head for the state legislature, their unions, and the newspapers. Parents threaten to take their children to private schools or other districts. Any of the parties, if they are angry enough, may take the school district to court or petition the governor. The system permits all those options.

The first characteristic of the system is freedom of conscience, which allows each a personal approach to the endeavor. The second characteristic is freedom of association, which allows individuals to create groups and coalitions and pursue their personal approaches. Thus the system is characterized, and thus it behaves.

THE FORMAL ORGANIZATION

Two tasks remain: first to discuss how the formal organization operates given the system, and second, to discuss the problems in the system and the formal organization. In both sections, the educational system is taken as uniquely American. What it is, it is, and school people must take it on its own terms. If education is as important as educators say it is, school is a logical place for Americans to exercise their rights of free conscience and association. Nor is it that schools are out of control or that school people regard their situation as impossible. Striving for rationality in the face of uncertainty is the normal condition of organizations, not just school organizations. School people accept the system's uncertainty on its own terms. Becoming a teacher means accepting students; being an administrator means accepting and working with parents and communities. People inside the organization have to take the system as it is and build an organization that operates with relative certainty in an uncertain world.

The answer to the uncertainty posed by the system is the school's bureaucracy, which makes regular and predictable what by nature is less regular and less predictable. Even fragmented by state and local governance, the bureaucracy is remarkably uniform, its processes duplicated across more than 15,000 school districts and 50 states. The bureaucracy gives sense to the coming and going of 38 million students from just past infancy to early adulthood. It enables the schools to assure the citizenry that their children are warm, dry, orderly, and fed. Its hours and credits express measures of effort and achievement and so add a currency, a medium of exchange, that extends easily throughout the system. Periodically, proposals float around for disestablishing schools or integrating students into communities where they would do their learning in more natural settings. But school people know that the citizenry does not want its children wandering around following their natural instincts. Parents will not give their children over to an organization that does not give the appearance of knowing what it is doing. The bureaucracy provides the appearance.

Several benefits are derived from the bureaucracy. Education is both a private and a public good. There is a difference between the private benefits that can accrue to individuals and the social benefits that accrue to society. The former are obtained privately, even within the public schools, by individuals, groups, and coalitions. The latter are protected by the bureaucracy that guarantees universalism and equality. It is true that the bureaucracy is coercive. It is equally true that if there were no coercive bureaucracy, the private interests would not, on their own, work toward education's public benefits. Rather they would exploit the larger system even more than they already do.

There are additional justifications for an educational bureaucracy. Beyond basic skills, abstract academic material is difficult to learn—more so than most educators admit. It takes personal commitment to read serious books and pay attention to math, science, and a foreign language. Few come by such efforts naturally and for the many who do not and who are not ensconced in an encouraging network, the bureaucracy with its requirements, tests, schedules, and sanctions provides a necessary incentive, a rolling agenda for students who come to school without one. It is the bureaucracy that ensures the education of the least advantaged, who if left to themselves, might not come to school. The bureaucracy makes regular what is by nature irregular. It manifests progress even in the absence of learning. It also keeps the possibility of learning open so that a student may, given some sudden energy or incentive, begin to take education seriously, at a point of her own choosing. Or after several years of marginal performance, one suddenly and for his own reasons decides to pick up needed courses and read required books; the bureaucracy is there, waiting and ready whenever he is.

The bureaucracy is less restrictive than it appears; it is also more flexible. From the days described in Middletown and Elmtown, it has accommodated vastly increased numbers of students, many of whom in former times might not have come to school or might not have stayed if they had come. It consistently opens itself to those with no formal status who bring ideas, energy, and resources into the schools. It is not a top-down organization, even though it looks, talks, and sometimes acts like a top-down organization. Its rules, regulations, and procedures do not supplant personal interactions, instead they provide a place and a framework within which the interactions take place. The bureaucracy gives students, teachers, and administrators wide latitude to make personal adjustments. Negotiation and accommodation go on all the time at every level, and in those two processes is the overlapping that creates the system from its separate collectivities. The bureaucracy also forces any suggested change to pass through several parties. Thus, while the bureaucracy is open to personal interpretation, it is also stable and prevents efforts at one level from overly disturbing efforts at other levels.

In addition to providing flexibility for individuals and stability in an uncertain environment, the bureaucracy gives groups private versions of this public endeavor. Those who want honors, magnets, special education, closed classrooms, experimental and alternative schools, and winning football teams get them. Growth and change are by specialization, co-optation, and accretion: processes that can take a long time.

That the bureaucracy is able to accommodate problems of society is evidence of its success. That it does so bureaucratically frustrates critics and reformers who see their lofty aspirations reduced to things the bureaucracy can do. Excellence is reduced to a state or federal testing program, equality to busing blacks and whites into the same schools, responsiveness to adding another speciality to its long list, and universalism to more detailed attendance policies. The bureaucracy gives form to abstract ideals, but it is a bureaucratic form, and is almost always less than what reformers want, particularly those who see the bureaucracy itself as the barrier to change and who see bureaucratic procedures devouring the time and energy that should go into teaching and learning.

But the bureaucracy is what it is. It cannot step outside its own nature and behave unbureaucratically. It cannot disestablish itself, dissolve into anarchy, or adopt nonbureaucratic solutions. It has to adapt to exigencies, but it has limited responses. Requiring changes to fit into the bureaucracy slows down the factionalizing that would result from the myriad groups following only their own interests. The persistence of the bureaucracy frustrates reformers who would like to see more change and who see the bureaucracy as stifling change. However, there are not many ways to organize a large collective endeavor obligated to respond to a diverse population. In the absence of consensus by the aggregated parties, bureaucracy is the easiest way.

The bureaucracy also allows schools to disassociate from negative outcomes. Along the way to failure, each dropout has been given help from reading and math specialists, counseling from the guidance office, progressive discipline from the vice principal, therapy from the school psychologist, and parent conferences with the principal. Special, vocational, and alternative programs have all been tried. "We've done everything we can" say the schools and indeed, within the confines of a bureaucracy, they have. In the end, student failure can be attributed to personal intransigence, negligent parents, or greater social problems such as poverty. Dysfunctions and failures are thus left to individuals who make their own decisions, pay their own price, and succeed or fail on their own merit.

The bureaucracy is not cavalier about failure, either personal or social. Indeed, its principal role is guardian of equality. It insists that children of the poor attend school for the same number of days that the more advantaged attend, that they take required credits, pass the minimum competencies, dress and behave in an acceptable manner, and learn to read, write, add, and subtract. The formal organization and its bureaucracy serve the function of government in a free society; they preserve the collective equality. The bureaucracy demands that students from classes and cultures least receptive to abstract academic material and majority values show up, behave, and take a credit of math, even if it is only fifth grade arithmetic and even if they have already failed it three times.

The bureaucracy demands in the face of resistance that students open themselves to things parents might not know, want to know, or want their children to know. It also spends the most money on the least able students. So it tries to and indeed does reduce the greater inequality that would ensue if each child's education were influenced only by her class and culture or only by associations he brought into school. Were it not for the bureaucracy insisting on equal treatment, equal time, resources, and teachers, the competing factions would balkanize the schools to death; the advantaged would run away with their advantages, even more than they already do. If the schools did not have the bureaucracy to control the competing factions, it could not direct resources to the disadvantaged.

It is true that the bureaucracy does not initiate reforms, but with the ethic of impersonality and rules and regulations, it lends itself naturally to reforms that argue for equality, as most do. Indeed, every one of the initiatives described in this book, the ESEA, busing, experimental schools, and open schools, were all argued from the view that education could increase equality, or put another way, decrease the inequality in the overall system. Each reform was based on the assertion that some group was being treated unequally and it was the schools' job to eliminate discrepancies. Without the bureaucratic ethic, female athletics might never have penetrated the schools. Were it not for the bureaucracy's impersonal standards, Elmtown's plutocrats would to this day be telling the principal that their own children are exempt from the rules, yet deserve the rewards. And when reformers pass to other concerns, the bureaucracy remains to ensure that the effort continues.

The bureaucracy sees that each student is getting the same resources, time, and attention. Unequal outcomes cannot be explained by the bureaucracy, but are evident from its weakness relative to the coalitions that operate within the school and in which a student's education takes place. The individuals, groups, and coalitions are unequal; so educational outcomes are unequal. If the formal organization were synonymous with the system, or at least coterminous with the system, one could expect more equal outcomes from schools.

But the formal organization is not a condensed version of the system; nor is it the sum of the system. It is the system's outward manifestation, a compromise, and a fragile compromise at that, among the system's myriad and competing parts. The formal organization spends a lot of time taking its pieces apart and putting them together in ways that it is hoped will increase equality. But the efforts are always under attack by groups that are already advantaged or who wish to accrue advantages and who use the schools for personal ends. The bureaucracy is the schools' defense against factionalizing. But it is a limited defense engaged in an always uphill fight against influential coalitions who press their privileges into the school to get what they want and what they want for their children. Nor is the bureaucracy as strong as it might be at the other extreme, against the coalitions that support deviant students who laugh off the teachers' efforts just as do their friends and just as did their parents when they were in school.

Thus the formal organization hangs together, conservatively to mask its diversity, bureaucratically in the name of equality, co-opting and specializing in the name of responsiveness, coordinating the numerous coalitions that operate freely within its walls: seeking a modest balance between those pressing for their advantages and those who if left alone would remain at the bottom of society.

WHAT IS WRONG?   WHAT IS TO BE DONE?

This is a book about the educational system. The tense is present; the mood in-dicative. This is a not a reform proposal or a treatise on how the system should work. But education having to do with improvement of self as well as the hu-man condition, any discussion of education has to finally come to the topic of improvement. So now, having described the system, we may address the matter of improving the system and improving the formal organization.

From the system's view, it is not clear that anything needs to change. That is not said cavalierly, but in recognition that the school-reform industry, so essential to the system's renewal, is busy and active and needs no further admonitions or advice. New ideas are being generated, new resources brought in. Coalitions of educators, policymakers, and business people are examining the curriculum, try-ing to increase tests scores and participation by minorities, to teach job skills, to elevate environmental awareness, and to improve health habits. State legislators are wrestling with textbooks, finance, testing, choice, and bilingual and sex ed-ucation. Citizens, boards, and administrators are trying to increase participation by teachers, compliance by students, and the power of the principal relative to both. Advocacy groups are pushing parental guidance programs, birth control, preschool, honors, advanced placement, and vocational, special, and alternative education. Vice principals are trying in-school suspension, timeout rooms, pro-gressive discipline, adult classes, and predropout counseling. Education's system is alive and busy hammering out its hopefully improved schools.

Furthermore, it makes little sense to criticize a system that so well reflects society. According to the description, the problem with the American educational system is that it is the American educational system. If it reflects Americans' lack of respect for authority and their maddening tendencies to do as and associate with whom they please, then so be it. To suggest the system change is to suggest that America alter its citizens' rights of free conscience and free association. That Americans play out these rights in schools is a tribute to their faith in education and a particular tribute to educators' success in convincing the public of education's worth. Perhaps too many people refuse to participate or participate on terms other than what the schools ask. But that is not a fault of the system. It is the other side, or perhaps, the underside of the same freedoms freely exercised.

It is true that there is too much inequality both in the system and in society and, because schools are charged with reducing inequality, there are problems with the educational system. But the system allows and encourages participation by individuals and associations. That people's efforts, resources, and visions are unequal ensures that the system will be unequal. In as open a system as described, a good part of the inequality that enters the schools will pervade the schools and emerge from them.

It can also be argued that there is not enough quality. But that is hard to discern, even with the aid of national measures and even compared to foreign countries, an absolute lack of quality. The schools are producing an annual crop of promising mandarins as evidenced by competitive colleges having more well-qualified applicants than they can admit. And with the exception of specialty occupations, which ebb and flow with market demand, businesses and industries that offer decent wages and working conditions do not lack qualified applicants. Not since the 1940s, when there was a booming war industry and 10 million Americans in uniform, has there been an overall and absolute shortage of qualified workers for decent jobs. The quality issue does not show up at the upper or middle levels of society or at the upper, middle, or even lower-middle levels of the school. It shows up at the lowest end of society and the lowest end of the schools' achievement scale where poor and disadvantaged students, many of them minorities, are not picking up enough literacy and technology to make themselves employable in a competitive market. The issue of quality is thus subsumed under the issue of inequality.

As a general problem, inequality gets played out in particular ways. The educated and advantaged and the uneducated but ambitious get what they want from public schools. The schools serve these people well. And these people serve the schools well. They wrap their children in supporting coalitions and push them from preschool on through K–12 and into the universities. They pick their schools, even their teachers. They support school events and vote affirmatively in millage elections. They help the teachers, support the principal, and tell their children to do what teachers and principals say to do. Subsequently, their children get the best teachers, or at least the teachers they want, the favored classes, the athletic teams, the yearbook and newspaper assignments, and the debate and chess clubs. The colleges are waiting for them on the other end with scholarships for the needy and qualified.

These coalitions of interested and appreciative citizens, students, teachers, and administrators keep the schools stable. They also make the schools hard to change, and as some critics assert, unresponsive. The first charge is correct; schools are hard to change. The second is incorrect; schools are not unresponsive. Schools are hard to change because each successful program is supported by a coalition of interested people, some from within, some from without, the schools. The coalitions are evidence that schools are not unresponsive. They are quite responsive to the people who demand a response. If the program protected by the supporting coalition is threatened, the coalition members will be up, organized, and marching. So the schools are hard to change.

Rarely do reformers, themselves part of the system, blame the educational system for inequality. Instead, they focus on the formal organization and blame the formal organization for unequal results. In a sense, that is unfair for all the reasons cited. But in another sense, the formal organization is the element in the system most amenable to policy. It is the part of the system that can be changed and thus is the fitting target of reform. The question then becomes how much can efforts to reform the formal organization offset the inequality in the schools and in the educational system?

Given the system as described, there are two avenues to reform. The first is to alter the formal organization. The second is to leave the formal organization as it is and to create more benefits for less-advantaged students. Let each be taken in turn, recalling that the important point about reform efforts is not that they are correct, incorrect, or likely to succeed or fail; it is that they are the system's and the schools' source of energy, initiative, and renewal, the vehicle by which interested and concerned people drive their views and ideas to the schools and open opportunities for students and staff. Reform joins those inside schools with those outside, and the system's classrooms with its periphery. Given the system, some reforms make more sense than others, but all make sense and all reflect the system at work.

Arguments for reforming the school organization usually begin with recitation of a set of problems, some directly tied to schools, some less so. The set includes dropout rates and particularly minority dropout rates, economic competition, poverty and welfare rates, teen pregnancy, current SATs relative to previous SATs, and American students' knowledge relative to foreign students' knowledge. The argument connecting all those to improved schools rests on the paradigm that evil, and these particular evils, result from ignorance, that ignorance can be cured through education, and therefore improved schools can solve these problems. And it can be demonstrated that people who stay in and do well in school suffer much less from those problems than those who do not.

The solution is reform of the school organization. The ways suggested are too numerous to list, but in general they take as their premise that the formal organization should be the educating entity. Students then should leave aside their groups and enter the classroom. Teachers should leave aside their personal ways of operating inside their classrooms and join a larger group of teachers and administrators. Teachers, administrators, and parents should join in a broad school collective. Reforms generally seek to defactionalize the schools: bringing people out of their self-interested groups and into the formally organized and larger collectives where, it is assumed, they will behave more rationally, work for broader collective goals, and garner just as many if not more of education's private benefits. As the argument goes, if the organization were the important educating unit, students could be more motivated, teachers more respected and harder working, administrators more attuned to management and less to control, and parents more active and supportive. If such efforts were to succeed, the principal would be the instructional leader as well as a school coordinator. Students and teachers would agree on and obey collective norms, distant planners could more readily connect their efforts to school and class-room events, and schools would take on the more appealing characteristics of communities. The correct application of organizational theories could improve student performance. The administrative entity would no longer be a container ship for the individuals and coalitions pursuing their varied perspectives. The school would be the educative unit, itself defining the endeavor. The formal organization would be strengthened. The power of individuals and groups relative to the formal organization would be reduced. The formal organization would become coterminous with the educational system and the system, as described it in this book, would be changed.

Organizational reform or as it is called, structural reform, is an appealing model designed to put the formal organization in charge of the system rather than behind and reacting to the system. It is also a control model designed to make people do less of what they as individuals and small groups want and more of what the formal collective wants. As such, it is prey to one of the system's two fundamental characteristics, the right of individuals to think and to a great degree do, as they please. Assumptions of collective rationality do not go very far in the educational system. The softness of the technology, the openness of the system, the myriad possible definitions of the endeavor, and the personal benefits promised by individual success give each person a reason to defy submission to a larger collective.

An additional barrier to organizational reform is that the more influential members of society, school reformers among them, are presently either getting what they want from the schools or are participating in activities designed to get what they want. Parents and teachers of honors and magnet students do not want reformed schools. They want a conservative school with a scholarly teacher lec-turing their children on Antigone and Oedipus Rex, and they want their children coming home, reading Shakespeare, studying calculus, and applying to (and get-ting accepted by) Stanford, Columbia, and the premier state universities. These people are organized. They collude with respected teachers, supportive princi-pals, competitive colleges, scholarship societies, and a network of school clubs wherein their children learn to publish newspapers, debate, play chess, study Latin, and take trips to France. If these influential and school-supporting people are ignored or discounted, if they see their children's future threatened, if they are not allowed to press their views into the school, they will activate their coalitions into opposition. These people are not unconcerned about collective benefits, about equality in schools, or distributive justice in general. But they are more concerned and personally active in seeing that their children get an education that will help them succeed in a competitive society, one that eval-uates individuals as individuals. The freedom of association that allows people to structure the education of their children as they wish and within the schools as presently organized is a second barrier to reforms that seek to weaken the groups and coalitions relative to the formal organization.

In addition to running counter to free conscience and association and be-ing of little interest to active and influential parents who want their children accepted into old conservative universities, proposals to change the formal organization are apt to misread or minimize the schools' most enduring problem, one that is most immune to policy. That is the problem of forcing a narrow definition of appropriate behavior onto society through its children. An inestimable gulf lies between teachers and administrators who deal directly with students and who understand the importance and difficulty of maintaining control and outsiders who do not deal directly with students and who do not understand the importance and difficulty of the task. The problems associated with keeping twenty-five students focused on literacy for fifty minutes and the problem of keeping hundreds or even thousands of young people coming and going in an orderly manner throughout a seven-hour day are real and enduring. School staff will subvert reforms that fail to understand the importance of control or threaten their personal and personalized ways of handling it.

Finally is the economic argument from Olson (1965), which explains why small groups are better at satisfying personal needs than large groups. Roughly paraphrased, Olson argues that (1) the larger the group, the smaller the benefit received by any single individual, (2) the smaller the benefit to be received, the less likely the individual is to bear the burden required by large group interaction, and (3) the larger the collective, the greater the organizational costs and the "higher the hurdle that must be jumped before any of the collective good at all can be obtained" (p. 48).

> For these reasons, the larger the group the farther it will fall short of providing an optimal supply of a collective good, and very large groups normally will not in the absence of coercion or separate, outside incentives, provide themselves with even minimal amounts of a collective good. (p. 48)

In effect, the structural reforms that ask individuals, groups, and coalitions to put aside their present affiliations and join the larger collective cannot promise that the benefits to be gained are either worth the effort or exceed the benefits they are receiving from their present and privately sustained affiliations. Unless coerced, students will not leave aside groups and enter classrooms, teachers will not leave aside classrooms and enter the school, or administrators leave aside the school and enter the district. Nor will the personally organized and personally maintained groups without formal recognition put aside their interests in favor of collective action. Indeed there is no empirical evidence to argue that if the formal organization were the educating entity, performance and effort would improve. From a cost-benefit view, there are good reasons why the educational system is factionalized and why individuals resist leaving aside personal interests and the groups and factions that satisfy personal interests.

A second avenue toward improvement is to leave the school organization as it is and concentrate instead on building stronger coalitions around poorer performing students. Because the most successful students are those ensconced in a supportive network, the effort would be to create a supportive network for less successful students. This is a conservative option; one that has been going on successfully for decades. The schools have grown by specializing and differentiating to handle diverse groups. Such an approach would work with rather than opposing the school bureaucracy and would tacitly recognize the bureaucracy as the advocate for less able and willing students and the guardian of the collective good. Such an approach would have the added benefit of keeping reform concentrated on students, where success is more likely to occur and away from the organization, where it is less likely to occur.

The effort to strengthen educating networks for students most in need would fit well with the system as it exists. System members who are getting what they want will not oppose reforms that seek to help students who are not doing well, as long as the new specialities do not threaten present arrangements. In that sense, this is less a reform proposal than a suggestion that the schools go on much as they have, with their bureaucracy intact, individuals continuing to make important decisions, and groups and coalitions continuing to exercise their influence. This is a modest approach, perhaps too modest for reformers who need at least some hyperbole to garner resources. It is a middle proposal that accepts both the intractability of factions seeking personal advantage and the need to offset the factions with a sometimes coercive collective. But it has the advantage of placing the schools in the context of the educational system and the system in the context of a democratic society. It recognizes that education is both a personal and a social good. With the personal benefits left to individuals, groups, and factions and the social benefits left to the collective, both the educational system and its schools will go on.

References

Adams, H. (1918). *The education of Henry Adams.* Boston: Houghton Mifflin.

Agee, J., and Evans, W. (1960). *Let us now praise famous men.* Boston: Houghton Mifflin.

A nation at risk: The imperative for educational reform. (1983). Washington, DC: The National Commission on Excellence in Education, The U.S. Department of Education.

Auletta, K. (1982). *The underclass.* New York: Vintage Books.

Bailey, S. K., and Mosher, E. K. (1968). *ESEA: The office of education administers a law.* Syracuse: Syracuse University Press.

Barnard, C. (1938). *The function of the executive.* Cambridge: Harvard University Press.

Bell, T. H. (1988). *The thirteenth man.* New York: The Free Press.

Brophy, J. E., and Good, T. L. (1974). *Teacher-student relationships.* New York: Holt, Rinehart and Winston.

Brown vs. Board of Education: 3407 U.S. 483 (1954).

Burnham, J. (1964). *Suicide of the west.* New York: The John Day Company.

Callahan, R. (1962). *Education and the cult of efficiency.* Chicago: University of Chicago Press.

Chandler, A. D., Jr. (1990). *Scale and scope: The dynamics of industrial capitalism.* Cambridge: The Belknap Press of Harvard University Press.

Clinton, C. A. (1977). *The politics of developmental change: A case study.* Cambridge: Abt Associates Inc.

Cohen, D. (1982, November). Policy and organization: The impact of state and federal educational policy on school governance. *Harvard Educational Review, 52,* 474–499.

Coleman, J. S. (1961). *The adolescent society.* New York: Free Press of Glencoe.

Coleman, J. (1966). *Equality of educational opportunity,* Washington, DC: U.S. Government Printing Office.

Colfer, A. M., and Colfer, C. J. (1979). *Life and learning in an American town: Quilcene, Washington.* Cambridge: Abt Associates Inc.

Conant, J. B. (1959). *The American high school today.* New York: McGraw-Hill.

Cremin, L. (1977). *Traditions of American education.* New York: Basic Books.

Crowson, R. L., and Porter-Gehrie, C. (1980). The discretionary behavior of principals in large city schools. *Educational Administration Quarterly, 16*(1), 45–69.

Cuban, L. (1975). Hobson vs Hanson: A study in organizational response. *Educational Administration Quarterly, 9,* 15–37.

Cuban, L. (1984). *How teachers taught: Constancy and change in American classrooms, 1890–1980.* New York: Longman.

Cusick, P. A. (1973). *Inside high school: the students' world.* New York: Holt, Rinehart and Winston.

Cusick, P. A. (1983). *The egalitarian ideal and the American high school: studies of three schools.* New York: Longman.

Cusick, P. A. (1985). Finding meaning in teaching. *Education And Urban Society, 17,* 355-364.

Cusick, P. A., and Peters, W. (1979). The secondary principal in the small town. *Secondary Education Today, 20,* 22–36.

Cusick, P. A., and Peters, W. (1979, field notes). [The secondary principal in the small town]. Fieldnotes.

Cusick, P. A., and Wheeler, C. (1987). *Improving education through organizational change* (Report no. 400-83-0052). Washington: National Institute of Education.

Cusick, P. A., and Wheeler, C. (1988). Organizational morality and school reform. *American Review of Education, 96,* 231–255.

Csikszentmihalyi, M. and Larson R. (1984). *Being adolescent.* New York: Basic Books.

de Tocqueville, A. (1969) *Democracy in America.* Garden City, NY: Doubleday & Company.

Donnelly, W. (1979). *Community and change in rural schooling: Constantine, Michigan.* Cambridge: Abt Associates Inc.

Everhart, R. (1983). *Reading, writing and resistance: Adolescence and labor in a junior high school.* Boston: Routledge & Kegan Paul.

Fitzgerald, F. (1979). *America revised: History schoolbooks in the twentieth century.* Boston: Little, Brown and Company.

Goffman, E. (1961) *Asylums.* Garden City, NY: Anchor Books.

Gold, B. A., and Miles, M. (1981). *Whose school is this anyway?* New York: Praeger Publishers.

Goodlad, J. (1984). *A place called school: Prospects for the future.* New York: McGraw-Hill.

Grant, G. P. (1988). *The world we created at Hamilton High.* Cambridge: Harvard University Press.

Green, T. F. (1980). *Predicting the behavior of the educational system.* Syracuse: Syracuse University Press.

Hamilton, A., Madison, J., and Jay, J. (1961). *The federalist.* Cambridge: The Belknap Press of Harvard University Press.

Harrington, M. (1963). *The other America.* Baltimore: Penguin Books.

Hayek, F. A. (1988). *The fatal conceit: The errors of socialism.* Chicago: The University of Chicago Press.

Hennigh, L. (1979). *Cooperation and conflict in long-term educational change: South Umpqua, Oregon.* Cambridge: Abt Associates Inc.

Hentoff, N. (1966). *Our children are dying.* New York: The Viking Press.

Herriott, R. E. (1980). *Federal initiatives and rural school improvement: Findings from the experimental schools program.* Cambridge: Abt Associates Inc.

Heilbroner, R. (1985). *The nature and logic of capitalism.* New York: W. W. Norton.

Hielbroner, R. (1990, September 10). Reflections: After communism. *The New Yorker,* 91–100.

High school and beyond: a national longitudinal study for the 1980s. (1986). Prepared for the Center of Statistics under contract 300-82-0273. Washington, DC: Office of Educational Research and Improvement, U.S. Department of Education, Center for Statistics.

Hollingshead, A. (1949). *Elmtown's youth.* New York: John Wiley and Sons.

Homans, G. (1950). *The human group.* New York: Harcourt, Brace and World.

Iannaccone, L. (1967). *Politics in education.* New York: The Center for Applied Research in Education.

Jackson, P. (1968). *Life in classrooms.* New York: Holt, Rinehart and Winston.

Johnson, N. B. (1985). *Westhaven: Classroom culture and society in a rural elementary school.* Chapel Hill: The University of North Carolina Press.

Kamminga, G. (1981). Reflections on the principalship in a small town. *Secondary Education Today, 22*(2), 14–18.

Kmetz, J. T., and Willower, D. J. (1982). Elementary school principals' work behavior. *Educational Administration Quarterly, 18,* 62–78.

Kidder, T. (1989). *Among schoolchildren.* Boston: Houghton Mifflin.

Knapp, M. S. (1986) *Legislative goals for the education block grant: Have they been achieved at the local level?* SRI Project no. 6684, Menlo Park, CA: SRI International.

Labaree, D. (1988). *The making of an American high school.* New Haven: Yale University Press.

Leonard, G. (1983) Car pool: A story of public education in the eighties. *Esquire, 99*: 58–66; *70, 72–73.*

Lightfoot, S. L. (1983). *The good high school.* New York: Basic Books.

Lortie, D. (1975). *Schoolteacher.* Chicago: The University of Chicago Press.

Lynd, R., and Lynd, H. (1929). *Middletown.* New York: Harcourt Brace.

Marshall, C., Mitchell, D., and Wirt, F. (1986). The context of state-level policy formation. *Education Evaluation and Policy Analysis, 8,* 347–378.

Martin, W., and Willower, D. (1981). The managerial behavior of high school principals. *Educational Administration Quarterly, 17,* 69–90.

Mazzoni, T. L. (1987). The politics of educational choice in Minnesota. *Politics of education association yearbook,* 217–230.

McNeil, L. M. (1986). *Contradictions of control: school structure and school knowledge.* New York: Routledge & Kegan Paul.

McNeil, L. M. (1987). The politics of Texas school reform. *Politics of Education Association Yearbook,* 199–216.

Messerschmidt, D. A. (1979). *Local-federal interface in rural school improvement: River District, Wyoming.* Cambridge: Abt Associates Inc.

Metz, M. (1978). *Classrooms and corridors.* New Haven: Yale University Press.

Meyer, J., and Rowan, B. (1975). The structure of educational organizations. Annual meeting of the American Sociological Association.

Mintzberg, H. (1980), *The nature of managerial work,* Englewood Cliffs, NJ: Prentice Hall.

Moore, G. A., Jr. (1967). *Realities of the urban classroom.* Garden City, NY: Anchor Books.

Murphy, J. T. (1974). *State education agencies and discretionary funds.* Toronto: D. C. Heath & Co.

Nelson, R. N. (1975). *A field study of the means by which the Michigan Department of Education reduces uncertainty in its environment.* Unpublished doctoral dissertation, Michigan State University.

Northwest Territories Act (1787). An ordinance for the government of the territory of the United States, Northwest of the River, Ohio. 1787, July 13, Congress of the Confederation.

Oakes, J. (1985). *Keeping track: How schools structure inequality.* New Haven: Yale University Press.

Okey, T. (1990). *The family's perspective on the individual's decision to drop out of high school.* Unpublished doctoral dissertation, Michigan State University.

Olson, M., Jr. (1965) *The logic of collective action.* Cambridge: Harvard University Press.

✳Parsons, T. (1951). *The social system.* New York: The Free Press.

Peshkin, A. (1986). *God's choice.* Chicago: The University of Chicago Press.

Popkewitz, T. K., Tabachink, B. R. and Wehlage, G. (1982). *The myth of educational reform.* Madison: The University of Wisconsin Press.

Powell, A., Farrar, E., and Cohen, D. (1985). *The shopping mall high school: Winners and losers in the educational marketplace.* Boston: Houghton Mifflin.

Richardson, K. (1981). Jackie of all trades in the fishbowl. *Secondary Education Today, 22,* 46–50.

Rossman, G. B., Corbett, H. D., and Firestone, W. A. (1988). *Change and effectiveness in schools.* Albany: The State University of New York Press.

Sapolsky, H. M. (1972). *The polaris system development.* Cambridge: Harvard University Press.

Sarason, S. B. (1982). *The culture of the school and the problem of change.* Boston: Allyn and Bacon.

School faces suit on volunteerism. (1990, September 22) *New York Times,* 22.

Silberman, C. E. (1970). *Crisis in the classroom.* New York: Random House.

Sizer, T. (1984). *Horace's compromise.* New York: Houghton Mifflin.

Smith, L. M., and Geoffrey, W. (1968). *The complexities of an urban classroom.* New York: Holt, Rinehart and Winston.

Smith, L. M., and Keith, P M. (1971). *Anatomy of educational innovation.* New York: John Wiley and Sons.

Smith, L. M., Kleine, P. F., Prunty, J. P., and Dwyer, D.C. (1986). *Educational innovators then and now.* New York: The Falmer Press.

Sproull, L. (1981). Managing educational programs: A micro-behavioral analysis, *Human Organization, 40*(2), 113–117.

Sproull, L., Weiner, S., and Wolf, D. (1978). *Organizing an anarchy: Belief, bureaucracy, and politics in the National Institute of Education.* Chicago: The University of Chicago Press.

Stinchcombe, A. (1964). *Rebellion in a high school.* Chicago: Quadrangle Books.

Thompson, J. (1967). *Complex organizations.* New York: Scott Foresman.

Trotsky, L. (1957). *The history of the Russian revolution.* (M. Eastman, Trans.). Ann Arbor: University of Michigan Press. (Original work published 1932).

Turnbull, B. J., and Marks, E. L., (1986). *The education block grant and intergovernmental relations: Effects at local levels* (SRI Project no. 6684). Menlo Park, CA: SRI International.

Tyack, D., and Hansot, E. (1982). *Managers of virtue.* New York: Basic Books.

Vidich, A., and Bensman, J. (1958). *Small town in mass society.* Garden City, NY: Doubleday and Company.

Waller, W. (1932). *Sociology of teaching.* New York: Russell & Russell.

Wax, M. L., Wax, R. H. and Dumont, R. V., Jr., (1964). Formal education in an American Indian community. *Social Problems 11*(4), 1–126.

Wax, R. H. (1967). The warrier dropouts. *Transactions, 4,* 40–46.

Westinghouse Learning Corporation. (1969). The impact of Head Start: An evaluation of the effects of Head Start on children's cognitive and affective development. Bladensburg, MD: PB184328.

Why socialism will never work (1989; January 28–Feburary 3). *The Economist, 310* (758), 85.

Willis, P. (1977). *Learning to labor: How working class kids get working class jobs.* Hampshire, England: Gower Publishing House.

Wirt, F., Mitchell, D., and Marshall, C. (1988). Culture and education policy: Analyzing policy in state policy systems. *Educational Evaluation and Policy Analysis, 10,* 271–284.

Wolcott, H. (1977). *Teachers versus technocrats.* Eugene, OR: The Center for Educational Policy and Management, University of Oregon.

Wolcott, H. (1978). *The man in the principal's office.* New York: Holt, Rinehart and Winston.

Index